THE KIBBUTZ COMMUNITY
AND NATION BUILDING

Paula Rayman

The Kibbutz Community
and Nation Building

PRINCETON UNIVERSITY PRESS

FOR MY PARENTS,
who gave me respect for tradition

FOR ROB AND ALYSSA,
who give me hope for the future

Contents

List of Figures and Maps

List of Tables

Acknowledgments

As this is primarily a case study, it owes its largest debt to the members of the kibbutz community. I want to take this opportunity to thank the havarim of Kibbutz Har for their generosity in sharing their home with me and for their considerable support during fieldwork. There are many individuals whose acts of hospitality, information gathering, and creative questioning gave me the energy to pursue my work fully. I hope that each of them recognizes the extent of my appreciation.

During fieldwork a number of members from other kibbutzim and Israeli academic institutions contributed to the study's progress. It is a pleasure to thank Menachem Rosner, Erik Cohen, Daniel Rosilio, Saadia Gelb, Dan Karmon, and Haim Barkai in this regard.

The critical comments and consistent support lent to the research project during its early stages by Severyn Bruyn, Martin Lowenthal, and Barry Bluestone were indispensable. In particular, I wish to thank Irene Gendzier for her exceptional ability to be a thorough critical advisor while, simultaneously, remaining a trusted friend.

Rosabeth Kanter provided very helpful comments early on regarding social change and community organization. Maurice Stein at a later stage offered generous encouragement and assistance. Gail Filion of Princeton University Press presented encouragement and expertise during all the stages of publication. Rita Gentry made important editorial suggestions. Others shaping the progress of the book, sometimes without knowing the extent of their contributions, include Everett Gendler, Kurt Wolff, David Riesman, Roland Warren, Bruno Bettelheim, Martin Blatt, Yair Svoray, Carmen Sirianni, Anne Rayman, Sol Levine, Joseph Singer, and the women in my women's group.

Joseph Bensman was a superb reader and I hope his elegant sense of language and subtle ideas are, at least, partly reflected in the final product.

The Department of Sociology of Brandeis University provided a supportive environment for writing and preparing the manuscript for publication. Marilyn Aaron, Muriel Hess, Gwen Whateley, and Ruth Kramer deserve special thanks for their efforts in the book's behalf and for their personal encouragement. Alan Arkush, Steven Klein, and Elizabeth Bouche admirably performed jobs of transcribing, typing, and proofreading.

Most especially, my husband and best friend, Robert Read, has continued to provide both the nurturance necessary to work during hard times and the hope of building communities based upon human solidarity.

THE KIBBUTZ COMMUNITY

AND NATION BUILDING

Setting the Stage

In the midst of current events, it is easy to become discouraged about the possibility for a communal model to produce and sustain democratic socialism. History has recorded an extensive catalogue of the extensive failure of small-scale communal ventures. But attempts to institute socialism on a larger, state scale have too often resulted in authoritarian forms of social control. The powerful forces of elitism, nationalism, and capitalism pose overwhelming odds against the emergence of genuine alternatives.

Yet, certain societies and communal experiments continue to offer the promise of new modes of social organization and social consciousness. The Israeli kibbutz has been one of those experiments. Its history presents a picture of the incongruities between communal norms and roles in the larger society, between ideology and material pressures. Learning how the kibbutz has resolved or has not resolved these incongruities provides lessons for the future.

Most studies of the kibbutz have focused on internal organization. In contrast, this book concentrates on the relationship between the kibbutz and external institutions. Primary attention is given to the effects of the dominant national and international systems of development and modernization on local communal patterns of resource allocation, social structure, and overall quality of life. In what ways have state policies influenced kibbutz autonomy, solidarity, and stratification? What is the nature of kibbutz regional relations, including those with other kibbutzim, the Palestinian-Arab population and Israeli development towns? These questions open the way for explo-

ration of issues important in political sociology and relevant to
the discussion of communal-based socialism, especially the relationship between nationalism and socialism and between
communal development and individuality. They are also central to the study of the community.

The future of communal experiments is dependent on a complex combination of internal and external forces. A major argument of the book is that the success of such experiments,
including the kibbutz, has been undermined because they fail
to resolve internal inconsistencies and because they exist in
conflict with their environment. For example, the limits of what
is meant by kibbutz socialism become clear from a study of the
community's earliest days. External national institutions greatly
aided kibbutz colonizing efforts, while simultaneously con-
straining internal kibbutz energies directed toward their traditional ideological goals.

Though some of the problems facing the kibbutz remain
unique to its history, its original quest for a new social order
reflects common threads in socialist thought and communal experience. The content of kibbutz socialist ideology, most
clearly articulated by A. D. Gordon and Martin Buber, is a
protest against the market mentality of the industrial order and
a movement toward an egalitarian human community. Rejection of the attitudes that reduced human labor to exchange
value and encouraged competitive antagonism was linked to
positive concern for individual freedom and social cooperation.
The fact that kibbutz reality often falls far short of its ideal will
soon be apparent. But the intrinsic difficulty of attempting to
realize a socialist vision must be remembered as the story un-
folds.

The book's methodology centers on a case study of a border
kibbutz. This approach permits an intensive examination of
community life from the prestate era until the present. Building
upon the sociological imagination of C. W. Mills, this study

relies on a historical perspective for the study of social change in relation to external events. Kibbutz Har was chosen for case study because its prestate establishment and recent economic expansion offer a wealth of historical material.[1] In addition, it was obvious during my initial stay at Har in 1970-1971 that the kibbutz was directly affected by the dynamics of national policy and that policy was shaping the community's internal organization.

The problem of conducting research within a volatile military-political situation deserves mention. As Eva Rosenfeld, an associate director of research of the Jewish Board of Guardians pointed out, the kibbutz "is not a quiet, stable, safe and secure place."[2] This is especially true for border kibbutzim. During my stay at Har in the spring and summer of 1975 increased military action along the Lebanese border affected a wide range of community activities as well as the general atmosphere in the kibbutz. It was impossible to ignore the situation and simply carry on research.

There were three primary ways in which the military-political events shaped my study. First, tension within the community noticeably increased, as men and women devoted more of their energies to security interests. When war practices were held or when night alerts kept members up into the morning, there was less energy left for regular work and for leisure routines. Moreover, the sounds of bomber planes and mortars, even after they became an almost daily occurrence, were reminders of conflict.

Secondly, because of the increased border tension in the area after the 1973 War, travel between Har and the outside world became more restricted. Leaving or entering the kibbutz in the evening could only be done with special permission

---

[1] The names of the kibbutz and the names of all of its members are pseudonyms.

[2] "The American Social Scientist in Israel: A Case-Study of Role Conflict," *American Journal of Orthopsychiatry*, 28 (1958), p. 567.

since the passage up and down the mountain was guarded by
soldiers at all times. The road from the kibbutz to the coastal
towns of Nahariya and Akko, leading to the larger cities of
Haifa and Tel Aviv, was also guarded at all times by a system
of roadblocks. The location of Har and the military restrictions
on travel prohibited access to other local communities and the
rest of the Israeli society in general. Since a majority of hired
laborers resided either in Shlomi, the development town at the
base of Har's hilltop, or in Nahariya, the closest seacoast town,
access to these workers was limited. Because the outside laborers had more difficulty entering the kibbutz, there were spo-
radic curtailments of the night shifts in Har's factory.

Under these conditions, there was also little opportunity to
meet with local Palestinian-Arabs in order to gather information
concerning their reactions to the kibbutz. A few of them worked
as hired laborers, usually in the fields or at construction jobs
within the kibbutz center. They were understandably reluctant
to discuss issues with a stranger. A discussion of the Palestinian-Arab perspective toward Har would add an important dimension to this study.

Since 1975 continuous cycles of tension along the Lebanese
border have affected Har's daily living. In the midst of the
Lebanese Civil War, Har participated in Israel's open border
policy, which allowed Lebanese Christians to enter the kibbutz
for shelter and medical supplies. This was the first time since
prestate days that residents of Lebanon have entered the kibbutz. In the beginning of 1979, Har went on alert after a guerrilla force entered Maalot, a nearby community. As recently as
May 1980, soldiers based at Har stopped a direct attack on the
kibbutz. Thus, the national military-political situation continues to have a significant impact on present kibbutz life.

Finally, as any traveler knows, it is not easy to feel at home
in a foreign society, to be accepted by the local population or
accept their way of living. This is particularly difficult when

the object of the visit is to conduct research on the life of the local community. Most people are wisely skeptical about how much foreigners can really learn about a different social reality. They correctly fear that the foreigners may, at best, be clumsy intruders and, at worst, distorters of the community's activities and dreams.

However, a researcher can bring to the study of a foreign culture a consciousness that provokes new questions, insights, and meanings not available to those totally immersed in the society. The personal struggles experienced during a surrender to the local society may produce a creative tension between critical thinking and sensitivity.[3] This was my hope during my stay at the kibbutz.

During its over four-decade history, Kibbutz Har has undergone transition from a struggling rural outpost with a population of 49 to a semi-industrial, well-established community with a total population of over 400 (see Tables 1 and 2). This growth reflects the influx of Jewish immigrants to the Yishuv, the Jewish community in Palestine, and after 1948, to the state of

TABLE 1. POPULATION OF KIBBUTZ HAR, 1938-1975 (total population including members, children, and candidates).

Year	Population '
1938	49
1942	126
1946	210
1955	308
1960	360
1963	410
1975	460

[3] The concept of surrender as part of community fieldwork was developed by Kurt Wolff, "Surrender and Community Study: The Study of Loma," in *Reflections in Community Studies*, ed. by Arthur Vidich et al. (New York: John Wiley & Sons, Inc., 1964) pp. 233ff.

TABLE 2. Jewish Population in Palestine/Israel, 1936-1975.

Year	Jewish Population	Total Population*
1936	384,078	1,366,692
1944	509,184	1,697,868
1949	1,013,871	1,173,871
1955	1,590,519	1,789,175
1960	1,911,189	2,150,358
1963	2,155,551	2,430,125
1975 (Jan.)	2,890,300	3,409,000

* SOURCES: For 1949-1975 *Statistical Abstracts of Israel* (Jerusalem: Central Bureau of Statistics, Government of Israel, 1949-1975). Figures for 1936 and 1944 are from Esco Foundation for Palestine, Inc., *Palestine: A Study of Jewish, Arab, and British Policies*, vols. 1 and 2 (New Haven: Yale University Press, 1947).
NOTE: Total population includes Christian, Moslem, and other non-Jewish population. The figure for 1975 does not include population in post-1967 Israeli Occupied Territories, which totals over 900,000.

Israel. While the first settlers were primary East European Jews from *shtetl*, or Jewish ghetto, backgrounds, more recent arrivals have come from France and the French-speaking countries of North Africa. The heterogeneity of national backgrounds exists within an emerging Israeli national identity and the use of Hebrew as the dominant public language.

An introduction to the place and people of Har must necessarily present a larger picture than that of the kibbutz itself. Har has been not only an isolated community but a part of a kibbutz movement. That movement has a complex ideological and historical background. There are currently 235 kibbutzim in Israel, constituting 3.3 percent (94,000 people) of the Israeli Jewish population. With its population of 400, Har is an average size kibbutz (kibbutz population ranges from less than 100 to over 1200). While the Sephardic Jewish population,

Jews from non-Western countries, of Har is nearly 20 percent, they make up only 7 percent of the total kibbutzim population.

The Ideology of the Kibbutz: Socialist-Zionism

The kibbutzim, as collectivist colonizing communities, were the historical vanguard of Socialist-Zionism in Palestine. The first kibbutz, Degania, was founded in 1909. During the prestate years, the collectivist orientation of the kibbutzim resulted in the establishment of national cooperative institutions in Palestine. These later became a major foundation of Israel's public and private sectors.

A crucial question confronting the early kibbutzim was whether a successful synthesis of socialism and nationalism was possible. Socialist-Zionism rests on a blending of various formulations in political and economic thought. Its iconoclastic perspective includes elements of Russian anarchism, bolshevism, social democratic Marxism, and bundism.[4] Zionist roots incorporated elements from a religious spiritual Zionism, but kibbutzim have been primarily linked to political Zionism and the foundation of a nation-state.

Spiritual Zionism dates back to the dispersal of the Jewish people from Zion (literally meaning, the city of Jerusalem) after the destruction of the second temple in 70 A.D. Since that event tradition links final redemption of the Jewish people to

[4] The best general accounts of the history of Zionism can be found in Ben Halpern, *The Idea of the Jewish State* (Cambridge, Mass.: Harvard University Press, 1969) and Arthur Hertzberg, ed., *The Zionist Idea: An Historical Analysis and Reader* (New York: Meridian Books, Inc., 1960). Other important related works include Henry J. Tobias, *The Jewish Bund in Russia From Its Origins to 1905* (Stanford: Stanford University Press, 1972); Leo Pinsker, *Auto-Emancipation* (Tel Aviv: Macabean Publishers, 1906); Theodor Herzl, *The Jewish State: An Attempt at a Modern Solution of the Jewish Question* (New York: J. Pordes, 1967); and Amos Perlmutter, "Dov Ber-Borochov: A Marxist-Zionist Ideologist," *Middle Eastern Studies* 5 (January 1969), 32-44.

a return to Zion. According to the spiritual view, Zionism could not be reduced to modern forms of nationalism: "it [Zionism] is a unique category extending far beyond the frontier of national problems . . . to the cosmic and Being itself."[5] Cultural rebirth of the Jewish nation depends upon the return to the sacred soil.

Modern political Zionism emerged as a force in the late 1800s in Western Europe. Its principal assumption was that Jews could not successfully live in the Diaspora. Jews could not hope for a normal existence within non-Jewish nations since the world of *goyim*, or non-Jews, was inherently hostile and suspicious. In a world of nation-states, Jews needed a nation-state where they would be the majority, where they could control their own destiny. The nation-state was thought to be a modern progressive institution. Among Western intellectuals, nationalism was seen as a means for self-determination and liberation.

This view was not a new one, but events in Europe during the late 1800s and early 1900s convinced many to uphold it. Overt anti-Semitism was also on the upsurge during this era. Many liberal Western Jews had believed that Jewish assimilation was both possible and preferred. However, the pogroms in Eastern Europe grew in intensity and drew attention from the West. The Dreyfus case in France revealed the prevalence of anti-Semitism even within Western Europe.[6] It was an especially important event in the history of political Zionism, as it moved Theodor Herzl, known as the father of political-Zionism, to write *The Jewish State*.

The response by Herzl to the Dreyfus case was shared by

[5] Martin Buber, *On Zion: The History of an Idea* (New York: Schocken Books, 1973), p. xx.

[6] A full discussion of the Dreyfus case appears in Hertzberg, ed., *The Zionist Idea*, pp. 202ff. For a provocative alternative view of Zionist history see Hannah Arendt, "The Jewish State: Fifty Years After," *Commentary* 1, no. 7, (19—), 1-9.

many other Western European Jews who eventually provided much of the organizational and financial support for the kibbutz movement. The early kibbutzniks' desire for self-determination was enacted as part of the quest for a society that would be free of the dictates of the non-Jewish world. As part of their search for a just society, however, the kibbutzniks attempted to integrate socialist concepts into the political Zionist ideology and they became the leaders of Socialist-Zionism.

Socialist-Zionism was the ideology of the majority of the Jewish settlers arriving in Palestine during the Mandate years and reflected the hard facts confronting Zionist efforts to build a Jewish nation-state. In order to create a Jewish state in Palestine, Jews had to create their own occupational structure and the foundation for an independent Jewish economy. Private capitalist endeavors allowed Jewish landowners in Palestine to rely on Palestinian-Arab labor and thus prevent creation of a separate, viable Jewish economy.[7] However, the harshness of land conditions, and political-military resistance by the Palestinian-Arab population, called for unified, mass action. Socialist-Zionism was a response to these needs of nation building.

The main function of the kibbutz was to create a material base for a Jewish state in Palestine: land had to be reclaimed, new immigrants had to be supported and frontiers had to be guarded. The ideological goal of the kibbutzim was to establish a Jewish farm class in Palestine as part of the effort to create a Jewish proletariat class that would insure Jewish control of the means of production. Only through direct Jewish control of the land in Palestine could the hope of a Jewish state be realized. This implied transfer of land settlement from Palestinian-Arab to Jewish hands.

Socialist-Zionism was thus an "ideology of materialistic ide-

[7] Halpern, *The Idea of a Jewish State*, pp. 127ff. describes the private endeavors of Baron de Rothschild in setting up colonies in Palestine at the turn of the century.

alism."[8] It was part of kibbutz development from its earliest days, approaching socialism from the pragmatism of national need. Socialist Zionist ideological formulations responded directly to the material conditions posing a threat to Jewish colonization in Palestine. In terms of the kibbutz, the most significant of these formulations were collective ownership, the religion of labor, and the principle of self-labor.

COLLECTIVE OWNERSHIP

Contrary to popular opinion, the Jewish collectives in Palestine did not emerge from a theoretical blueprint but rather from the concrete needs of Zionist colonization. The technique of group settlement was more advantageous than individual endeavors since it was less expensive, more efficient and guaranteed greater security. Dr. Arthur Ruppin, Director of Land Colonization for the Yishuv in Palestine, has emphasized the necessity of collective action: "The question was not whether group settlement was preferable to individual settlement; it was rather one of either group settlement or no settlement at all."[9]

Economically, the Zionist organization could not afford the type of individualist colonization that had previously characterized Palestinian-Jewish settlement. Most Jewish immigrants did not have any agricultural training. It was far cheaper to have an expert train an entire group than a series of individuals. Group settlement often meant a savings on human labor and a decrease of the initial capital outlay. The building costs for a

---

[8] Yonina Talmon, *The Family and Community in the Kibbutz* (Cambridge, Mass.: Harvard University Press, 1972). Additional sources on Socialist-Zionism include Dov Ber-Borochov, *Nationalism and the Class Struggle* (Jerusalem: Poale Zion, 1937), and Aaron Samuel Tamaret, "Zionism, Judaism and World Well-Being, Three Unsuitable Unions" (unpublished, translated by Rabbi Everett Gendler, Andover, Mass., 1969).

[9] Arthur Ruppin, *The Agricultural Colonization of the Zionist Organization in Palestine*, (London: Martin Hopkinson and Company Ltd., 1926), p. 8.

group settlement were substantially less than the cost of constructing a corresponding number of individual quarters.

Environmental conditions were a significant factor. Deforestation and erratic rainfall had caused erosion.[10] Water was a severe problem. It existed in swamps in the northern areas and was almost completely absent in the desert. The only good sources of water irrigation in mandated Palestine were wells, most of which needed repair. Group efforts were necessary to clear the swamps, clean the wells, and build a network of roads. Many early Jewish collectives were founded by the members of such group efforts.

The swamps bred malaria and other diseases, including cholera and typhoid. The collective settlement offered the individual security in times of personal crisis. When illness occurred, the collective member did not have to worry about losing his or her economic base; other members would take care of the rest of the family. Avraham Ben-Shalom, an early kibbutz member wrote of the relative tranquility of his hospital experience during a typhoid sickness:

> It is possible for me to lie quietly here and enjoy reading the encouraging letters of my comrades of the Kibbutz. Without worry I wait patiently for the crisis. . . . My companion, however, sighs deeply, spends sleepless nights. . . . His illness attacked him in the most critical season for his farm; all the care of it has fallen upon his wife. He joined a Moshav rather than a Kibbutz because he did not want to be a slave to the collective. . . . To me, however, he seemed to have put his head under the yoke of a greater slavery.[11]

Collectives were also a preferred form of settlement for purely defense reasons. They facilitated quick mobilization,

[10] Henrik Infield, *Cooperative Living in Palestine* (New York: Dryden Press, 1944), pp. 39ff.

[11] Avraham Ben-Shalom, *Deep Furrows*, trans. Frances Bunce (New York: Hashomer Hatzair Organization, 1937), p. 215.

smooth organization, and a high degree of solidarity. Their circular, defensive plans are reminiscent of the American covered-wagon arrangement.

Collective form of settlement implied values of mutual aid, direct democracy, and egalitarianism important to Socialist-Zionists. When implemented, these values had social-psychological as well as political-economic consequences. Collective ownership bound individuals together through mutual responsibility and gave the kibbutzniks an added sense of protection in the face of external threats.

To Socialist-Zionists egalitarianism meant equality of opportunity and was expressed by a sharing of the fruits of labor. Distribution of goods was not related to the individual's output or status, but was allocated according to need. Additionally, job rotation was proposed so that no one person would assume special powers. Direct democracy meant that all collective members would be involved in community decisions. Each member was expected to attend the weekly General Assembly, which had principal authority in the community. Issues were decided by majority rule. Members of subcommittees concerned with different areas of community life were determined by a system of rotation. In the subcommittees consensual decision making was encouraged. Since they were a voluntary group, the collectives had no legal or formal system of punishment. Members could leave as they chose, and the strongest coercion was public opinion.

THE RELIGION OF LABOR

A second significant tenet of Socialist-Zionism, the religion of labor, provided a moral dimension to Jewish colonization in Palestine. Unlike collective ownership, the concept of the religion of labor reflected ideological rather than strictly pragmatic concerns. Since the majority of kibbutzniks were not guided by traditional religious maxims, a substitute moral incentive was deemed necessary to strengthen the settlers' perception that their colonization efforts were just and right. A spiritual approach to labor stressing the importance of agrarian labor as the spiritual link between the settler and the land met this need.

A. D. Gordon, known as the religion's principal teacher, asserted that national rebirth depended upon Jews recognizing the sanctity of labor. In the major collection of his writings, *The Nation and the Work*, he expresses the thought that the Jewish people can earn the right to a cultivated Palestine only if they do the work themselves. As a person becomes fulfilled only working directly with nature, the Jews would become whole as a nation only by working directly with the land. Gordon also stressed that physical labor emancipated the individual from inner slavery. Social order was dependent on such liberation. The individual was the "basic unit of the kibbutz" while work in the name of the kibbutz freed the individual. The individual and kibbutz, in turn, were linked to the larger national colonization movement. In this way, the individual, the community, and the national movement were tied to the same ideological goal.

The religion of labor clearly was an essential factor in the kibbutzniks' ability to overcome unfavorable material conditions. It united the individual's convictions with the idea of national redemption and it allowed secular-minded kibbutzniks to feel the strength of moral conviction within a Socialist-Zionist context.[12] Similar to other community movements, the sacred quality given to laboring promoted a sense of physical and mental unity within the community.[13] It provided a common bond during the actual process of land settlement. This was

---

[12] This can be compared to Mao Tse-Tung's success in equating ideological training with moral training in the context of the Chinese Revolution. See William Hinton, *Fanshen: A Documentary of Revolution in a Chinese Village* (New York: Vintage Books, 1966).

[13] Rosabeth Kanter, *Commitment and Community: Communes and Utopias in Sociological Perspective* (Cambridge, Mass.: Harvard University Press, 1972), p. 49.

especially significant since there was continued hostility from the native population to the process of Jewish colonization. The principle of religion of labor provided the kibbutz movement with the "universality of a religious cause."[14] Working for the economic development of the kibbutz linked individual devotion to labor with a commitment to a nationalist system of values. Curbing individual personal needs led to a unifying form of asceticism characterizing kibbutz solidarity. It was not at all unlike the Protestant ethic and the rise of capitalism.[15]

SELF-LABOR

The single most important tenet of Socialist-Zionism was self-labor, a policy of utilizing only Jewish labor. While collectivist ownership provided the form for land colonization and the religion of labor provided a moral dimension, the concept of self-labor provided an economic and political formulation for Zionist labor policies and linked socialist ideals with Jewish national and economic interests. There could be no Jewish state in Palestine without Jews relying on their own labor. Abraham Granovsky, a Zionist agrarian and land development expert, noted that the realization of the Jewish national home was "intimately bound up with the application of the principle of Jewish labor."[16] Zionist leaders also understood that continued reliance on Palestinian-Arab labor by Jewish urban and rural institutions would undermine the attainment of Jewish autonomy.

The effect of Socialist-Zionism on the development of the political economy of the kibbutz mainly centers on the issue of autonomy. The essential goal of Socialist-Zionism in the pre-

[14] Edgar Snow, *Red Star over China* (New York: Grove Press, 1961), p. 353.

[15] See Max Weber, *The Protestant Ethic and the Spirit of Capitalism* (New York: Charles Scribner, 1958).

[16] Abraham Granovsky, *Land Policy in Palestine* (New York: Bloch Publishing Co., Inc., 1940), p. 100.

state era was the founding of an autonomous Jewish state in Palestine. In 1907 Arthur Ruppin wrote a paper entitled "Memorandum on the Future Work in Palestine" outlining three conditions for obtaining Jewish autonomy in Palestine: a Jewish majority in Palestine; Jewish ownership of the majority of land; a will for autonomy on the part of the Jews.

The kibbutzim embraced the self-labor formulation in both their labor and land colonization practices. They aspired to change the Jewish occupational structure through the proletarianization of Jewish immigrants and through voluntary deurbanization. Hired labor, employment of nonkibbutz members by the community, was taboo within the kibbutz economy. By prohibiting hired labor, the kibbutzim hoped to open employment opportunities for new Jewish immigrants, while creating a rural labor economy separate from that of the existing Palestinian-Arab agarian economy.

The expression of Socialist-Zionist ideology on the part of the early kibbutzniks was a strong indication of the will for autonomy. Through putting into practice the religion of labor and norms of self-labor the kibbutz created job possibilities and sustenance for Jewish immigrants. The kibbutz movement was the key instrument for attaining Jewish land ownership. The collective ownership of the kibbutz's land and its labor policies shaped its internal political economy and produced a collectivist system of consumption and production.

Finally, the Socialist-Zionist ideology of the kibbutz has had profound implications for the social development of the community with respect to solidarity and national leadership. The solidarity achieved in the kibbutz through ideological commitment allowed the kibbutzim to achieve great influence in leading the way of Socialist-Zionist practices. Acting as a vanguard of the nation-building efforts and setting the pace for the realization of substituting national priorities for personal material interests, the kibbutzniks were recognized as moral as well as political and economic leaders. External confirmation of the elite position of the kibbutz in the Yishuv provided an important sense of reward and pride for their members. The kibbutz attachment to voluntary idealism aided members in overcoming material difficulties with the conviction of belonging to a "chosen" group of the chosen people.

The Historical Setting of the Kibbutz

The existence of the kibbutzim as the vanguard of Socialist-Zionism depended upon the development of the Jewish institutions in Palestine during the British Mandate years.[17] Between the two world wars, the growth of the Yishuv society resulted in the foundation of various economic, social, and political institutions that were to become the basis of the future Jewish state of Israel. The major Yishuv institutions—the Jewish Agency, the Histadrut, and the Jewish National Fund— served as direct links between the worldwide Zionist organizations and the Jewish colonial settlements.

In addition to the goal of building a Jewish state in Palestine, the Yishuv institutions were united by the view that Jewish development of Palestine would be beneficial for the country and the entire Middle East region. This reflected their support for Western conceptions of progress and technological devel-

[17] For a full discussion of the history of the Mandate period refer to Esco Foundation for Palestine, Inc., *Palestine: A Study of Jewish, Arab, and British Policies*, vols. 1 and 2 (New Haven: Yale University Press, 1947); Christopher Sykes, *Crossroads to Israel* (New York: World Publishing Co., 1965); Walter Laqueur, ed., *The Israeli-Arab Reader* (New York: Bantam Books, Inc., 1971); Y. Porath, *The Emergence of the Palestinian-Arab National Movement: 1918-1929* (London: Frank Cass, 1974); Doreen Ingrams, *Palestine Papers 1917-1922: Seeds of Conflict* (London: John Murray, 1972); and F. Jabber and A. Lesch, *The Politics of Palestinian Nationalism* (Berkeley: University of California Press, 1973).

opment that specifically complemented British imperial interests.

The Yishuv existed within the political and economic realities of the British Mandate government. It also had to deal with
the increasingly hostile reaction of Palestinian-Arabs to Zionist
colonization. The combination of British colonial policies and
the conflicting forces of two emerging nationalisms set the stage
for continual turmoil, which has continued until the present
time. The kibbutzim were founded and developed in Palestine
as it underwent the difficult transition from semifeudal conditions to a Westernized nation-state.

What was happening in Palestine during the Mandate years
had international as well as local significance: British interests
reflected political struggles between nations with imperial concerns; Palestinian nationalism was linked to other Arab nationalist struggles; and Yishuv institutions reflected the concerns
of the worldwide Zionist movement. It is especially important
to keep in mind the regional and international dimensions when
attention turns to Kibbutz Har. The kibbutz movement population was never more than 7 percent of the Yishuv population,
which during the Mandate years was never more than 35 percent of the total population in Palestine.[18] Although the development of the kibbutz has been correctly viewed as a highly
significant event during the history of Mandate Palestine, its
existence and expansion has always been tied to larger circles
of social, political, and economic activity.

BRITISH INTERESTS IN PALESTINE

At the San Remo Conference in April 1920, the British government was assigned the Mandate for Palestine under the jurisdiction of the League of Nations. From that time until May
1948, the British government was responsible for carrying out
the provisions of the Mandate, which included the establish-

---

[18] Esco Foundation, *Jewish, Arab, and British and Policies*, vol. 2.

ment of a national home for the Jewish people in Palestine. The events leading up to the British assumption of the Mandate, and Britain's eventual role in influencing conditions in Mandate Palestine, demonstrate the centrality of imperial interests in British Mandate activities.

In September 1923 the League of Nations ratified the British Mandate for Palestine. The twenty-two articles very loosely defined the terms of the Mandate and gave Britain a wide range of responsibilities. The most important aspects of the Mandate's structure for the development of the kibbutz were its clear support of the Balfour Declaration and its reference to the native majority population as citizens entitled to minority rights.[19] Articles 4 and 5 established organizational ties between the Mandatory and the Yishuv national institutions, represented by the Jewish Agency and supported Jewish immigration to Palestine and Jewish land colonization:

> Article 4: An appropriate Jewish agency shall be recognized as a public body for the purposes of advising and cooperating with the Administration of Palestine in such economic, social and other matters as may affect the establishment of the Jewish national home. . . .
>
> Article 5: The Administration of Palestine, while ensuring that the rights and position of other sections of the population are not prejudiced, shall facilitate Jewish immigration under suitable conditions and shall encourage in cooperation with the Jewish Agency referred to in Article 4 close settlement by Jews on the land. . . .

While Britain did offer significant support for Zionist endeavors during the Mandate period, implementation of policies ultimately depended on what was perceived to be in Britain's

---

[19] Articles give the Mandatory responsibility for citizenship laws, guarantee of religious freedom, security of holy places, and control of natural resources and international relations.

interest. The British government was never consistent in interpreting the Balfour Declaration: while some British officials felt Britain had definitely promised a Jewish state in Palestine, others felt bound by a much more limited pledge. Perhaps with the awareness that Britain had less and less to gain in Palestine, the Mandatory in 1937 issued the Peel Commission Report advocating a partition plan. After first rejecting the commission findings, the British government, ten years later, finally gave up on Palestine and left the two-state plan in the hands of the opposing sides (see Map 1).

THE PALESTINIAN-ARAB COMMUNITY

Until World War I Arabs residing in Palestine considered themselves part of an area broadly defined as Syria, with Palestine itself divided into a number of smaller districts. At first, after British occupation in Palestine, many of the local inhabitants looked to the Damascus government of Amir Faysal that supported the inclusion of Palestine within an independent Syria. After Faysal's fall in 1920 Palestinian-Arabs turned their nationalist aspirations toward an independent Palestine and consequently became more concerned with Zionist colonization.

According to the 1922 census of Palestine there were 668,- 000 Palestinian-Arabs with 589,000 Moslems, 71,500 Christians, and 7,500 Druzes. On the eve of World War I and throughout the Mandate period, the overwhelming majority of Palestinian-Arabs lived in the rural areas, and almost two-thirds of the Moslem population worked as peasants.[20]

There was a clear economic division between the agrarian peasant class, or *fellaheen*, and the landowning class, or *effendis*. The *fellaheen* were farmers of Palestine under a semifeudal system of land ownership surviving during Ottoman rule from earlier periods. Land was usually owned by the elite class of

[20] Porath, *Palestinian-Arab National Movement*, p. 19.

absentee landlords and farmed by the tenant-farmers. The *fellaheen* farmed the land within the framework of the *Mesha'a*, an Islamic community land organization code, which encouraged joint agrarian responsibility. The *fellaheen* were those most affected by kibbutz land colonization, since Jewish ownership of the land inevitably meant an end to Arab tenant-farming. By the time of the 1936 Palestinian-Arab strikes, the *fel-*

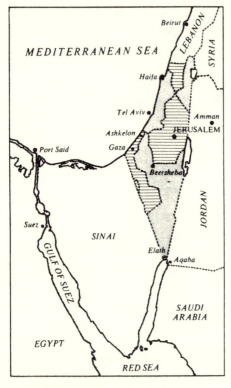

MAP 1. United Nations Partition Plan for Israel

▨ ISRAEL
under 1947 UN partition plan.

☰ Palestinian Arab State
proposed in 1947 UN partition plan.

laheen had become the hardcore of the nationalist resistance movement.

YISHUV INSTITUTIONS

Before the Mandate period, Jewish settlement was limited in Palestine; it grew only from 24,000 in 1822 to 60,000 in 1917.[21] Jews were primarily settled in the large towns of Jerusalem, Tiberias, and Safed. At the turn of the century, motivated by Zionist considerations, Jews began settling in rural areas. The principal Jewish rural communities prior to the Mandate period were colonies privately financed by Baron de Rothschild and Rishon le-Zion and started by the BILU pioneers.[22] Ottoman law made it difficult for non-Ottoman subjects to own land, and Jewish buyers were often represented in land deals by Arab or Sephardic-Jewish agents.

With the establishment of the British Mandate and its support for the Balfour Declaration that encouraged Jewish immigration and land settlement, the Jewish population in Palestine sharply rose and was accompanied by significant gains in Jewish rural land ownership (see Tables 3 and 4). Efforts to secure a Jewish state in Palestine were coordinated through three major Zionist institutions, the Jewish Agency, the Histadrut, and the Jewish National Fund. Each of these institutions and their subsidiaries played a critical role in the development of the kibbutz.

The institutions setting the policies for the developing national homeland in Palestine were divided into two cooperating sectors. The Yishuv society had its own National Council that focused on social welfare and educational and health needs. This internal government was linked with the Jewish Agency,

[21] Esco Foundation, *Jewish, Arab, and British Policies*, vol. 1.

[22] BILU are the Hebrew initials of the phrase, Beth Yaakov Lechon Vehelechu ("House of Jacob arise and let us go"). It was the name of an early Jewish pioneer group.

TABLE 3. Real Property in Jewish Hands in Palestine.

Year	In Jewish Ownership (dunams)	In J.N.F. Ownership	% of J.N.F. in Jewish Ownership
1914	418,100	16,400	4
1922	557,000	77,400	13
1927	864,700	196,700	23
1932	1,007,500	296,900	29
1936 (March)	1,231,800	364,700	30
1939 (Sept.)	1,356,200	471,100	35

SOURCE: Abraham Granovsky, *Land Policy in Palestine* (New York: Bloch Publishing Co., Inc., 1940), p. 91.

TABLE 4. Percentage of Rural Jewish Population in Total Jewish Population.

Year	Total No. of Jews	Jewish Pop. in Rural Areas	% of Rural Pop. in Total Jewish Population
Oct. 1922	83,790	15,170	18
Dec. 1927	148,000	30,500	20.6
Nov. 1931	174,600	42,200	24
Dec. 1934	300,000	72,000	24
Dec. 1936	404,000	96,829	24
June 1939	460,000	125,000	27

SOURCE: Abraham Granovsky, *Land Policy in Palestine* (New York: Bloch Publishing Co., Inc., 1940), p. 11.

regarded by the British as the major Jewish public body. In this way, the Yishuv community and the international Jewish community were joined in their Zionist goals.

The internal politics of the Jewish Agency largely shaped the dynamics of the Yishuv community and the eventual Jewish state. Within the Yishuv, the population voted for a National Council which sent representatives to the biannual Zionist Congress and the General Council which met every six months. Rather than vote for specific candidates, Yishuv constituents voted for party lists. In the Mandate period, the Yishuv political parties represented the various perspectives prevalent in the world Zionist organizations. They included capitalist and socialist, religious and nonreligious, and binationalist and revisionist platforms. By the mid-1930s, the Labor Party, known as Mapai, became the dominant political force in the agency and in the Yishuv. Originating from the merger of the Poale Zion and left-Zionist groups, the Mapai Party continues today to be the single most powerful political party in the Knesset.

Kibbutzniks' party affiliations depended upon their kibbutz federation membership. In the 1920s three major kibbutz federations were formed reflecting different interpretations of kibbutz functions and development.[23] Each federation, in turn, was closely affiliated with a particular national political party. Kibbutz Hameuchad, which emphasized large kibbutz groups, affiliated with Ahdut Ha-avoda; Kibbutz Artzi Hashomer Hatzair, the Socialist-Marxist Federation, associated with the Mapam; and the Hever Hakvutzot (later Ichud Hakvutzot V'Hakibbutzim), which stressed small-family groups, affiliated with Mapai. Each of these parties originally stood left of center in the Zionist political spectrum. Although an individual member of a kibbutz was free to vote for any party, the choice usually coincided with the kibbutz's federation affiliation.

The Histadrut was founded in 1920, with its principal goal the transformation of middle-class Jewish immigrants into an organized working class. It was a fusion of the two Socialist-Zionist parties, Poale Zion and Hapoel Hatzair, and combined the socialist tendencies of the first with the national emphases

[23] For a history of the kibbutz federations see Harry Viteles, *A History of the Cooperative Movement in Israel*, vols. 2 and 3 (London: Vallentine, Mitchell & Co. Ltd., 1967).

of the latter.[24] Its intentions were to create jobs for Jewish workers in Palestine, to develop the Yishuv economy, and to promote Jewish immigration based upon productive labor. The Histadrut represented the synthesis of Socialist-Zionist ideology and political pragmatism. David Ben-Gurion was elected General Secretary at its first convention.

Kibbutzniks joined as individual members but the benefits and responsibilities of membership were dealt with by the kibbutz as a group. Many of the services necessary for a viable community were provided to the kibbutz through the various Histadrut agencies. In turn, the kibbutz movement provided the Histadrut with many of its leaders and workers. The hope to build a Jewish state on the basis of Socialist-Zionism united the Histadrut and the kibbutz.

The Jewish National Fund, operating under the political auspices of the Jewish Agency, was the land trust of the Zionist movement. From 1922 to 1939 its holdings rose from 77,400 *dunams* (one *dunam* is equivalent to one-quarter acre) to 471,100 *dunams*, or from 13 percent to 35 percent of Jewish-owned land in Palestine. All kibbutzim were settled on land of the Jewish National Fund.

As the land trust of the Zionist movement, the Jewish National Fund closely adhered to the self-labor principle and kibbutzim were expected to follow its charter. Jewish National Fund officials usually bought land indirectly from Arab *effendis* through agents. The history of the organization reflects the implementation of land settlement policies of the Zionist move-

---

[24] A recent publication, Zvi Sussman, "Wage Differentials and Equality within the Histadrut," *Massada* (1974), argues against the myth that the Histadrut's wage structure was based on egalitarianism. Sussman's research concludes that pay scales were based upon work performance and that while within individual groups such as kibbutzim pay was equalized, there was wide pay discrepancy between groups. In fact, wage disparities were perhaps larger in the Histadrut in the 1920s and 1930s than in Israel in the 1960s. Reported by Moshe Ater, editor, *Jerusalem Post*, April 14, 1975.

ment with the kibbutzim as the prime agent of actual colonization.[25]

The history of Jewish military forces in Palestine and development of the kibbutz movement were tightly interwoven.[26] The very existence of such forces in Palestine indicates both the success of Jewish nationalist efforts during the Mandate and the Mandatory's partial support for their establishment.

In the first days of the kibbutz, Hashomer, or the watchmen, was organized as a nationwide group of volunteers ready to defend Jewish settlements, especially in isolated areas. From 1921 to 1929 as Jewish colonization efforts increased so did the intensity of Arab-Jewish conflict. Jewish settlers came to rely upon their own militia, the Haganah, or the Jewish defense force, established in 1921. The Haganah's membership during this period included persons of the third and fourth *aliyah*, or immigration groups, who had had paramilitary training in Europe for defense against pogroms.

Yigal Allon, both an Israeli military hero and statesman, explains the interlocking military, economic, and political functions of kibbutz settlement in the Yishuv and how these functions determined its character as a pioneer outpost:

The planning and development of pioneering Zionist settlements were from the start at least partly determined by the politico-strategic needs. The choice of the location of the settlements, for instance, was influenced not only by considerations of economic viability but also and even chiefly by the needs of local defense, overall settlement strategy (which aimed at ensuring a Jewish political presence in all parts of the country), and by the role such blocks of settlements might play in some future, perhaps decisive in all out struggle. Accordingly, land was purchased, or more often reclaimed, in remote parts of the country. The settlements—ordi-

[25] For a history of the Jewish National Fund see Arthur Ruppin, *Three Decades of Palestine* (New York: Schocken Books, 1936).

[26] Yigal Allon, *The Making of Israel's Army* (London: Sphere Books Ltd., 1971), presents a revealing history of the Haganah.

nary villages, kibbutzim and moshavim—thus came to be isolated from one another by geographic distances, topographic barriers and demographic differences, not to speak of political obstacles created by the Mandatory regime. Consequently, every Jewish settlement had to be also a Haganah fortress.[27]

The growth of kibbutz settlements from 11 in 1920 to 28 in 1929 with a total population of 2,690 reflected the increased push for Jewish colonization during the period. As the political-military situation became more tense in the 1930s, a concerted kibbutz settlement operation known as the Tower and Stockade movement was put into effect to secure Zionist claims in Palestine. The program bore this name because the settlements were built in one day and featured a watchtower and stockade.

The Birth of Kibbutz Har

The northern border had been the scene of continual military activity during Mandate years. A barbed wire barrier, several feet thick had been built along this border from the Mediterranean to Jordan. Known as the Tegard Wall after its inventor, it had not been able to keep out the guerrilla units. A decision was made by the Yishuv leaders to build a settlement on the upper Galilee border as part of the Tower and Stockade program.

This settlement, which became Kibbutz Har, was set up in the spring of 1938 and populated as a community in the fall of the same year. Its birth occurred at the height of conflict in Palestine.

[27] Ibid., pp. 18-19.

CHAPTER ONE

The First Years

When travelling to Kibbutz Har, one realizes it is an outpost. The kibbutz is marked by its distance from the nation's city centers and its position atop a rocky mountain range that straddles the northern Israeli-Lebanese border near the Mediterranean Sea in the Western Galilee. Haifa, a city of 250,000, is 50 kilometers away. Nahariya, a resort town 12 kilometers away, has a population of 35,000.

The sense of geographic separation and self-containment is furthered by the winding, steep road bringing travellers from the main roadway to Har and the difficulty of reaching it by public transportation. The only efficient way of getting to the kibbutz is by private car or by arrangement with the community's own transport schedule. Public transportation is by bus and the schedule is very limited during daytime and non-existent after dark. The one-hour car drive from Haifa can take 3 to 4 hours more by bus. In addition, the bus usually leaves the rider at the base of the mountain road. Getting a ride up to the kibbutz depends upon one's fortunes hitch-hiking.

On entering the kibbutz, one has a panoramic view of the sea to the west, the plain to the south, Lebanese villages to the north and the extending mountain range to the east. Because of the sparseness of greenery in the rest of the country, the lushness of evergreen forestation and foliage growth is surprising. An average of 60 rainy days a year more than doubles that of the Negev desert area. Temperature ranges of 40 to 60 degrees Fahrenheit in January and 70 to 90 degrees Fahrenheit in August resemble those of the southern United States and California. Har's rural character is particularly evident during the rainy season lasting from November through February when constant precipitation turns pathways into muddy streams.

A circular pattern of building, initiated in prestate days, has been continued until the present period. Surrounding the center tower are the principal communal buildings: the main dining hall, the laundry, the community store, administrative offices, and utility operations. One and two-story housing units radiate from this center to the borders of the community. Small gardens frame each of the units and a network of paved and unpaved paths connect the entire community. There is a feeling of balance between the carefully designed buildings and the ruggedness of the mountains.

When Har was originally founded, the attempts to develop an agrarian economy were limited by the area of its hilltop position. Since statehood, however, the kibbutz has extended its farming to the fields lying in the plain approximately a twenty-minute drive from the kibbutz center. The geographic separation is unusual for a kibbutz and necessitates a well-arranged transport schedule for those members who commute daily to the fields.

Although Har receives more rainfall than most other locations in Israel, its agriculture is still dependent upon irrigation systems. Every effort is made to conserve water that is nationally regulated and shared with other kibbutzim having adjacent fields. The irrigation system together with straight rows of crops and orchards give the plain a very well-tended appearance.

The military-strategic character of the kibbutz is also apparent. Trenches line certain areas and bomb shelter entrances stand nearby all major buildings. A large communal shelter was built under the newly expanded dining hall during the 1970s. Atop the original tower structure stands an electric menorah, a candelabrum that is a symbol of the border kibbutzim. At night, the menorah lights of Har and other kibbutzim in the neighboring plain create a silent message of kibbutz unity and strength.

Since the establishment of Kibbutz Har in 1938, the settlement has faced the paradox of being geographically isolated and yet an integral and important part of the Zionist colonial movement. The experiences of isolation and interpenetrations has affected each community member and the development of the kibbutz as a whole.

Because of its border and mountaintop position in the midst of an all-Arab region, Har's initial significance was as a military outpost. Its role as a border fortress limited its ability to serve as a model for agrarian socialism in the region. Before the foundation of the State of Israel in 1948, the kibbutz was not able to farm land in the adjacent plains. Agricultural was restricted to the mountaintop locale and the achievement of economic viability was difficult. While the kibbutz successfully fulfilled its military-strategic role as directed by national Yishuv institutions, its economic situation by 1948 was precarious.

The community's primary role as a military outpost also influenced its social development. The original settlers were young men, all single, identifying themselves as pioneering soldiers. They held ideological attachments to Socialist-Zionism and had immigrated to Palestine via political youth groups and kibbutz federation networks. The entrance of women and families into the social structure of Har did not occur until after the first settlement battles had been won. During the entire prestate period, the continual existence of external military threat created an internal cohesive environment. It was not until military priorities were overshadowed by economic developments, especially the increasing division of labor due to industrialization, that social stratification marked kibbutz social reality.

Thus, during its first decade the kibbutz was primarily concerned with military security and issues of political economy: How would Har survive within a hostile environment? How would vital resources be guaranteed and developed? In what

ways would Socialist-Zionist ideals be realized? The response
to these issues reflects the interconnection between Har's internal organization, national Yishuv institutions, and the political realities of military threat. By specifically examining the
interconnections, we can see how the activities of the Yishuv
institutions—the Jewish Agency, the Jewish National Fund,
and the Haganah—related to internal community stratification
and economic development.

Military Significance

The colonizing plans for Kibbutz Har reflect political-military
factors in the national Tower and Stockade movement. Prior to
1936 Yishuv settlement efforts stressed economic development.
In fact, in 1929, when the land of Khirbat Hanoutab (later Har)
was offered to Yishuv officials, the offer was refused because
they did not think that security could be maintined in that
region. Moreover, they had little experience with mountain outposts. After that date, Yishuv leaders recognized that the British would eventually divide Palestine between Jews and Arabs
according to population concentrations of these two contending
groups. The population of the Western Galilee region was primarily Arab and had not yet been targeted for Jewish settlements as is reported in the *Igeret Hashayahu Bakibbutz*: "According to the discussions of the Royal Commission [the Peel
Commission] the Western Galilee was to be given to the Arabs.
The function of the land laws issued by the British Government
which denied its commitments of the Balfour Declaration, was
to narrow Jewish penetration to additional areas."[1] Yishuv officials, therefore, decided that the establishment of Jewish settlements in the Western Galilee were imperative if there was to

[1] *Igeret Hashayahu Bakibbutz*, 1 February 1962, p. 32. This issue was
published as a joint venture by the three main kibbutz federations commem-
orating the Tower and Stockade movement.

be a Jewish claim to that area of Palestine. Kibbutz Har became the object of Jewish conquest and settlement in that region; its purchase and settlement became, after 1937, the major national colonizing event in Palestine.

A review of the actual land purchase of Har sheds light on the controversies surrounding settlement of the kibbutz and shows how Yishuv colonizing policies were finally reconciled. The Jewish National Fund's caution conflicted with the policy of the Jewish Agency. This internal Yishuv policy dispute occurred as opposition by local Arabs to all Jewish settlements was steadily increasing.

Both Chaim Weizmann and David Ben-Gurion, representing the Jewish Agency, recommended Jewish settlement in the upper Western Galilee to correspond to the international border. Ben-Gurion stated, "if there are between four to five Jewish settlements on the frontier this will reinforce our rights on the upper Galilee."[2] Abraham Ussiskin, head of the Jewish National Fund, was a pragmatist who was not certain Jewish colonies could be successfully established along the Lebanese border. He had steadfastly refused to purchase land in mountain areas.

The conflict over Har's land purchase between the Jewish National Fund and Jewish Agency was finally settled in 1938 by the intervention of Joseph Fein. Fein, born in Metualla, was well acquainted with the Galilee region and knew many local Arab inhabitants. He recognized that the border Galilee area was one of the "principal passages for entering and leaving Palestine."[3] It had been a main thoroughfare from Syria to

---

[2] Zionist Archives S/25/2810 (Jerusalem), cited an unpublished report in French, "Har [pseudonym] 1938-1962" given to the author by a member of Har. The report, referred to hereafter as the French Report, is an ethnography written by a French student during her stay at Har. It presents an excellent history of the kibbutz that was of great benefit to this study. The French Report now has a home in the archives of Kibbutz Har.

[3] "Joseph Fein's Journal," Har Archives.

Haifa and was now on the crossroads of Arab raiding bands. In addition, he felt that settlement of a Jewish colony in the region was of political significance. Because of his excellent relations with both the Jewish National Fund and agency officials, he was able to effect an agreement for the purchase of land for Har.

The Jewish Agency put into motion its "psychological strategy" for insuring the maximum level of cooperation from Arab officials. First, the agency developed reciprocal ties with the Christian Arabs who had traditionally had tense relations with the Sunnite Moslems of the area. Next, as a diplomatic move, the agency informed Abdullah of Transjordan of its proposed settlement intentions. Finally, and perhaps most significantly, a communication was sent to the Lebanese government from the agency stating plans for Har and expressing the hope for future relations of mutual respect and peace.[4]

All of these actions demonstrate the function of the Jewish Agency in the Yishuv. It acted as if it were a government of an independent state, equal to other governments with political and diplomatic functions. During the 1930s, its political efforts were aimed at securing an environment conducive for its colonizing activities. The Har experience demonstrated a measure of the Jewish Agency's success in dealing with ruling neighbor governments, but Har's creation did not result in a lessening of local Arab resentment. During the negotiations internal conflict arose between Yishuv institutions because of the tense atmosphere surrounding the sale of Arab land to Jews. The case of Har aroused particular fear and resentment among Arabs because it marked the first time a settlement was planned "at the heart of a hostile Arab community."[5] In such an environment, the Jewish National Fund chose to operate in secrecy,

---

[4] Cited in the French Report: from *J.N.F. Dossier 2956*, Zionist Archives, Jerusalem.

[5] *Igeret Hashayahu*, p. 32.

finding an Arab agent to represent it to the Arab *effendi*, or seller.[6]

An incident concerning the land purchase specifically indicates the extent of the antagonism between the policy of Jewish colonization of the Zionist institutions and the sentiments of the indigenous population. It involves the role played by a Jewish National Fund representative, Joseph Sinigaglia. With the Weinshall brothers, Sinigaglia agreed to offer a loan to the Jewish National Fund to help purchase Har. When he came on an inspection visit to the future kibbutz site, the Arab land agent, Abyad, started a rumor to conceal the transaction. The rumor, based on the Italian sound of Sinigaglia's name, presented Sinigaglia as a representative of the Catholic Church who wanted to purchase the land to establish a monastery. When the truth became known, the Arab agent was tried and killed by a guerrilla band of Arab nationalists.[7] The agent, as a servant of both Arab absentee landlords and Zionist agencies, represented the interests of two enemies of the local Arabs.

The relationship between the agency and the British over Har was also marked by tension. After the 1936-1939 period of turmoil, the British demanded that all future Jewish colonizing efforts be announced in advance. They hoped they would be able to stop Jewish settlement by declaring that the security of the colonies could not be guaranteed. The British wanted to maintain order in Palestine and realized that escalation of Jewish settlements, particularly in all-Arab regions, would fuel rising hostilities.

The Jewish Agency had already implemented a policy of disregarding the British demand when it created the kibbutzim of Kfar Ruppin and Nevetan. Wishing to enlist whatever cooper-

[6] Cited in the French Report: letter from Weitz to an official of the Jewish National Fund, from *J.N.F. Dossier 1198*, Zionist Archives, Jerusalem.

[7] Ben Zion Dinur, ed., *Toldot Ha-Haganah (The History of the Haganah)*, in Har Archives, p. 879.

ation possible, the agency sent a Haganah representative to meet with the British police at Safed for the purpose of requesting military protection for the establishment of Har. The British replied that Har's settlement should wait until conditions in Palestine were more calm.

During the months leading up to a proposed March 1939 settlement, the Jewish Agency had already worked out its conflict with the Jewish National Fund and made financial arrangements for purchasing the land. In joint coordination with other Yishuv institutions it had prepared volunteers and material resources for Har's establishment. The land deed, dated 3 February 1938, registered the purchase by the Jewish National Fund and Joseph Sinigaglia of 25/40 and 15/40 shares respectively of the land sold by Assad Daoud Zoroub through his agent, Aamil Abyad. Five thousand Palestinian pounds were paid for the thirty-six plots of Miri land that included Har and Ein Hur.[8]

Beside the actual land purchase, the agency's organizational activities for Har's settlement included the gathering of people and materials. The Jewish Agency's funds were very limited and three of its leaders, Ben-Gurion, Sharett, and Weizmann, personally solicited financial support for Har's establishment. A combination of Yishuv organizational coordination and direct help from the Diaspora resulted in final preparation for the actual settlement. The agency supervised political action; the Jewish National Fund, the financial administration, and the Haganah, the military security. Roadbuilding, like other external difficulties, helped to create closer ties between Jewish feuding factions. A road was needed to join Har to the main Basa-Kedesh road since the three hundred meters separating Har from the main road were still held by Arabs. The agency and

---

[8] *Miri* lands, or statelands, is one of the land categories of the Islamic land system. For an explanation of the value of the Palestinian pound see Appendix One.

the Jewish National Fund decided to push jointly for the road's eventual construction. The original tension and controversy between Yishuv institutions regarding Jewish settlement in the Western Galilee region thus was resolved.

THE HAGANAH

Once tensions were overcome, the plans for securing Har as a Jewish outpost were developed and implemented by the Tower and Stockade movement of the Haganah. As Rami Don, a member of Har, states, "it was the first time that the Haganah moved towards a genuine mobilization for an extended period; before it was content to mobilize for several days and no longer."[9] For the Haganah the settlement of Har also reflected a change in policy and practice from defensive operations toward a more active offensive posture.

Organized in response to the increasing Arab opposition to Jewish colonization in Palestine, the Haganah operated as the semisecret militia and was the forerunner of the Israeli Defense Force. Its policies were directed toward "the end that we [the Haganah] should one day become a foundation for an effective defense force of a free and sovereign people."[10]

Until the 1936 outbreak of hostility and the resultant Tower and Stockade movement, the Haganah's policies were *haganah*, or self-defense, and *havlagah*, or self-restraint. The first concept meant Jews would defend themselves from attacks, using arms when necessary. The second referred to a refusal to permit indiscriminate reprisals against Arabs or to be provoked into mindless counterattacks.

The 1930s marked a change in the political atmosphere in Palestine and a transformation of Haganah policies. The attitude of the leadership shifted from adherence to a slow evolu-

[9] From a conversation with Rami Don as reported in the French Report.

[10] Munya M. Mardor, *Haganah* (New York: New American Library, 1964), p. xviii.

tionary pragmatic strategy to militancy. In fact, political Zionism was redefined as an ethos of "the state on the way." As the Yishuv institutions assumed more of the functions of an independent government, the state on the way began to emerge and the militancy within the Yishuv community became more accepted. The switch of control from Weizmann, who preferred the evolutionary strategy, to Ben-Gurion, who backed militancy, indicated a political change within the Zionist organization.[11] And the new atmosphere of militancy fostered a Haganah shift from a defensive to an offensive posture. As Munya Mardor, Yishuv commentator, reports:

> It became equally obvious that passive defense alone from within the "stockade" was not enough to deter the attacker or halt the growth of terror. . . . The Haganah would have to take matters into its own hands and move outside the "stockade." It would have to carry its defensive operations beyond the limits of the Jewish settlements into the strongholds of the assailants. . . . the realization grew that a strategy of simple defense could have no permanent effect and might even be taken by the Arabs as evidence of a lack of confidence in our defense forces.[12]

New tactics required intense training, more refined planning, and the acquisition of better armaments. The movement away from voluntarism as the primary mode of activism was another indication of the movement toward the institutionalization of a shadow nation-state.

Har's settlement provided the Haganah with a golden opportunity to put the new strategy into practice: from its mountaintop, the site of Har had a commanding and spectacular view and offered an excellent strategic stronghold. In cooperation with the Jewish Agency and Jewish National Fund, the Ha-

---

[11] An interesting discussion of the differences between Ben-Gurion and the revisionists appears in Jay Gonen, *A Psychohistory of Zionism* (London: Mason-Charter, 1975).

[12] Mardor, *Haganah*, p. 4.

ganah planned the settlement of Har to proceed in two stages. A Haganah camp would first be fortified halfway up the mountain and only after military conditions permitted would an actual agricultural settlement be established on top of the mountain, which was then inhabited by Arab bedouins.

Despite supposed secrecy of the operation, volunteers from the Haganah, kibbutz federations, worldwide Zionist youth groups, and local Yishuv residents far exceeded the demand. The plan called for ninety volunteers, who would undergo military training camp and then a year's service fortifying Har. Moshe Bet, an early Har member recalls: "At that time it was important for everbody to be at Har—in the Haganah or later in the settlement."[13] This can be explained by the heroic purpose the operation symbolized at that time: the conquest of a mountain in the midst of an Arab region; a joint, year-long planned effort by the chief Zionist, Yishuv institutions; a high risk venture in the name of building the future Jewish state. It is no suprise that the event inspired poems and songs that became known throughout the entire Zionist world and even served as the plot for an opera (see Appendix Two).[14]

A sense of unity contributed to the enthusiasm for the operation. The choice of a group to carry out the conquest was given great attention, not only among the cooperating national institutions but throughout the Yishuv and Diaspora. The final ninety-person force represented the major political factions of the Zionist organizations, and each kibbutz federation was allowed an equal number of delegates.

THE *Aliyah* TO HAR

The volunteers were supplemented by a force of four hundred men organized by the Haganah. This force included

[13] Fieldwork interview with Moshe Bet, 28 June 1975.
[14] There were poems and songs by J. Urland, S. Shalom, and Abraham Levinson; an opera was composed by Max Brod.

110 members of the Mobile Squads, a part of the Jewish Settlement Police known as the M.G.'s who were the most active
and experienced Haganah units. At the time each bloc of Jewish settlements was assigned a Mobile Squad unit, its size
being determined by local needs. Mobile Squad tactics were
"to prevent attack and any form of terrorist activity against the
Jewish settlements or vehicles and to serve as immediate re-
inforcements in case of attack."[15] As part of the Jewish Settlement Police, these units were under the joint command of both
the British authorities and the Haganah.

A history of the Haganah in referring to the heroic Har *aliyah*, or migration, states that the entire conquest group was led
by Yitzhak Sadeh and two young deputies, Yigal Allon and
Moshe Dayan. The presence of three key Haganah leaders in
the operation is another indication of the significance of the
event.

The ninety elect volunteers were assembled at Kiryat Haim
Kibbutz near Haifa to receive intensive training and to become
organized into an effective military unit. As training progressed
it became clear that the British would not give approval for
Har's establishment and concern was felt that the large camp
would attract British and Arab suspicion. Restlessness began
to pervade the camp and the decision was made to disband if
an expected order to initiate the *aliyah* was not forthcoming.
At this moment Weizmann, having secured the funds necessary
for Har's establishment, sent the anxiously awaited telegram:
"Go to Har regardless of the cost."[16] Jews, he went on, would
take the risk of Har's establishment no matter what the British
did; each man, woman and child would fight for survival in
Palestine. March 21 was chosen for *aliyah*.

Before dawn on March 21, the convoys of trucks carrying

[15] Shabtain Teveth, *Moshe Dayan* (Jerusalem: Weidenfeld and Nicolson,
1972), p. 95.
[16] Har Archives.

men and materials reached the base of the mountain. From there, all materials had to be carried on camels, donkeys, and people's backs up to the lower base of Har: "Young and old, united in spirit, began the shuttle from the road to Har, sacks on the back, guns in belts. While groups continued to go up and down, others began digging trenches, and raising tents. Night fell, most volunteers returned home, ninety remained to guard Har."[17] A contingent of workers from Solel Boneh, the Histadrut's public works company, began building a road from Basa to Har and laying a waterpipe. An airplane made reconnaissance flights.

Accounts of the *aliyah* note the "stupification" of the local Arab residents at so much *aliyah* activity. But if the Arabs were in a stupor, it was quite brief, for by midnight they undertook their first attack on Har. Attributed to the Quassmite nationalists, the attack resulted in the death of two Jews and six Arabs, with others wounded.[18] While the first attack was repulsed, it was only the beginning of a series of attacks during the first months. The local Arab population continued their resistance to the Jewish settlement of the area, but their efforts lacked both resources and coordination necessary to resist the well-organized Zionist movement.

The period of Haganah fortification of Har not only left its imprint on the kibbutz, but deeply affected Haganah's future strategy. A major influence on the new strategy was the forceful example set by Orde Wingate at Har.

Orde Wingate, a Scottish Artillery Captain, arrived in Palestine in September 1936 to organize the defense of oil pipelines of the Iraq Petroleum Company, which passed through

---

[17] Interview with Chaim in the French Report.

[18] Fieldwork interview with Micah Lebon during the author's first stay in Har during 1970. Anne Lesch in *The Politics of Palestinian Nationalism* (Berkeley: University of California Press, 1973), p. 33, describes the Quassamites as revolutionary cells of Palestinian-Arab nationalism that were begun by Shaykh Izz al-Din al-Quassam before 1929.

the Galilee on its way to the port of Haifa.[19] As part of this task, Wingate undertook a survey of the organization and methods of Arab guerrilla forces. His work gained him the full confidence of the Haganah leadership and he, in turn, became an ardent supporter of Zionism. Wingate was very impressed with the Tower and Stockade movement and set up one of his principal training camps at Har. After his arrival at the settlement, Wingate questioned the lack of military operations beyond the fortification's perimeters. He commented that fences were useless unless one "goes out and meets the enemy." Utilizing his authority to conduct survey work, Wingate began leading Har patrols across the border into Lebanon.

In June 1938, Wingate submitted a memorandum to his British commanding officers on "the possibility of night movements by armed forces of the Crown with the aim of putting an end to the terror in North Palestine."[20] This proposal to set up the Special Night Squad was approved and Wingate trained and led the squad. Three squads were formed, with the first headed by Wingate consisting of 18 British soldiers and 24 Haganah men, mostly from Har. The duty of the squads was to defend the oil pipeline and its surrounding environment. By putting into effect Wingate's notion that the Special Night Squad was the best night fighters and the Arabs were afraid of the night, the Special Night Squad carried out surprise night raids on Arab guerrilla forces and suspected village hideaways. The squads became elite combat units and Wingate's exploits became the basis of a great many legends throughout the Yishuv. From then on, the Haganah's leaders, Sadeh, Dayan, Allon (who later became commanders of the Israeli Defense Force)

---

[19] Background on British and other government and corporate interests in the Iraq Petroleum Company is given in *Memorandum* submitted to the Special Session of the General Assembly of the United Nations, April 1948, by the National Associates, New York, including "The British Record on Partition."

[20] Teveth, *Moshe Dayan*, p. 99.

used a strategy of retaliatory raids that fundamentally changed the strategy underlying the defense of kibbutz settlements and other Yishuv communities.

Wingate's personal presence at Har had a strong effect, producing such confidence in its military security that Har's first leader, Joseph Fein, suggested that no one was afraid anymore. Military operations involving factors of secrecy and surprise were increasingly carried out, and the continued battles of the first weeks diminished.

The Tower and Stockade plan called for the completed construction of a fortified square camp of 35 by 35 meters, surrounded by a wall and barbed wire, circling the center Searchlight Tower to be constructed before settlement began. Construction was not finished before the first stage of the Har *aliyah*. On the night of the first attack, the wall was not completed around the tower and tents. A completion of the physical plan, which greatly resembled American frontier settlements, did not occur until the move was made to the top of the mountain. The original date for the transfer was set for March 1939, one year after the *aliyah*. An immediate change of plans occurred when it was learned that a group of Arabs were planning to join the Arab farmers who had been living on the mountaintop in order to strengthen the Arab case of ownership.

Joseph Fein, the leader of Har, had been negotiating with the Arab farmers. He offered them compensation for their homes. They refused even as the news that others would join them reached the lower base from a Jewish guard stationed in their midst. Within a few hours, a decision was made to occupy the top immediately. A squad, later augmented by a Wingate unit, went to the top and demanded that the Arabs leave. After taking over the Arabs' stone house, it repulsed an Arab attack and within a week constructed the beginnings of a Tower and Stockade kibbutz. The lower camp continued to serve as a Haganah training post. And by September, the first group of *ha-*

varim, or kibbutz members, had arrived to take over from the volunteer guards and to construct a stable settlement to guard the frontier. But the *aliyah* to Har with the seven-month presence of the Haganah left an important mark on both the kibbutz and the Haganah. The kibbutz reaped the benefits and paid the price of achieving an heroic image, and the Haganah became more sophisticated in its offensive operations.

Social Structure

The enormous task of creating viable social structures to sustain a developing community confronted the first permanent settlers of Har. Geographically isolated from other Yishuv communities due to its function as a military outpost, Kibbutz Har was nonetheless tied to Jewish national political and economic institutions. These organizations had a significant impact on the shaping of Har's internal social structure.

Beginning as a military outpost, Har was initially composed of young adult members who had either immigrated as part of Diaspora youth groups or come to Har from Yishuv communities. Difficulties arose between Sabra and non-Sabra groups with separate, often clashing cultural backgrounds. These difficulties emerged and were resolved in the context of a "community on the way"; Har in its first years was not yet a fullfledged community, since its youthful population lacked family and institutional structures.

The first decade can be viewed as a transition period from an intimate, soldier-pioneer *kvutza*, or settlement, to a larger, more complex community. In moving from a differentiated, one-generation group to a multigenerational, multicultural community, Har gained stability, but also faced new questions of scale, stratification, and loss of intimacy. During this process, a significant change occurred regarding members' kibbutz identification. At first the kibbutz was personalized; it was spoken of in terms of "we are the kibbutz." By the end of the 1940s the kibbutz became an external object. Members began speaking of the kibbutz as an entity outside themselves: "the kibbutz does this or does not do that." This change is partially explained by the increasing stratification within the community that set members apart from each other despite the overall sense of solidarity manifesting itself in participation in communal activities.

The stratification, demonstrated by cultural group segregation, the formation of leadership elites, and the development of occupational and social hierarchy, reflected the community's response to changing material conditions. However, the community has continually been able to maintain a level of solidarity necessary to continue its economic, social, political, and security functions for its members.

The articulation of Har's social structure began with conflict among the first settlement, or *garin*, groups. Although sharing a similar Socialist-Zionist perspective, wide differences in the backgrounds of the groups impeded immediate mutual acceptance; their ideological agreement was not sufficient to create trust in each other. In September 1938 the first settlers, from Shimron, arrived. The group was a successful fusion of two *garin* sections, the Sabras from Nahalal, a moshav, and a group, originally from Germany, who had already been in Palestine a number of years.[21] Erin, still a Har resident, was a member of the latter section and his background is typical of others in that group. He came to Palestine in 1934 and attended the Mikva-Israel agricultural school.[22] Once he sup-

[21] Nahalal was the first moshav, or cooperative family-centered settlement, formed by dissenting members of the first kibbutz Degania. Shmuel Dayan, one of Nahalal's founding members provides a personal history of the moshav's beginning in his autobiography.

[22] Mikva-Israel was founded as the Jewish Agricultural Training School in 1870 by the Alliance Israelite Universelle of Paris. It was a center of agricultural training for immigrants during the Mandate period.

ported the political right, but contact with the Ha Noar Ha
Oved, or the Young Workers—a Histadrut-sponsored youth
movement—moved him toward the kibbutz movement. Young
Germans, like Erin, from the school groups joined together to
form a *garin* group. The group tested commitment to nationalist
goals: each member had to renounce his or her studies and
spend years of preparation at Kibbutz Degania.

The group of thirty who completed their studies eventually
joined the youth of Nahalal who previously had rejected the
moshav in favor of the "purity" of the kibbutz. Some of the
Nahalal members were volunteers for Har's *aliyah*, so a tie
between Shimron and Har existed. Though they began working
at Kibbutz Shimron, they wanted a more "heroic" experience.
About fifty of them moved to Har in September and replaced
a similar number of guards.

The German members of the Shimron group had been
quickly able to integrate with the Sabras since they had been
in Palestine for a while and, more importantly, knew Hebrew.
The knowledge of Hebrew was a crucial factor in separating
Sabras or those "sabratised" from other groups. Union between
Shimron sections was also made easier as each group respected
unique aspects of the other; those of German origin recognized
the prestige of Palestinian birth and the Sabras respected the
intellectual achievements of those from Germany. The integration of the sections was further assured by their joint desire to
"fight on the front line."

The conflict between the Shimron group and the second
garin group, Garin Segev, was harder to overcome. The Segev
garin came from the Gordonia youth movement united in a
religious quest for a new society in a Jewish homeland in Palestine. After arrival from Roumania, they studied agriculture
in Degania and they prepared for Har. At Har they were seen
as a separate *kvutza*, or organic group, from the Shimron
kvutza; each spoke its own language and had its own culture.

The clash over language that developed indicates the generally superior attitude of Sabra groups toward non-Hebrew speakers and reveals what Spiro has termed, "the anti-Semitic component of Zionism."[23] He suggests that the Zionist movement rejected the culture of the ghetto, which included stereotypes of Jewish behavior and physical appearance, as well as the Yiddish language. The rejection of ghetto life has been utilized to explain the insistence of the kibbutz using communal structures to perform functions usually ascribed to traditional family units. In any case, the Shimron group of Har clearly did not welcome the Segev *garin* members enthusiastically.

The tense daily atmosphere of the first months was evidenced in a continuing series of hostile incidents. In the dining room the Sabras mocked those knowing no Hebrew. This resulted in the refusal of the new Roumanian group to learn Hebrew. If a woman from the new Segev group showed interest in a Shimron member she was criticized by her group for being "Hebratised." Erin commented, "We saw many painful days. I truly believed it was the end of Har and I recall myself speaking at the *Assafa* [General Assembly] of a new anti-Semitism."[24]

A long-term result of this conflict was the emergence of the Shimron in kibbutz leadership positions. Having arrived first, they achieved leadership roles and justified their clinging to them with the rationale that they knew the language of the Jewish homeland. Only those who spoke Hebrew headed Assafa meetings and committees. The lowest work tasks were given to the new Europeans. Years later, they still monopolized the job of driving the tractors.

The conflict was resolved through the intervention of the Hever federation and federation members. The federation

[23] Melford Spiro, *Kibbutz: Venture in Utopia* (New York: Schocken Books, 1970), p. 41. See also Yehezkel Kaufman, "Anti-Semitic Stereotypes in Zionism," *Commentary* 7 (1949), 239-245.

[24] Conversation with Erin cited in the French Report.

urged mediation of difficulties, stressing the special role of
Har's settlement in the Yishuv. The Shimron group over time
became impressed by the hard work of the Segev group, which
gradually learned Hebrew. Later arriving members spoke both
Yiddish and Hebrew, and this also helped to ease the tensions.
The unifying force of nationalism and the *chalutz*, or pioneer,
spirit ultimately prevailed. The Segev group became "Hebratised."

The integration of other groups into Kibbutz Har became
easier as internal social structures were established and family
groupings developed. From 1938 to 1946 the population of Har
went from 49 to 210 (see Figure 1). The increase was due to
a number of causes: the newly absorbed *garin* groups, the birth
of children, and the arrival of dependent parents of members.

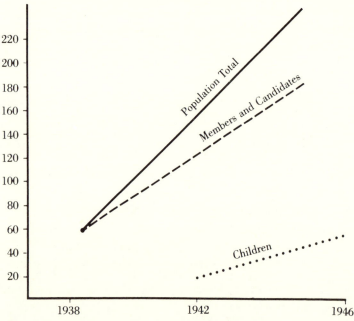

FIGURE 1. Population Increase at Har, 1938-1946

Age and sex differentiation developed in the community after the original youthful age group approached their thirties. Following the formation of couples, family units appeared and the first child was born in 1939. The formation of family units stabilized the population and precipitated the creation of more formalized community patterns and institutions. For example, a doctor arrived at Har in 1942 and an educational system was initiated in the same decade for the children. The fact that members began to bring their parents into the community was based on their recognition of Har's growing stability.

The basic socio-political framework for Har's community affairs was provided by a constitution. This document largely followed the Constitution of the Jewish Communal Villages that was a codification of the Co-operative Societies Ordinance of 1933. The constitution set forth guidelines for the objectives and purposes of the kibbutz, qualifications for membership, financial provisions, obligations of members, and administrative structures.[25] The latter included procedures for the General

---

[25] An outline of the major provisions of the Constitution follows:

1. General Assembly
   a. The supreme authority shall be vested in the General Meeting of the Society. . . .
   h. The presence of at least two thirds of the members shall be necessary for the disposal of any business. . . .
   j. Every member shall have one vote only and no member shall be entitled to appoint a proxy.
2. Management Committee
   a. The Committee of Management shall consist of not less than — members of the Kibbutz who have completed their twenty-first year [specific number left to discretion of each kibbutz].
   b. The members of the Committee shall be elected at the annual General Meeting for a period of one year. . . .
   e. Meetings of the Committee shall be held when necessary and in any case not less than every — days [specific number left to discretion of each kibbutz].
   k. The Committee shall exercise all the powers of the Kibbutz, except

Assembly (the *Assafa*); the kibbutz secretary (the *maskir*), the treasurer (the *gizbar*), and the Secretariat or Management Committee (the *maskiroot*).

In practice, the General Assembly decisions were made generally by consensus rather than voting in Har's first decade. This was due to the desire to maintain a communal atmosphere. Meetings were held each Saturday evening after dinner as they still are today and almost all members attended. In the early days most members fulfilled their communal responsibilities. The General Assembly, therefore, provided a setting that promoted community cohesion; its use of consensus eased community stratification.

Full participation varied among members depending upon extent of commitment and personal characteristics. Frequent absences indicated that a person probably intended to leave Har. Participation in public was mostly limited to those comfortable in speaking to large groups. Many members were said to be overwhelmed by the ailment of silence. Dora, a Har member, wrote in 1945: "If the comrades only knew the suffering of those who don't know how to express themselves, the ones who think and feel as they do, but lack the courage and habit to sort out and express their thought and what weighs on their

---

those reserved for the General Assembly. . . .
3. The Secretary
   a. The Committee of Management shall appoint from their number a Secretary.
   b. The Secretary shall be responsible for the conduct of the routine business of the kibbutz. . . .
4. The Treasurer
   The Committee of Management shall appoint one of their members to be Treasurer of the Kibbutz, who shall be responsible for the safe custory of all money received by the Kibbutz and for the disbursement authorized by the Committee of Management. . . . He shall produce the cash balance whenever called upon to do so by the Committee of Management of the Audit Union. . . .

hearts."[26] In a society where participation rested heavily on an individual's ability to be articulate, the less verbal members' views often remained unheard.

The daily business of Har was carried on by three main persons: the British-appointed *mukhtar*, the kibbutz-elected secretary, and the treasurer. The *mukhtar* was held responsible for maintaining relations with the British authorities. The British had previously used the *mukhtar* system in Arab villages where the village mayor was nominated by the British at the suggestion of the villagers. In the case of the kibbutzim, the British asked the members to select their own representative. Joseph Fein, the first *mukhtar* of Har, met with representatives from Arab villages, dealt with matters concerning the British, and served as the notary public for the kibbutz.

While the *mukhtar* performed duties typical of a president of government, the daily operation of the kibbutz was in the hands of the secretary and treasurer. The secretary's functions included maintaining social order, arbitrating personal disagreements, and administering daily affairs. The role thus involved administrative and interpersonal skills. The Secretariat, or Management Committee, was both an advisory and coordinating body that helped in the selection of committees dealing with various aspects of kibbutz life such as health issues, cultural affairs, and children's education.

The treasurer was the principal intermediary between the kibbutz and the Jewish Agency, Histadrut, and other financial institutions of the Yishuv. Because he needed to travel to meet with members of these institutions, he had the most frequent use of the kibbutz vehicle. He spent a good part of each week in Tel Aviv where the kibbutz kept a room for him. As the only member who regularly visited the outside world, he was expected to provide detailed descriptions of movies, concerts, or

[26] From 1945 *Har Newsletter*, Har Achives.

plays. Narrative ability thus became a criteria necessary in the choice of a treasurer. It was also the treasurer's responsibility to obtain loans, to handle purchases and cash from kibbutz sales, and to meet regularly with the Histadrut's Audit Union to review and plan the kibbutz' budget. The Audit Union provided the Histadrut, kibbutz federations, and other Yishuv institutions with a direct means of assessing the development of a kibbutz and a way of determining what types of support were necessary.[27]

Both the dining hall where community meetings were held and the living quarters reveal the intimate style of the internal administration and the general kibbutz solidarity. Dan Leon, a kibbutz sociologist, has remarked that a study of kibbutz development could be traced by focusing on the changing role of the dining hall. As the only substantial structure in the community, it served as the setting for all business, social, and cultural gatherings. Sleeping quarters in the early years were of minimal standards; they were one-room huts, often shared by a number of people. For washing there was a common shower room. A lengthy dispute arose regarding whether members could have teapots in their rooms. It was felt by some that "a teapot in every room" would destroy the communal atmosphere. The stress on the public over the private was so strong that Yaakov Gan recounted hanging red handkerchiefs on the door if privacy for sexual relations was desired. The individual was expected to respond to the needs of the group.

Aside from the teapot dispute, other critical events occurred during Har's first decade: These included conflicts over sleeping quarters for children and a decision on whether to join the British effort in World War II or remain uninvolved.[28] Both

[27] In Audit Union of the Workers' Agricultural Cooperative Societies, Ltd. also, *The Cooperative Villages of Palestine in 1938* (Tel Aviv: 1940).

[28] A questionnaire was distributed to Har's members during the author's fieldwork asking them to list, according to historical periods, events in the kibbutz's history that they thought most affected the development of the community. These events are called critical events.

conflicts, in part, reflected the economic condition of Har. The issue of children's quarters was common to the entire kibbutz movement and was related to the issue of the women's role in the kibbutz and the socialist ideological aspirations concerning the dignity of labor. The call to join the British war effort raised questions of ties to the Mandate government.

The role of women in the kibbutz and the child care structure reveal the existence of social stratification according to gender even in the community's early days. Moreover, the "masculinization" of women, without a similar male role change, reflected the norms of the greater kibbutz movement with its emphasis on a military-pioneer ethos. Contrary to the prevailing notion, communal child-care facilities were not an assumed element in the kibbutz institutional structure. In Degania, the first kibbutz, children have always slept in their parents' home, though day-time communal care is maintained. In Har's first years there were few childen, so child care was relegated to women whose jobs were defined as nurse-mother aides, *metapelet*. The strongest argument for communal child care was that it would free women to work in equality with men. This view was consistent with the Socialist-Zionist ideology of egalitarianism for the sexes. Women were given equal political rights and access to participation in community affairs. However, informal sources suggest that even from the beginning women did not participate as much as men in the General Assembly. Key leadership positions were most often held by men, with women heading those committees dealing with social, cultural, and child-rearing concerns. Yet, women superficially strived to take on men's roles. They dressed in baggy shorts, refused to wear make-up, and prided themselves on physical strength.

At the same time that women attempted to perform manual tasks, they were also expected to fulfill traditional women's roles in the domestic and service areas. Men did not attempt to perform these roles as their part of the egalitarian ideology of labor exchange. Thus, no male "feminization" balanced the

female "masculinization." By 1946, Har had forty-nine children, constituting 32 percent of its population. Women had
been busy in reproductive labor, breast-feeding, and staffing
the service branches of Har's labor force. They were the *metapelets*, cooks, ironers, and dining hall workers.

According to one woman member of Har, part of the push
for a communal child-care center originally came from the
training received in Zionist Diaspora, a youth movement that
urged women to reject the traditional roles of their mothers.
One way of achieving this would be for mothers to separate
themselves voluntarily from their children. The time saved
would enable them to cultivate their own talents. But the member noted that, from the start, mothers had ambivalent feelings
about this arrangement. Still, the children's houses were more
modern and better equipped than were the parents' barracks.

No doubt the double role placed upon women members of
Har helped cause these ambivalent feelings. While mother and
child were separated soon after birth (this was changed to a
six-week period in the mid-1950s), a mother was expected to
breast-feed the infant.[29] Since she was on call day and night
for breast-feeding, she had to be close to the children's house
at all times. Her workplace, when she gradually resumed full-
time work after the birth of the child, necessarily had to be
close by. In most kibbutzim, including Har, the fields were too
far away to be the workplace for nursing mothers. Thus, when
children were born in the community, women gave up agricultural work.

The argument that communal child-care arrangements resulted in work equalized between the men and women of the

[29] Breast-feeding was seen as part of the natural role of women and important for the child. Even in Hasomer Hatzair kibbutzim where babies were
given bottles at night, mothers breast-fed during the day. Mothers breast-fed
for at least eight months; this allowed for a great deal of contact between
mother and child. For more on nursing in the kibbutz see Bruno Bettelheim,
Children of the Dream (New York: Avon Books, 1971).

kibbutz is, therefore, not true. The communal children's houses erected by Har's members did free women to work at full-time jobs and to provide necessary services to the community. But women were expected to fulfill the role of the pioneer by doing physical labor while, simultaneously, fulfilling traditional female roles. The pioneer-settler ethos of the kibbutz movement was predicated on masculine norms of physical power and aggressiveness.[30] Women worked in areas given lesser status, the consumer-service roles rather than income-producing, productive roles; and women's roles were clearly seen as being less important. It is not surprising that men did not see taking up "women's work" to their advantage. It is also not surprising that three decades later, women led the campaign to have children sleep in the parents' home.

In the early years of Har, however, the prevailing argument was that communal child-care centers would free women to work. Moreover, Har residents believed with this decision they were upholding a socialist principle that the community should replace the family. The kibbutz and not the parents would provide for the child. The removal of the role of individual as family provider was aimed at eliminating economic dependence on the family. It was, however, one thing for single adults to talk about replacing the family, but it was another thing to hold this view once these same youths became parents. While economic dependence on the family was minimized, the community did not find substitutes for family functions, and these functions became more important as Har became a multigenerational kibbutz.

FEDERATION AFFILIATION

We have seen that political and military considerations of

[30] On the relationship between militarism and sex roles see George Lakey, *Strategy for a Living Revolution* (San Francisco: W. H. Freeman & Company, Publishers, 1973).

Yishuv institutions had a significant impact on Kibbutz Har's internal social structures. One national organization especially important to the community's future development was the Hakvutzot, one of the three principal kibbutz federations. The choice of affiliation to a federation by a kibbutz was a reflection of ideological struggle and choices among Zionist factions. The struggles were as much a part of Jewish land colonization as pioneering heroism. In the prestate era, the federations primarily represented political and religious, rather than economic and social, differences. While each federation had its own organizational structure, all existed within a Socialist-Zionist framework. Differences centered on such questions as kibbutz size, degree of centralization, and the interpretations of ideology. Each federation sought the membership of new settlements. Much politicking occurred in the federation-affiliated youth groups in the Yishuv and Diaspora since the youth groups supplied many members for kibbutzim. The pattern of development of a kibbutz was strongly influenced by the federation, since critical aid for the young settlements was obtained by the federations from the Yishuv institutions.[31]

Hever Hakvutzot, Har's movement federation, also maintained a close working relationship with the kibbutz administration. During the Mandate years it was particularly active in setting up agricultural training programs, securing loans for member kibbutzim, and providing cultural events. The federation's successful role as mediator between Har's conflicting social groups has already been mentioned. In addition, A. D. Gordon's concept of religion of labor was emphasized in Hever kibbutzim more than in kibbutzim of other federations. The economic, political and overall social administration of Har continually reflected its Hever ties.

The choice to join the Hever Federation came after intense discussion within Har and within larger Yishuv circles. During

[31] Eliyahu Kanovsky, *The Economy of the Israeli Kibbutz* (Cambridge, Mass.: Harvard University Press, 1966), p. 26.

the Mandate period three principal kibbutz federations existed, along with three smaller religious federations. Each of the federations was linked in various degrees to a national political party (see Tables 5 and 6). The Hashomer Hatzair party chiefly relied on the Marxist federation, Kibbutz Artzi Hashomer Hatzair. All members of this federation were expected to support the Hashomer Hatzair party. Its "collectivist rayonit," or communal ideology, policy demanded strong identification with the party line. Kibbutz Hameuchad allowed more voting freedom to its members. Originally part of the left-wing faction (Poale Zion) of the Mapai Party, it formed its own party, Ahdut Ha'Avodah, in 1944.[32] The largest of the federations, it also promoted large

TABLE 5. KIBBUTZ FEDERATION AND POLITICAL PARTY LINKAGE.

Kibbutz Federation	Political Parties
Hever Hakvutzot	Mapai
Kibbutz Hameuchad	Achdut Ha'avoda
Kibbutz Artzi-	
Hashomer Hatzair	Mapam

TABLE 6. STATISTICS ON THREE PRINCIPAL KIBBUTZ FEDERATIONS, 1940.

Kibbutz Federation	No. of Settlements	No. of Members
Chever Hakvutzot	34	2,819
Kibbutz Hameuchad	38	8,957
Kibbutz Artzi-		
Hashomer Hatzair	42	4,902

SOURCE: Esco Foundation for Palestine, Inc., *Palestine: A Study of Jewish, Arab, and British Policies*, vols. 1 and 2 (New Haven: Yale University Press, 1947), 1:358-359.

[32] Ahdut Ha-Avodah took its name from a merger of Labor-Zionist factions in 1919. After the state's establishment, it became part of the Mapai-led coalition government. For a full picture of political party institutions, see Leonard Fein's *Politics in Israel* (Boston: Little Brown and Company, 1967).

kibbutzim in the hope of attracting the greatest numbers to the land settlement movement. The third federation, Hever Hakvutzot, supported the right-wing Hapoel Hatzair faction of Mapai. It focused on the ideology of the religion of labor and was the least concerned with issues of class struggle. Its settlements were kept on a small scale so that a more family-like atmosphere could be maintained.[33]

The considerable prestige of Har made the factional conflict more intense than usual. Because Mapai was the strongest party in the Socialist-Zionist movement, its kibbutz federation affiliate, Hever Hakvutzot, won Har. Mapai's program emphasized a pragmatic orientation to nation building rather than the more Marxist ideological approach of Hashomer Hatzair. In the 1930s Mapai gained control of the Jewish Agency, the Yishuv National Council, and the World Zionist Organization. Most of the Socialist-Zionist factions, including other kibbutz federations, supported the coalition with Mapai, which has stayed in power since statehood. The close relations between the kibbutzim and Mapai have provided an important vehicle for the strong kibbutznik influence in the political life of the Yishuv and the state.

Despite its affiliation with Hever Hakvutzot, Har did not receive all the direct political benefits other kibbutzim enjoyed from their party affiliations. This was because Mapai did not depend on its kibbutz federation for organizational support as much as other parties did. The Histadrut gave Mapai its major organizational constituency, and much overlapping of leadership occurred between the two institutions. However, Har did benefit during the Mandate from power exercised by Mapai on

[33] Originally the term *kvutzot* defined the smaller, more family-like Jewish communal settlements as compared to the larger kibbutzim. When the Hever Hakvutzot Federation, to which Har belonged, became Ichud Hakvutzot V'Hakibbutzim, the distinction was no longer held and the term kibbutz covered the category of communal settlements.

such matters as immigration when members were provided for the Chever Federation and its settlements.[34]

The Hever Hakvutzot (in 1951 it became Ichud Hakvutzot V' Hakibbutzim) established a reciprocal economic, social, and political relationship with its settlements. It functioned primarily as an intermediary between Har and other member kibbutzim and between Har and the Yishuv institutions. The close reciprocal relationship between Har and Hever Hakvutzot existed within the context of the larger ideological, political framework of the Yishuv. The success of the federation and its member settlements was dependent on the achievements of the Zionist movement in Palestine. The conflicts characterizing the Yishuv ideological and political scene often threatened to destroy efforts toward the creation of any social order. Observers of kibbutz development have commented on this fragmentation while arguing for the need for kibbutz unity: "the great danger of any sort of collectivist group in a free enterprise society is sectarianism . . . great portions of the Kibbutz Movement allowed themselves to be driven into the blind alley of a sectarian dogmatism. The consequences of this mishap will . . . prove an incubus upon the back of the kibbutz until the day it is thrown off."[35] Har was especially dependent upon larger Socialist-Zionist organizations and was thus deeply affected by their ideological conflicts. The Hever Federation played a strong role during the Mandate years in defining the nature and direction of Har's resolution of factional disputes and the nature of the community's social organization. After 1948 the influence of the federations on member kibbutzim waned, sectarianism diminished, and kibbutz practices increasingly reflected state policies.

A critical decision for Har of whether to join the British war

[34] Harry Viteles, *A History of the Cooperative Movement in Israel*, vols. 2 and 3 (London: Vallentine, Mitchell & Co. Ltd., 1967), 2:207.

[35] Ibid., 2:509.

effort reflected both conflict between federations and other Yishuv institutions and an extension of kibbutz involvement in the larger world beyond Palestinian politics.

Ben-Gurion and Moshe Sharett urged the Jewish Agency to form Jewish batallions in the British army and enlist the aid of Yishuv residents. The kibbutz federations opposed this call on two grounds: it reduced Jewish colonization to a secondary level and it would deplete the ranks of the kibbutz-based Haganah, thus weakening kibbutz security.

At Har, the reaction was mixed. The older Europeans, already separated from their families, wanted to enter the war on the British side. Others believed that the chief enemy confronting Har was its failing economy: Har was losing its war against rocky soil, lack of water, and geographic isolation. The General Assembly decided to expel any members who joined the war effort without its express permission. Several members of the German origin section of the Garin Shimron did leave to enter newly formed Jewish legions in the British army, but the vast majority of members were committed primarily to the interests of Har. They did not view British interests, aside from battling the German forces, as necessarily tied to those of the Yishuv. Inside the kibbutz, the British were viewed with suspicion. They were thought by many members to be the allies of the Arabs and not of the Jews. In addition, the primary economic links of the kibbutz were not unilaterally with Britain; they were with the worldwide Jewish community of the Diaspora. The General Assembly decision concerning the war effort reflected this central concern for Har's economic welfare as part of the Zionist movement.

Economic Environment

The economic organization of Har has retained the same basic form throughout its history with changes due to increased complexity and bureaucratization. Like other kibbutzim, it was divided into production and consumption branches. The productive branches have been the income-producing sectors and include field crops, vegetables and fruits, dairy, poultry, farm animals, carpentry, a rest house, and industrial units. The development of the productive sector has been upon the natural conditions of the area, capital investment, and members' skills. A limited labor force has continually caused the issue of hired labor, which was prohibited by the kibbutz ideology of self-labor, to be raised. The collective consumption branch has been divided into kitchen and dining hall, laundry, central clothing and ironing, shoe repair, landscape gardening, child care, and education. While the productive branches of Har took years to develop, the consumer branches necessarily came into existence at the beginning.

During its first decade, Har experienced a series of unsuccessful attempts to build a stable economic foundation. Problems of land, labor, and capital were troublesome and were not resolved until after the establishment of the state. The kibbutz was able to survive through the financial support of the Zionist organizational network and its members' commitment to carry on what they considered a heroic economic struggle.

A major goal of the economic activity of the kibbutzim was to help form a Jewish agrarian labor force in Palestine, which in turn was part of building a Jewish working class. A proletariat is usually created in two ways: (1) as an organic development of the workers' class in societies where modern industrialization has already occurred and (2) as a product of a rapid shift of population from village to town. The hope for a Jewish working class in Palestine could be based on neither of these factors since the Yishuv society was based on recent immigration and depended upon the building of a new, separate economic order other than the one that already existed in Palestine. The Zionist colonization effort in Palestine, of which the kibbutzim were the vanguard, was aimed at building the new Jewish economy.

The Zionist economic efforts in Palestine benefited from the country's general prosperity during the 1932-1935 period: revenue of the Palestine government grew by 91 percent, industrial production by 61 percent, imports by 30 percent, exports by 77 percent, and the consumption of electricity by 335 percent.[36] This growth took place when the rest of the world suffered from the Great Depression and can be attributed to internal and external conditions: the increase in Jewish capital in Palestine as investment conditions elsewhere deteriorated; the lessening of import costs for Palestine as a buyer country; and a new booming citrus industry accounting for four-fifths of Palestinian exports in the 1930s. Most important was an increase in purchasing power caused by a great influx of both Jewish immigrants and Jewish capital. As economist David Horowitz stated: "Purchasing power had no opportunity to flag as it was being continuously reinforced from abroad" (see Table 7).

Just prior to Har's establishment, economic prosperity declined. Import costs rose: the citrus growers of other nations flooded the market with their produce and the influx of immigration and capital declined in 1938 to about half of its 1935 level. Competition from the Syrian agricultural market was especially stiff.

The effects of this reversal were experienced very differently by the Jewish and Arab populations of Palestine. The 1936 Arab general strike allowed Jewish farmers to benefit from curtailed Arab market deliveries and Jewish employment increased due to the creation of new public work jobs brought on by increasing security needs. The Arabs, meanwhile, lost jobs as Jews filled what had previously been Arab-dominated oc-

[36] David Horowitz and Rita Hinden, *Economic Survey of Palestine* (Tel Aviv: Jewish Agency for Palestine, 1938), chap. 1. Most figures cited for this period come from this chapter.

TABLE 7. Jewish Investment in the Yishuv, 1932-1935.

	1932 LP.*	%	1933 LP.	%	1934 LP.	%	1935 LP.	%	Total 4 years LP.	%
Land	149,000	5	855,000	15	1,648,000	18	1,700,000	17	4,352,000	15
Citri-culture	1,090,000	38	1,390,000	25	1,509,000	16	943,000	9	4,933,000	17
Mixed Farming	—	—	—	—	—	—	—	—	1,000,000	3
Building	1,094,000	39	2,884,000	51	4,554,000	50	5,730,000	56	14,262,000	50
Industry Transport	500,000	18	500,000	9	1,500,000	16	1,800,000	18	4,300,000	15
Total	2,833,000	100	5,630,000	100	9,211,000	100	10,173,000	100	28,847,000	100

* Palestinian Lira.
SOURCE: David Horowitz and Rita Hinden, *Economic Survey of Palestine* (Tel Aviv: Jewish Agency for Palestine, 1938), p. 13.

cupations such as port workers. Arabs, of course, were unable to benefit from the credit policies of Zionist financial institutions available to the Yishuv to help overcome the economic slump. These credit policies helped the Jewish settlements to diversify crops and lessen dependency on citrus crops. To support Jewish mixed farming activity, for example, 7,000,000 Palestinian pounds were invested in cooperative settlements largely by Yishuv public institutions not expecting profitable returns. Such investments were seen as necessary to advance the growth of the Jewish economy.

Thus when Har attempted to deal with its serious land, labor, and capital difficulties, it did so with the support of the Yishuv network. As part of the new Jewish labor economy in Palestine, its fortunes were directly and indirectly linked to the success of the Zionist movement. The fact that the Jewish proletarianization effort preceded any major capitalist development in Palestine gave the Jewish labor economy the opportunity to establish itself in areas as yet not attractive to private investment, especially in farming and transportation. The growth of

Histadrut membership demonstrates the steady growth of the labor economy sector. Even when private enterprise became a greater factor in Palestine, the labor economy held its own by developing mechanisms of competition and cooperation. Both sectors of the dual-economy were primarily concerned with the successful development of a Jewish economic structure. By 1973, 14,060 people or 13 percent of the entire Jewish labor force was involved in cooperative land settlements.

Eliyahu Kanovsky has noted that the early kibbutzim were motivated by "the fulfillment of Jewish nationalist goals rather than by the profit motive."[37] He suggests that the abolition of private property and the tenet "from each according to ability to each according to need" are antithetical to the profit maximization concept. It was also clear that the primacy of nationalist motives held true for Har: its geographic location alone testifies to the importance of security and strategic, rather than economic, considerations.

At the same time, Har's members wanted to become a stable community and never opposed opportunities for raising the standard of living and acquiring capital. The economic difficulties of Har's first decade were thus viewed as social as well as financial barriers. In the midst of its land, labor, and capital restraints, the kibbutz tried to colonize the land; increase production, especially agricultural production; expand agricultural population; and attain a decent standard of living for its members.[38]

LAND

Har's location on the mountain range in the Western Galilee was the result of a policy decision to place national interests before economic considerations. Its site presented serious

[37] Kanovsky, *The Economy of the Kibbutz*, p. 31.

[38] I. Shatil, *The Economy of the Communal Settlements in Israel: Principles and History*, p. 100.

problems with soil and climate conditions and lack of water resources and transportation. These problems were exacerbated by the lack of sufficient planning for the kibbutz's agricultural development. The persistence of the difficulties through the first decade was cushioned by the continual encouragement of the national Yishuv institutions to maintain the settlement.

The Jewish National Fund leased 5,500 *dunams* (a *dunam* is about one-quarter acre) to the kibbutz in 1938. The estimated cost of the land plus amelioration in 1943 was 15,100 Palestinian pounds. Har held a forty-nine-year renewable lease under the policy of "the inalienable property of the Jewish people" and under an agreement of the lessee to cultivate the land. These were key provisions of the Jewish National Fund that owned over 50 percent of Jewish-owned land in Palestine by 1947.[39] The lease provisions were designed to prevent the fragmentation of Jewish farm units and the growth of a class of large land-owners renting land for profit.

Although Har received 5,500 *dunams*, only 340 were easily available for cultivation in the first years. The soil, climate, and water limited agricultural expansion. The soil consisted of chalky layers, two hundred meters thick, above porous rock. Rocks and pebbles covered the area. In 1938-1939 members spent uncounted hours clearing rocks, which were eventually used to build stone huts. Kibbutz members at first had thought that the proximity to the Mediterranean Sea would benefit agriculture, but the winds from the sea were dry and helped to erode the land. Fruit trees and poultry could not flourish under the dry winds. Moreover, the scarcity of water was a great difficulty. Irrigation was essential for successful agriculture, but Har barely had enough water for its basic domestic needs. The kibbutz relied upon a pumping station located at the lower

[39] Baron de Rothschild's foundation owned 25.1 percent of the land; 21.1 percent was privately held, mostly in citrus plantations. Kanovsky, *The Economy of the Kibbutz*, p. 33.

camp that provided only twenty cubic meters of potable water daily, twelve of which went to Har. The other eight went to Kibbutz Matzuba. Har asked for water from well-supplied Kibbutz Eilon, but the situation was not substantially improved until the 1950s.

Conservation of water was, therefore, crucial. The number of showers per year was strictly counted. Water for bathing was collected in ancient Byzantine cisterns, which also collected rainwater. One basin was used by three persons to bathe. The same water was then used to clean their three rooms and, then, to water the locust trees providing shade.

In spite of the constraints and perhaps motivated by their challenge, the members expanded the arable land to 597 *dunams* in 1942 and 3,793 in 1946. The original subdivision of cultivation is presented in Table 8. Throughout kibbutzim in Palestine during the late Mandate years there was a similar shortage in arable property. In 1929 kibbutzim had 70.3 *dunams* per family, but by 1947 it had decreased to 30.9 because of restrictions on land purchase increasingly imposed by the British, though these were offset by the rising availability of irrigated land. The situation was greatly altered for the kibbutzim, including Har, after 1948 when the lands that the state took over were distributed to Jewish settlements.

TABLE 8. ORIGINAL LAND USE AT HAR.

cover crops (i.e., wheat)	240.0 *dunams*
vines	3.0 *dunams*
fruit trees	12.0 *dunams*
vegetables	8.0 *dunams*
oranges	0.5 *dunams*
cabbages	25.0 *danams*
greenhouse	1.5 *dunams*
buildings, roads, etc.	10.0 *dunams*
other cultivable land	40.0 *dunams*

During the first decade, the attempts at new agricultural projects were almost entirely failures. Economic Plan I called for unirrigated tree terraces including plums, apples, almonds, olive trees, and grapevines. They were planted in 1938-1939, but by 1944-1945 their harvest was negligible. Orange trees fared no better. The same results held true for cultivation of field crops and vegetables.

To compensate for the crop failures, a major effort was made to establish farm animal husbandry projects including goats, cows, and poultry. The goats and cows were primarily raised for dairy production, but lack of adequate transportation facilities made it cheaper to bring milk from Haifa than ship the milk for processing. Cheese making, hen raising, and cattle breeding were equally unsuccessful despite an Economic Plan II that called for mixed farming centered around the cowshed.

Today the stories regarding other early agricultural attempts reveal an overwhelming lack of forethought and planning due both to the members' original military concern and to their relative inexperience. The list of attempts include raising bees for honey, selling flowers, quarrying marble, making perfumes, selling wood, and packaging sausage.[40] One example of the lack of planning, is that on the advice of a dry laurel leaf buyer the kibbutz decided to distill aromatic oil from laurel leaves for export to Australia. A great still was purchased but it had such a large capacity that the local supply of leaves was insufficient. Supplies had to be brought in by camel from Lebanon. In the end, two and one-half liters were produced, which never were sold to Australia because of the outbreak of World War II.

Other examples of unsuccessful agricultural efforts demonstrate the resistance of the members to accept Arab methods of cultivation where European methods were clearly unaccepta-

[40] The historical accounts of each of these attempts, while often humorous, also demonstrates the deadly combination of ignorance of agricultural processes and inability to investigate the project before beginning.

ble. While the Arabs planted trees according to the curves of
the hills, the members tried plowing in straight furrows. When
the rain came, the young trees were uprooted and washed
away. They also refused to exploit the natural plantation of
carob trees in the Arab way and used the fruit only to replace
feedstock during the war years. This dismissal of Arab agrarian
procedures reflected arrogant attitudes of the European and Sabra newcomers that the kibbutz could ill afford.

The location of Har presented another severe constraint on
the effort to achieve economic stability. There was no regular
means of transportation from the kibbutz to a nearby town. The
Yishuv transportation association had refused to serve Har, cit-
ing the scarcity of spare parts and bad road conditions as reasons. An agreement on one daily scheduled round trip to Har
was finally reached. At the time, the kibbutz had only one car
at its disposal and arranging truck transport was a complicated
matter. Even with transport a trip to its main market town,
Haifa, took a full day for the round trip; and the time it took
to walk to Nahariya, the nearest small town, was at least two
hours.

Har's distance from the markets was a particularly hard
problem for milk delivery, and ideological considerations also
affected the situation. A private company, the Straus Company,
had set up a milk-processing plant in Nahariya. Often the milk
arrived curdled at Nahariya because of the delays in shipping:
cream was separated from the milk at 3 A.M., but Har did not
have the electricity for the refrigeration necessary to store
cream. The truck could not leave with only one load so it
waited until 9 A.M. to depart. By then, the cream curdled.
Meanwhile, Tnuva, the Histadrut's central agricultural marketing cooperative, was located in Haifa. Har had to maintain
good relations with Tnuva to insure its loans and credits from
Histadrut institutions. The cooperative in Nahariya serviced
only non-Histadrut affiliated settlements, as a result Har had

to bypass both it and the Straus Company and deliver its milk and cream to Haifa. The milk by then was guaranteed to be bad.

Yet, the location benefited Har. First, it was beautiful, if not amenable to cultivation, and a guest house for Yishuv residents and visitors became a money-making venture after it opened in 1945. Secondly, the kibbutz's isolated geographic position from the rest of the Yishuv demanded reliance on the internal production of food supplies particularly during wartime when local Arabs often closed the road leading to Nahariya. Har residents experienced a sense of pride that their efforts at self-reliance were successful in the face of an external threat. One resident recalled that, "For several months the Arabs closed the road [to Nahariya]. . . . in two places there were very strong Arab villages—Basa, it's now Schlomi, and Achziv, now a kibbutz. . . . If they imagined they could force us out by hunger, we never ate so much . . . milk, cheese, all we had."[41] Making do with whatever they could produce gave the members a sense of heroism in building an organic community. And hardships with the land were seen as a necessary, integral stage in the colonization process.

LABOR

The organization of labor at Har revealed a continual struggle to reconcile ideological norms of self-labor with the practical considerations of raising the economy above a survival level and coping with a geographic isolation from the rest of the region. Moreover, the labor structures of the kibbutz were modeled along those developed at other kibbutzim and on the federation level. Thus, labor conditions were another factor of kibbutz life demonstrating the simultaneous existence of community isolation and national affiliations.

Each sector's daily activities are directed by a branch man-

---

[41] Interviews with Moshe Bet and Yaakov Gan during fieldwork.

ager who in turn reports to the *sidron avodah*, the head work manager. The *sidron avodah* is in charge of labor organization and works together with the economic manager of the kibbutz.

The economic management committee deals with overall planning, efficiency of the branches, and resource allocation. The committee includes the economic manager as chairperson, the *sidron avodah*, the treasurer, and the heads of the most important productive branches. A separate committee of personnel includes the consumer branch managers. The economic manager sits in the Secretariat that controls the kibbutz purse strings.

In addition to the consumption and production branches, the kibbutz has had to take care of what usually would be considered municipal functions such as water supply, sanitation, and local defense. In recent years, these functions were organized on a regional basis; until then, they added to the stress on the kibbutz labor shortage.

Ideological attitudes had a strong impact on determining how Har organized its response to more material requirements for the organization of labor. The tenets of self-labor, job rotation, and the overall reverential attitude toward work itself, however, were not rigidly enforced. While the ideological commitment to these concepts remained constant, various practical arrangements were made that reflect the dominance of material factors in struggling with ideology.

Self-labor was viewed as critical to the development of a Jewish proletariat in Palestine. According to this principle of Socialist-Zionist ideology, all work done in the kibbutz should be done by members. When some of the older members of Har first arrived in Palestine, they derived their income as hired help for private farmers. Many early kibbutzim relied for income upon the pooled earnings of members holding outside jobs. Har was largely able to avoid this due to an original settlement budget from the Jewish Agency. Members did work outside the kibbutz in jobs within the Hever Federation and Zionist institutions, but this did not violate the canon of self-labor. However, the hiring of both Jewish and Arab outside labor that took place at the beginning of Har's history was a serious ideological deviation. The use of hired labor became more prevalent after statehood when industrialization increased the community's labor shortage and when the Israeli government pressed the kibbutzim to create jobs for new nonmember immigrants.

A number of events during the first decade illustrate this problem with the tenet of self-labor. In conversations with a number of the older members, the margarine incident was recalled. A member had brought a large amount of margarine to the kibbutz that another promptly threw away in the garbage on the grounds that it was a foreign product and not made by Jewish labor. Arab laborers were contracted for specific jobs. For example, in an attempt to utilize the oak trees surrounding the kibbutz, a plan for making handles for work tools was adopted. Trees were cut and the job of cutting them up was given to an Arab resident of Alma, a nearby Lebanese village. The project, therefore, was dependent on outside labor for completion and violated the norm of self-labor.

Job rotation was to be a means to insure the ideological commitment of socialism to equality between workers. In Har's first decade when there was no great differentiation in the work skills of members, job rotation was largely actualized; within each branch the position of branch manager was rotated. However, job rotation was not attempted between the service and income-producing branches. Service branch specialization existed primarily along sex-role lines. In addition, as in any community, some members became more skilled in certain work areas than did others and they tended to advance to and remain in leadership positions. The problem of job rotation became more severe as Har became industrialized and jobs required specialized training. The kibbutz could only afford to send a few members at a time to gain the required education. This affected the service branches as well when they too became more mechanized and when teacher-training courses began.

To be a good kibbutznik meant to be a good worker. Good workers received special recognition from other members and enjoyed a certain prestige in the community. The increased status ascribed to a good worker was only one factor motivating work. Another was the realization that as the kibbutz became more successful economically personal welfare would also be improved.

The kibbutz laborer could also count on long range economic security. As long as one remained a member, at least the fundamentals of economic well-being would be provided. There was no fear of unemployment, lack of an old-age pension, or inability to get health care. These must be considered a primary factor in commitment to the kibbutz.

The total number of workdays remained fairly constant during the first decade. A labor-intensive community, the kibbutz provided little time for relaxation and in the initial years, no regular vacation time. In 1942 members worked an average of 310 days and in 1946, 309. Saturday, the Jewish Sabbath, was traditionally the rest day but on some occasions, especially during crop seasons, members also worked on Saturdays. This is still true during the picking seasons at Har, though it is less frequent.

The division of labor between the income-producing and service branches largely depended upon the ratio of children to the adult population: As the number of families grew, the service branches increased, women became concentrated in the service sector, more pressure was placed on income branches, and the workday structure was altered. A few women in pre-state days continued to work in the orchards; and men worked in the laundry until it was mechanized. Otherwise sex-division in the branches was largely maintained. In 1942, Har had a total of 115 residents, 103 adults and 12 children; in 1946 the population total was 205, with 156 adults and 49 children. The ratio thus changed from approximately 1:8 to almost 1:3.

Har has utilized the kibbutz system of *yom avodah*, or workday, to determine the labor cost of the income-producing branches. The cost of a workday is defined by the ratio of the total number of workdays in the productive branches to consumption expenditures. It is also used to determine the earnings of a particular income-producing branch by dividing the net income of the branch by the number of labor days of the branch.

As more members had to work in the service branches due to the increase in children, the cost of a *yom avodah* had to be at least twice the cost of maintaining a person in the kibbutz. Interest on debts and loan payments also had to be covered. Branches were expanded according to their income-producing level. By the end of the 1940s, however, Har's problem was not which branch to enlarge but to find a branch that could become economically solvent. In 1943, they had not been able to pay back any part of the 31,877 Palestinian lira debt to the Keren Hayesod.

The increase in the child-adult ratio also brought about a change in the structure of the workday. In Har the workday was divided into eight sections including the hours for eating and resting. As children became a more significant element in the community, the work lists were revised to read, "8th section—time reserved for the children." Since children did not sleep with their parents, this was an important period of the day for family gatherings.

When there were only a few children, the nonparents were a majority and felt the children were the responsibility of the whole community. They did not mind working the extra section when parents joined the children. This changed when the majority of members became parents: then the nonparents felt exploited. A new labor schedule was established with eight sections for work and a ninth one when everyone might be called for work but otherwise could be free to do what he or she pleased.

Workplace conditions were determined by the harsh physical environment and lack of mechanization. The climate with its long, very hot season and chilly rainy season made outdoor work difficult. The service branches, which were mainly indoors, suffered from the subsistence economy that did not provide much use of electricity or needed machines. The exception to the austere work settings of the service sector was the children's houses; these were built with the best materials available and kept in model shape. As the future of the kibbutz, "the children of the dream" were accorded the best the community could offer.

The workday for Har members did not end with the nine section schedule. Members were expected to commit themselves to extracurricular committee work of kibbutz life in the evenings. Being a good worker included participation in these community activities as well. Job rotation ideally also was supposed to be carried out, but in practice committee organizational leadership continually fell within a particular circle of members. During the initial years that circle consisted primarily of members of the Shimron *garin*.

CAPITAL

Kibbutz Har would not have been established or been able to survive without the continuing investment of capital from Zionist Yishuv and Diaspora institutions. Starting in the 1940s, capital investment also came from private sources. At all times, capital investment was limited. But as economist Eliyahv Kanovsky has pointed out, capital was the most constant of the three traditional factors of production. Land became more plentiful after statehood while labor shortages grew.

Har started out without any capital of its own. Its first loan was for 6,000 Palestinian lira on a long range at 2 percent interest.[42] The Jewish Agency raised these funds from the worldwide Jewry. Loans from the agency as well as other public Zionist institutions were not commercial and were deferrable in case of hard times. The interest rate was appreciably lower than the commercial rate, which during the Mandate was 10 percent or higher.

After its initial establishment, Har received a major development investment loan from the Keren Hayesod. The cost of settlement was 20,733 Palestinian lira and the first loan from the Keren Hayesod was 31,877. This was considerably more than most other kibbutzim received principally because of Har's remote geographic location and its difficulty in establishing a stable economy.

The Jewish National Fund completely subsidized Har's reforestation project. Conceived to improve the existing oak forest and add new tree varieties, the project consisted of planting plum trees on the steep inclines and carob trees on the smoother terraces. A member of the kibbutz went down the mountain to Har's fifty *dunam* of valley land each day under military protection to water 7,000 seedlings. In kibbutz reports of 1942 and 1946, Jewish National Fund funding was recognized as the key factor in improving the community's environment. The forest land grew from 200 to 1,957 *dunams* during this period.

The financial benefits did not occur without costs. The kibbutz was dependent on outside sources for its production and working capital so it had to turn to less favorable capital investors when the public funds became tight. Har was forced to

[42] *Twenty-fifth Anniversary Issue* of internal kibbutz journal, Har Archives, p. 1.

carry a heavy interest burden that increased production costs and depressed its standard of living. The 1946 economic reports testify to the struggling budget problems. It was not until 1955 that a reserve of 747 lira suggested a less constrained economic era.

Restrictions on the Yishuv market also affected demand and sales possibilities. The self-labor concepts and the virtual separation of the Palestinian economy into Jewish and Arab markets limited kibbutz trade possibilities. Har was affected by this situation as well as by poor planning in developing production areas. One example of lack of adequate planning was the community's yoke-making endeavor. Utilizing the surrounding woods, the kibbutz produced fine wooden yokes only to discover that another kibbutz, Yad Mordachai, was already meeting market demands. Worms devoured the unused wood before another project could be created.

Har also made use of other sources of capital, including aid from the Histadrut's Workers' Bank and Hever Fund of the federation. After they had rejected certain utopian concepts, private sources became an important source of capital for the kibbutzim. In 1938 private sources provided 38 percent of the total credit of the older kibbutzim. By 1943 Har had received 4,029 Palestinian lira from private sources and only 2,068 from its own resources. A substantial increase in private investment in Har's economy occurred when its factory became a major factor in its total production.

THE BEGINNING OF INDUSTRY

The beginning of Har's industrialization again reveals the community's link to military needs of the Yishuv and national political considerations. An emphasis on agriculture prevailed in the kibbutz economy during the prestate period, but factories began to be built in the kibbutzim during the last decade of the Mandate. By 1943 the older kibbutzim, those established before 1927, employed 11 percent of their labor force in industry. These accounted for 21.3 percent of their gross income. For among those established between 1936-1938, the percentage of their labor force in industry was 10.3.[43] This was due in part to the personal efforts of individual members, partly to provide tools for the agricultural work, and partly, and perhaps more significantly, in response to conditions created by World War II. The constraints of insufficient land and an oversupply of labor for agriculture made the shift to manufacturing attractive.

The three major federations adapted different attitudes toward the conversion to manufacturing on the kibbutzim. Hashomer Hatzair and Meuchad climbed onto the industrial bandwagon early in the period, sometimes to appeal to their affiliated kibbutzim. Hever Hakvutzot, to which Har belonged, was more resistant to industrialization; since it supported the *kvutza*, or smaller community unit, it feared the changes industry would bring. However, even its kibbutzim started small-scale factories in the 1940s.

World War II stimulated kibbutz industrialization in two ways: difficulties in importing manufactured items created a favorable environment for local production and secondly, factory products were demanded by Allied forces stationed in the region. In this environment, kibbutz factories no longer served purely agrarian needs.

Kibbutz members with industrial skills often pushed for factory construction on a kibbutz. In the case of Har, one individual and a romantic attachment was the initial cause for the setting up of a factory branch. A woman member fell in love with a machinist from Haifa who worked clandestinely for the Haganah. The couple were married in 1940, but the husband agreed to stay on the kibbutz only if he could continue to employ his industrial skills. The General Assembly, after heated debate, decided to begin a machine workshop employing five

[43] Kanovsky, *The Economy of the Kibbutz*, pp. 59-60.

to six of the kibbutz's members. However, the Haganah strongly objected to losing a good worker. A compromise between the Haganah and the kibbutz was reached in 1942: the Haganah sent its machine tools to Har where it could start a secret factory producing weapon parts. From 1941-1947, Har had eight members doing clandestine work under the sheep pen in its community factory. This was the predecessor to the current Har metal works, which is the principal income-producing branch of the entire kibbutz.

This collaboration between the Haganah and Har established another link between the military-political and economic factors in the kibbutz's development. Members took a substantial risk in establishing a secret Haganah weapon factory and further demonstrated their dedication to national purposes.

The military-political context in which the kibbutz developed affected the economic and social reality of the community in ways other than in the creation of the factory. Members were directly involved in community defense and some played important roles in the Haganah. The Haganah, in turn, stationed nonmember representatives and Jewish Settlement Police at Har. These Haganah-affiliated forces were closely watched by the British authorities who from time to time conducted unannounced army checks in the settlement.

The military dimension affects the employment of labor and capital in production in several additional ways. A number of situations exemplify this impact on labor. First of all, in 1942, ten members, including one woman, enlisted in the British army; the decision to do so, as mentioned above, was part of a critical debate in the community's General Assembly; in 1946 the figure rose to twelve. Secondly, all of Har's members were considered part of the Yishuv's defense forces. They had learned to use arms and participated in training. They were responsible for guard duties in the watchtower and went out on patrols. Since the plain area between Har and Haifa was dark at night, a light signal system was instituted between the kibbutz and the port city. A woman with a guard escort had a nightly assignment of being on watch for signals. Labor energies were thus channeled to military duties on a regular basis. Thirdly, a number of Har's members were active in Haganah activities outside of the kibbutz. One member played a particularly significant role in Iraq as part of the Haganah's security forces. Others took part in raids into Lebanon and Syria, one member being on the raid of Syria when Dayan lost his eye.

Although the General Assembly debate had stressed the need to concentrate on shoring up Har's failing economy, members felt deeply attached to the larger nationalist struggle. Provision of labor and participation in the Haganah and local defense efforts were viewed as a continual and necessary responsibility to maintain the internal economy. However, the decision to allow its members to join the British army rather than the Haganah was the bone of contention.

Capital investments also reflected the military-political status of the kibbutz. Har's well-known heroism attracted financial support. This support did not end Har's struggle for economic stability in the first decade, but may have sheltered it from collapse. When the state of Israel was established, special loans, grants, and gifts were earmarked for settlements like Har in high risk areas.

The military-political impact on the daily life of the kibbutz was pervasive. As a border outpost, it was a constant host to Haganah troops. When the world war broke out, many Jewish students in Palestine enlisted in the British army but the Haganah retained thirty of them for special missions. Since Har bordered on Lebanon, then influenced by the Vichy regime, the kibbutz became an important Haganah base of operation. A Haganah representative stayed at Har, as a regular working volunteer, while performing his security duties. Only later did many of the members learn of his Haganah role.

The British, who were largely interested in maintaining order in Palestine, kept up surveillance, if often at a distance, of Jewish defense forces. This included watch of the Jewish Settlement Police who kept a border guard at Har. The settlement police were under a dual British-Haganah authority but were allowed to carry arms only under British command. The British would regularly come on surprise searches for unauthorized weapons. If caught with such weapons, the Jewish policemen forfeited pay and other crucial supplies. Occasionally, strict penalties were imposed, but Har's members were skilled in negotiating terms with the British.

Har existed within an area of a suspicious but politically negotiable relationship with the British and of a threatening, militarily hostile relationship with the Arab population. The members were isolated from and yet dependent upon outside institutions.

On the Eve of the 1948 War

By the 1948 War and the establishment of the state of Israel, Har had achieved its political and military goals but was still an economic failure. Attempts to attain economic growth and stability were severely hampered by the constraints of the political and military factors such as its location, military drains on its labor, and the lack of time for sufficient planning. Socially, however, the kibbutz benefited from the type of solidarity resulting from a focused national commitment. An increasingly cohesive internal structure was being built. Differences between *garin* groups were reconciled, families replaced the single adult population, and stable administrative processes were developed.

A consistent ethos of heroism, of being part of a national colonization effort and of being "bridgehead soldiers," enabled the community to struggle through the limits imposed by a barely subsistence economy. The sense that history was on its side was a critical, forceful factor in the development of the new community.

Throughout the period, Har's economic failures were eased by its attachment to the external Zionist institutional framework. Land, labor, and capital resources were provided by the Jewish National Fund, the Histadrut, the Jewish Agency and the kibbutz federations. Har received support for its leadership role in securing Jewish defense boundaries and for creating a class of agrarian Jews in Palestine. Unlike most utopian communities, it did not reject its national community or maintain a local, inward posture. Har derived confidence and strength by perceiving itself as others in the Yishuv perceived it, as a leader in nationalist endeavors despite its geographical isolation.

At the same time Har remained relatively isolated within its local region. It had limited dealings with local Arab villages and nonkibbutz settlements. This was mainly a result of Har's attempts to adhere to the Socialist-Zionist principles of self-labor. Even new members who were not yet "Hebraized" were subject to this form of isolation.

Most local communities establish social and economic networks with other established communities in their region to pursue common interests and to provide for common necessities. For agrarian communities intraregional ties are usually more utilized and intimate than are their links to the national economy. However, the role Har played in nation-state building reversed this pattern. It maintained closer ties with national institutions than it did with neighboring villages. Har's role as a border fortress limited its ability to serve as a model of agrarian socialism for the region.

At the end of the first decade, Har had accomplished its mission as a Tower and Stockade kibbutz. It served as the home for over two hundred people who were committed to the struggle of building a permanent settlement. Its economic problems were serious but did not seem insurmountable. The main issue remained the role Har would play in the larger society once the state was established: Would the kibbutz lose its prestigious role? What changes would the new situation bring to the various aspects of kibbutz life? In what form would the community continue?

Ben Ami, a Har member, urged members to remain true to the "conquering, pioneer framework" and continue "the willingness to perform any role in support of the nation."[44] The next chapters examine in what ways Har fulfilled this call.

[44] Ben Ami, "Six Years 1938-1944," in *Twenty-fifth Anniversary Issue*, p. 23.

CHAPTER TWO

The Transition Period

The establishment of Israel in 1948 marked the end of the kibbutz's role as part of a military vanguard and the beginning of its role as an important economic unit for the state. From 1948-1967, Har's internal organization underwent a transition from an agrarian to an industrial producer, from a subsistence economy toward affluence, from communality to instrumentality, from homogeneity to generational and cultural differentiation. Incongruities between communal egalitarian norms and the demands of national policies stressing modernization became sharper. The responses by the community to these demands determined future development.

Har's push to meet the requirements of the new economic order undermined its ideological commitments to self-labor, asceticism, and manual labor. Agriculture was mechanized in order to produce cash crops for export, and as industry developed, hired workers were needed to fill labor needs. Community processes originally designed to preserve egalitarianism, such as job rotation, gave way to specialization and the emergence of management positions. As classes emerged in the "classless community," each group started pressing to maintain its own interests.[1] Har experienced increasing tension between communality and Westernized economic rationality. The kib-

---

[1] Eva Rosenfeld ("Social Stratification in a 'Classless' Society," *American Sociological Review*, 16 [1951] 766ff.) reported the emergence of "class interest" differentiation in the kibbutz as early as 1951: "The managerial stratum, strongly identified with the communal enterprise and immune from many tensions, acts as a whip for inducing greater effort in work. . . . The rank and file on the other hand, press for the elimination of the discomfort and dependency inherent in some of the institutional structures."

butz's withdrawal from ideological commitment reflects a process common to communal groups as they prosper. Weber comments on this pattern in *The Theory of Social and Economic Organization*: "Communistic systems for the communal or associational organization of work are unfavorable to calculation and to the consideration of means for obtaining optimum production, because . . . they tend to be based on the direct feeling of mutual solidarity."[2]

While socialist, ideological considerations suffered, Har's economy began blooming. Clothing and food consumption, building construction, cultural activities, and increased leisure time all demonstrate the rapid rise in the community's standard of living. Simultaneously, there was a movement away from emphasis on the community to a new emphasis on the individual and family group. Individualized budgets, individual savings accounts, and eating at home rather than in the communal dining hall are evidence of this change.[3] The word "home" came to mean the individual apartment unit instead of the communal dining hall.

Patterns of hierarchy became institutionalized with the incorporation of hired laborers as part of the internal economy. Moreover, stratification developed among the members between the Sephardic, French-speaking group newly arrived at Har and the older, Western-oriented group. And the ensuing rift between the European and North African groups shaped internal arrangements of housing, leadership, and cultural practices. Har became one of the few kibbutzim with a very large Sephardic Jewish population after 1948 when the Jewish pop-

---

[2] Max Weber, *The Theory of Social and Economic Organization* (Oxford: Oxford University Press, 1947), p. 205.

[3] Yonina Talmon, the kibbutz sociologist, did an in-depth study of twelve kibbutzim in the Ichud Federation in the 1950s on the question of new consumption patterns. See Harry Viteles, *A History of the Cooperative Movement in Israel*, vols. 2 and 3 (London: Vallentine, Mitchell & Co. Ltd., 1967), pp. 363ff.

ulation of Israel rose to 2,400,000, with most of the immigrants coming from non-Western countries.

Yet even after 1948, Har's community development continued to be tied to nation building, reflecting the increasingly capitalist patterns and policies of the economy of the state of Israel. The network of national institutions that supported kibbutz development assured its adaptation to the changing conditions of Israeli modernization. The Jewish Agency, Histadrut, and the government directed this network and channelled a new influx of foreign capital into the public sector of the economy and to the various Zionist party factions in the country. In this way the state and Zionist institutions controlled the direction of nation building in general, and the development of the kibbutzim, specifically.

The distributed funds indicate the extent of Israel's dependency on foreign capital to maintain its economy. Oscar Gass, an American economist, comments on the uniqueness of the situation:

> What is unique in this development process . . . is the factor of capital inflow. . . . During the 17 years of 1949-65 Israel received $6 billion more of imports of goods and services than she exported. For the 21 years 1948-68, the import surplus would be in excess of $7½ billion. This means an excess of some $2,650 per person during the 21 years for every person who lived in Israel (within the pre-June 1967 borders) at the end of 1968. And this surplus from abroad . . . only about 30% came to Israel under conditions which call for a return outflow of dividends, interest or capital. This is a circumstance without parallel elsewhere, and it severely limits the significance of Israel's economic development as an example to other countries.[4]

During the 1949-1965 period, the capital influx came from three main sources: 60 percent from worldwide Jewry, 28 per-

[4] Oscar Gass, an American economist, in *Journal of Economic Literature* (December 1969), 1177.

cent from the German government, and 12 percent from the government of the United States.[5] An investment rate of 20 percent of the gross national product continued despite the absence of any net savings within the internal Israeli economy. Thus Israel's economic growth completely rested upon foreign support.

Har's development in many ways reflected what was happening on the national level. Its autonomy had always been limited by its fulfillment of national functions. In the post-1948 years, the centralization of national planning increased the kibbutz's dependence on external institutions for internal growth. As these external, national level institutions became increasingly tied to the worldwide capitalist economy, to the United States' economy in particular, so did the kibbutz. The industrialization of Har is a clear example of how the kibbutz fits into this pattern of economic expansion.

During the 1948-1967 period, these trends were accompanied by an increasing subordination of socialist ideological concerns to the needs of nation building emphasizing economy efficiency and growth. Patterns of self-reliance were further reduced while regional and internal economic and social developments caused increased internal stratification.

Military-Political Situation

A shift in Har's priorities from military-political considerations to economic development followed the establishment of the Israeli state when the state took over control of military defense from the kibbutz-based Haganah. However, during the events

---

[5] Haim Hanegbi, Moshe Machover, and Akiva Orr, "The Class Nature of Israel," *New Left Review* (1971), 6. The 60 percent includes United Jewish Appeal funds collected in the United States, which are tax-deductible, and the 28 percent represents German reparation money that was compensation money to those suffering losses from World War II.

leading up to the state's foundation in 1948, the upper Galilee region, in which Har existed, was excluded from the proposed Jewish state and Har waged an active battle so as to be included in it.

In 1947 Britain was losing control of Palestine when its foreign secretary, Ernest Bevin, proposed that the issue of Palestine be brought before the United Nations. In April 1947, an International Commission of Inquiry appointed by the United Nations recommended the end of the Mandate, the establishment of two independent Arab and Jewish states and a transition period of two years after the joint surveillance of Britain and the United Nations. Under the Partition Plan all of the Western Galilee, including Har, was included in the future Arab state. Har was to be under Lebanese jurisdiction.

The Zionist organizations accepted the Partition Plan, although many of its members had proposed other plans, including binationalism.[6] Their acceptance reflected their general, strong desire to establish finally a Jewish state in Palestine and to offer a place for refugees from the Holocaust. The Arabs' rejection of the Partition Plan indicated their refusal to accept any division of what they considered their homeland.

The Jewish military forces from November 1947 to May 1948 were determined not to retreat from any Jewish settlement. During the battles the Haganah supported Har by sending convoys across the predominantly Arab areas surrounding it. These convoys brought supplies of arms ordered from Europe and the United States. When the Arabs attacked the convoys, the Haganah conducted a series of reprisals against Arab attackers of the convoys. On 15 February 1948 twenty houses were blown up in the Arab village of Sasa, near Har. The Arabs continued

[6] See Hashomer Hatzair Worker's Party *The Case for a Bi-National Palestine* (New York: Shulsinger Bros., 1947); and Esco Foundation for Palestine, *Palestine: A Study of Jewish, Arab, and British Policies*, vols. 1 and 2 (New Haven: Yale University Press, 1947), vol. 2.

to cut off communication and transportation lines from the Galilee to the rest of the Yishuv. Roads from Har to Haifa were closed. In March 1948, three convoys, bringing supplies to the four Jewish settlements of the "Har Block"—Har, Eilon, Matzuba, and Yehiam—were attacked, leaving Har isolated from the rest of the Yishuv by the Arab town of Tarshiha (today Ma'alot). Members of Har managed to reach Nahariya, borrow a boat, and bring in supplies from Haifa.

The eventual link of Har with Yishuv forces was the result of efforts in the eastern Galilee by the Palmach known as the Yiftah operation. Set in motion two weeks before the British departure date, the operation was headed by Yigal Allon and was intended to capture key positions, to free roads, and to prepare Galilee for invasion of Jewish forces.[7] The principal towns of Safed and Rosh Pina in the eastern Galilee were captured. This prevented Syrian and Lebanese troops joining those of Transjordan in the Galilee.

With the eastern section secured, attention turned to the western city of Akko that had been evacuated by the British on May 14. A force set out from Haifa, already in Jewish hands, captured two Arab villages near Har, and reached Har and Yehiam. At the same time, along the Mediterranean coastline near Har, the railroad from Gaza to Beirut was destroyed to prevent a Lebanese invasion. Har's inclusion in the future Jewish state was assured.

With the establishment of the state of Israel, Har became part of a continuous line of border settlements that were part of the national defense network. The Lebanese border remained calm until 1967 and the kibbutz no longer functioned in the military vanguard. However, it still remained closely tied to security and defense policies.

From 1948 to 1967 the community was largely responsible

---

[7] Cited in the French Report. See Chapter One, Note 2 for a description of this report.

for its own defense. A kibbutz security committee was formed to oversee security needs. In consultation with the Economic Committee it scheduled rotation of guards with each member making night rounds for about a week each year. During guard rotation the member slept during the day. The Security Committee in consultation with the Construction Committee also supervised the construction of shelters financed by the state. Each section of the kibbutz has had one or two shelters built near its place of work, while children's houses were directly connected to shelters. Communal areas such as the dining hall had their own shelter areas. Members were divided into teams to clean and be responsible for each shelter. Before 1967 the system of shelters was inadequate and trenches were used as an alternative. After the 1967 War a more sophisticated shelter system was built, which was further improved after the 1973 War.

The state and the Histadrut contributed to the security costs of the kibbutz. After deducting government grants, the Horowitz Committee Report noted that security costs for each kibbutz averaged 21 lira per capita in 1954.[8] In 1956 during a meeting of Ichud Hakvutzot V'Hakibbutzim (the successor to Hever Hakvutzot), it was estimated that member kibbutzim spent over five million dollars for security measures, which was partly refunded by the two national institutions.[9] The burden of security measures was thus still too great for Har to carry alone.

Members of a border kibbutz like Har are usually assigned to the community in times of war rather than being sent elsewhere. Specially trained members, however, such as paratroopers, are mobilized, and some of Har's members are high ranking military figures. Among them are two one-star generals of

[8] Israeli Government, *The Position of Agriculture in Israel* (Jerusalem: 1960) pp. 258-289. It is known as the Horowitz Committee Report after its chairman, David Horowitz, governor of the Bank of Israel.

[9] Viteles, *Cooperative Movement*, 2:555.

the Israeli Defense Forces. Many of those who served in the Haganah and Palmach have continued to serve in special leadership roles. All of Har's members are members of the Israeli Defense Forces. Thirty-months service is required for men and twenty months for women. It usually begins at eighteen years of age. Members are part of an active reserve system until they are forty-nine. Since members can be called for reserve training at any time, the distribution of labor can be disrupted within the kibbutz. In times of peace, a kibbutz can arrange to delay the call-up for any member whose job is critical. Women are not called into the reserves in almost all cases, but since the rising of Lebanese border tension they have been training inside Har. An example of a successfully requested delay was the postponement of the poultry manager's call-up during a critical growth period of the chickens.

As an integral part of the kibbutz movement, Har continues to reap the prestige of the important role played by the kibbutzim in the Israeli Defense Forces. A number of writers have commented on the special role kibbutzniks have had in the armed forces and their overrepresentation in the high-risk military positions. This is often related to an emphasis in the kibbutz on group responsibility, individual leadership skills, and a commitment to do more than the minimum. Harry Viteles in his *History of the Cooperative Movement in Israel* praises the success of the kibbutz's values: "This bears witness to our success in molding a new type of Jew—with an unusual alertness, intelligence and other attributes, able to assume responsibility."[10] And Dan Leon comments that "the spirit of volunteering and pioneering makes kibbutz youth 'a natural' for leadership in a land where security is so much a part of the national need . . . they play a role quite out of proportion to their members in every military action which requires a special initiative, staying power and readiness to make quick and independent

[10] Ibid., 2:562.

decisions."[11] Five of Har's members have been killed in warfare since the state was established. Others have been wounded, including a young man who lost his leg. In a war-related incident, a teenage girl lost her eye when a horse she was riding stumbled over a mine laid near the perimeter of Har. In addition to close family and friendship networks among Israeli-Jewish citizens, members of Har have deeply experienced deaths and injuries occurring to others outside the community.[12]

Since the creation of the state, the military and political situation continues to affect Har's economic and social reality—its land expansion programs, labor needs, sources of capital, its patterns of immigration, internal stratification, and the overall rhythm of daily life.

Toward Economic Expansion

For Har, the statehood period of 1948-1967 was one of soaring success in a number of its economic branches and an appreciable rise in the standard of living. The improved economic situation reflected the increased acreage, the mechanization of the agrarian sector, and the very successful development of the industrial sector. The growth of both sectors was largely a result of support from the government, the Histadrut, the Jewish Agency, and the Ichud Federation.

Immediately after the state's establishment, the government adopted a policy calling for rapid agricultural expansion—a policy that was consistent with the agricultural bias of the kibbutz. The possibilities of land for expansion and improved irrigation made possible the actualization of this policy. By the

[11] Dan Leon, *The Kibbutz: A New Way of Life* (New York: Pergamon Press, 1969), pp. 141-142. He cites a study by Dr. Yehuda Amir published in *Magamot*, a quarterly of the behavioral sciences in Israel (August 1967).

[12] For a very important and sensitive accounting of the effect of the 1967 War on kibbutz soldiers see *The Seventh Day*, ed. Andre Deutsch (Tel Aviv: Steimatsky's Agency Ltd., 1970).

mid-1950s, however, national economic policy began to emphasize industrialization as agriculture produced surpluses and the state increased its need for industrial goods.[13] Har's own economic development benefited from both emphases, but the success in agrarian and industrial sectors also brought about new problems for the community, including a larger number of hired laborers and a greater degree of job specialization.

THE AGRARIAN SECTOR

In the statehood years Har's agrarian development reflected government directed policies including a number of long-range plans, the distribution of land previously farmed by Arabs, and a series of special support benefits to the cooperative settlements. Har became linked to a new bureaucratic network of the government, the Histadrut, and the Jewish Agency.

Until 1952 a Committee for Joint Agricultural Planning consisting of representatives of the Jewish Agency's Land Settlement Department and Ministry of Agriculture was in charge of agrarian planning.[14] Its Four-Year Plan for 1951-1954 called for national self-sufficiency in food production, other than grain and meat and an increase in rural population from 13.1 percent in 1950 to 26 percent in 1954. In 1953 a Joint Planning Center took over the role of the committee and issued a new Seven-Year Plan that at first greatly resembled the former plan. However, several national realities necessitated modification of its goals:

(1) immigration in 1952 was less than emigration, and new

[13] Between 1958 and 1964, national income from agricultural goods declined from 13.6 percent to 9.9 percent; manufacturing income rose to 25.4 percent.

[14] Dorothy Willner, *Nation-Building and Community in Israel* (Princeton: Princeton University Press, 1969), chap. 5. It is important to note that the Jewish National Fund lost its autonomy in 1958 when it became part of the state-controlled Land Authority.

    immigrants were not primarily interested in rural settlement;

(2) irrigation improvement would be slower than anticipated;

(3) Israel had an extremely poor balance of trade record preventing actualization of self-sufficiency.

Mixed farming plans gave way to promotion of crops suitable for mass export.

This policy of turning away from mixed farming had several implications for Har. First, it violated the kibbutz ideology of supplying the food needs of the community; the emphasis on cash crops increased Har's dependence on the external economy to meet even its basic food supply. Next, the shift marked a movement away from "the religion of labor" to greater concentration on production for the market. It undermined the emotional value of work. Finally, production of cash crops demanded mechanization of the agrarian sector. This further cut off the agrarian worker from the soil and increased the need for specializing training. Job rotation, therefore, became less feasible.

The single most important factor in the increased success of Har's agrarian sector was the additional land the kibbutz received from the state after 1948. Until this time the community was restricted to the fifty *dunams* of valley land below its hilly mountain site. In 1951, in exchange for a small piece of its land, Har received 2,900 *dunams* with 2,500 of that 12 kilometers away on the valley floor and ready for cultivation. The new lands were split up into two sections of 270 and 2,230 *dunams*. Transportation was thus necessary to reach the fields from Har. One hundred fifty *dunams* of the remaining 400 *dunams* were planted as a forest; the remainder was reserved for building and future use. At first the land had been given jointly to Har and two other kibbutzim in the region. In 1952, Har obtained sole use of the land. At this time intensified agrarian development at Har started because the members, as is suggested by Mica Lebon, could identify the land that was theirs: "The banana . . . plantation began in 1953, and the *pardess* [citrus grove] in 1953. Why in 1953? Because the government [at first] gave an amount of land to three kibbutzim together. The kibbutz did not know what would be its land. Only in 1952 was it decided that that section will be for Har, that for Matzuba, that for Eilon. So we began to be attached not only to work on the land, but to the land which was ours."[15] Even though the land was still legally owned by the Jewish National Fund, kibbutz members felt it was their land to farm and that they owned it.

The land was part of Arab refugee land reclaimed by the state under the Development Authority Law of 1950 and put at the disposal of Jewish land settlements.[16] Until 1948, Zionist organizations had only been able to acquire 6.6 percent of the land in Palestine. The redemption of land formerly held by Palestinian-Arabs came under state control primarily through the Absentee Property Law of 1950. Owners declared as absentees would have their land placed in custodianship until ownership rights could be settled. After 1948, state land of 15,025,000 *dunams* together with Jewish National Fund land of 3,570,000 *dunams* became known as national land and constituted more than 90 percent of all Israeli territory. Near Har, land that had belonged to the Arab villages of Umm al Faraj, Basa, and Ikrit was taken over by the state. Part of the lands surrounding Basa became Har's.

The expansion of Jewish cultivation in the Galilee after 1948 was an important factor in the government's "Judaization of the Galilee" policies. In 1953 Joseph Nahmani, one of the originators of these policies and head of the Jewish National Fund

[15] Interview with Mica Lebon, 24 April 1975.

[16] Sabri Jiryis, *The Arabs in Israel* (New York: Monthly Review Press, 1976), chap. 4. Also A. Granott, *Agrarian Reform and the Record of Israel* (London: Eyre Spottiswoode, 1956).

from 1935-1965, writing to the current Minister of Defense David Ben-Gurion, recognized that for kibbutz settlement to be successful a large Arab population would have to be moved: "Though Western Galilee has now been occupied, it still has not been freed of its Arab population . . . in all, there are 84,002 Arabs, not counting Akko, controlling 929,449 *dunams* of land . . . most of them farmers, who make up 45% of the Arab minority in the country. They are living in a self-contained area stretching right up to the borders of Arab Lebanon. The Arab minority centered here presents a continual threat to the security of the nation."[17]

The land made available to Har allowed a successful expansion of the kibbutz's internal economy. Without Jewish ownership of the Western Galilee plains and valleys, the kibbutzim in the area would not have been able to develop their agrarian sector. Moreover, Jewish land ownership and removal of Arab farmers eased the immediate military threat to the kibbutzim.

The newly acquired lands of Har would have been at best a mixed blessing if it were not for the improvement of irrigation in the area (see Tables 9 and 10). During the Mandate years the level of water necessary for large-scale cultivation at Har could not be guaranteed. The Mekorot Water Company, established in 1936 by the Jewish Agency and the Histadrut, began the first efforts for a national water plan based on G. B. Hayes' outline in *Tennessee Valley Authority on the Jordan*. The outline called for water to be brought from the Jordan River to the Negev desert. Until 1948 only temporary installation of pipes could be made.

With the foundation of the state, intensive water planning efforts were initiated, and overcoming the water limitation was seen as a major factor in developing the national economy. In 1952 Tahal, the Israel Water Planning Corporation, was set up

---

[17] Joseph Nahmani, *A Man of Galilee* (Israel: Ramat Gan, 1969).

by the government to plan the nation's water, sewage, and draining systems. The government holds 52 percent of Tahal stock and the Jewish Agency and Jewish National Fund each hold 24 percent. A 1959 law passed by the Knesset gives all water rights to the state; they are administered through the Water Commissioner of the Ministry of Agriculture. The administration of the water supply is thus quite well established.

Har, as do all kibbutzim, benefits from a discount rate on water. Water prices are regulated by the water commissioner and vary according to nature of use and distance from the source of supply. Har's height above sea level and distance from the main water system would make its water supply expensive if it were not for its kibbutz status.

In the 1960s, Har's water needs were about 1,205,000 cubic meters per year, but the exact amount available depended upon

TABLE 9. PERCENTAGE OF TOTAL IRRIGATED AREA IN ISRAELI KIBBUTZIM, 1949-1960 (in thousands of *dunams*).

Year	Israel	Kibbutzim	Kibbutzim % of Total
1949	300	82	27.3
1950	350	101	28.9
1951	470	123	26.2
1952	340	130	24.1
1953	650	198	30.5
1954	760	212	27.9
1955	890	169	30.2
1956	965	295	30.6
1957	1,100	331	30.1
1958	1,185	391	33.0
1959	1,235	418	33.8
1960	1,305	427	32.7

SOURCES: *Statistical Abstracts of Israel* (Jerusalem: Central Bureau of Statistics, Government of Israel, 1949-1960); Audit Union of the Workers' Agricultural Cooperative Societies, Ltd., *Statistical Manual* (Tel Aviv: 1940).

TABLE 10. Division of Water among Har's Agricultural Branches (in thousands of cubic meters).

Agricultural Branch	Number of Cubic Meters
Padess (citrus)	300
Avocado	350
Bananas	450
Potatoes	35
Cotton	120
Total	1,255

SOURCE: Economic Management Office of Kibbutz Har.

the yearly rainfall, the available national supply, and other changing factors. The cost during the period varied from 5 to 10 *agarot* per cubic meter (an *agarot* is equivalent to one one-hundredth of a lira).

At first water was brought to Har through a system of aluminum pipes turned on and off at irregular hours. These were replaced by polyvinyl pipes that did not rust, a single command system at the head of the network, and a time clock that would automatically shut off water. Watering took place through a system of aspersion. Only in the 1970s did the new drip irrigation system appear at the kibbutz.

Har's water planning is done on a yearly basis by the Economic Committee in consultation with the agricultural branches and those concerned with house management. Plans reflect maximum water conservation, optimal management of resources, and careful consideration of allocation. The decision to grow avocados and cotton establishes a balance between a crop that requires much water with one demanding less.

The shift of responsibility for irrigation from each agricultural branch indicates a growing concern with efficiency at the expense of decentralized decision making. Until the 1970s, each branch was responsible for planning for its own irrigation.[18] The Economic Committee, wanting to make it more efficient, decided to send a kibbutz member to take a special course in irrigation so he could be responsible for all the branches. Each branch, however, wanted to maintain some control over its share of water and a compromise was reached: one trained expert would coordinate branch irrigation but the actual execution of the yearly plan would be the responsibility of each branch. Despite the increased efficiency, the change in irrigation diminished branch autonomy and increased job specialization.

The discount in charges for water irrigation that Har received was only one of the financially important supports given to the kibbutz. Agricultural subsidies in the form of grants and loans by the government, the Jewish Agency, the Histadrut, and the Ichud Federation were crucial to Har's agrarian development after the state emerged. The availability of support for agricultural expansion was largely due to the government's reaction to the closing of markets by the Arab states and the increase of new immigrants who settled in urban areas. In prestate years, agricultural supplies in Palestine were partly met by trade with Lebanon, Syria, and Transjordan. After the state's foundation, these sources of food were closed off to the area. At the same time, the new immigrants arriving in the state era were less idealistic about land settlement than the *Ashkenazi* Socialist-Zionists.[19] The urban centers and newly planned development towns became the major sectors of population growth, and the need for greater agricultural production became intensified.

Har benefited from the 35 million dollar loan given by the Export-Import Bank of the United States government to the Israeli government. The loan was solely for agricultural devel-

[18] Interview with Moshe Kadimah, economic coordinator of Har, 22 June 1975.

[19] S. N. Eisenstadt, *The Absorption of Immigrants* (London: Routledge & Kegan Paul Ltd., 1954).

opment and was used principally for mechanization and irrigation. Har received sorely needed irrigation equipment and agrarian machinery. Tractors that could be used for hauling as well as fieldwork were especially useful. Kibbutzim as a whole had 41 percent of all tractors in Israel in 1959, 64 percent of the grain combines, and 53 percent of the balers.[20] They cultivated over 33 percent of all cultivable land in Israel though their population then was only just over 4 percent of the total Israeli-Jewish population.

The "conversion loans" of the government, Jewish Agency, and Histadrut replaced reliance on short-term, high interest commercial loans. The new credits helped Har reduce its interest payments and put more capital investment into agrarian development. Economist Eliyahu Kanovsky has estimated that "conversion loans" of the Jewish Agency saved kibbutzim founded before 1948, 3.5 million lira in 1961 and double that amount in 1962.[21]

Har also made use of loans from Keren HaIchud, the Bank Fund of the Ichud Federation. The Keren HaIchud serves as the credit guarantor for the individual kibbutz that borrows from commercial banks and has its own fund as well. The interest rate for federation members is far lower than the commercial rate, that is, 12 pecent compared to 20 percent. Har pays a one-half-percent service fee to Keren HaIchud for the service. The federation used its funding relationship to the kibbutz to implement its ideological goals. For instance, it maintains a tax on those kibbutzim using hired labor, which is against the federation's and the kibbutz's economic principles. The taxes collected are placed in a fund to purchase agricultural machinery for member kibbutzim to help them eliminate the need for the hired labor. In addition to its agricultural sup-

[20] Eliyahu Kanovsky, *The Economy of the Israeli Kibbutz* (Cambridge, Mass.: Harvard University Press, 1966), p. 54.

[21] Ibid., p. 120.

ports, the Keren Halchud services Har with old-age pension and other welfare benefits.

Har additionally received the advantages of reduced costs for fertilizer and drought and disease relief. These are part of the government support policies for the cooperative settlements, and in cases of a bad season, Har's loan payments have been postponed. The assured backing of the government and other national institutions has made Har a good credit risk in its quest for the financial support necessary for its economic expansion. The treasurer of Har comments that "the reputation of the kibbutz is good. It's like General Motors. The kibbutz is reliable. We have good backing. They know Keren Halchud can also pay. The banks like the kibbutz. They know we are no risk."[22]

Without the gifts, loans, and overall support of the national government and national and international institutions, Har would not have been able to expand its economy in the way it did after 1948.

The principal agricultural branches of Har that were begun in the early 1950s are the *pardess* or citrus grove, and the banana plantation. At first Har practiced mixed farming to produce its own food needs. As mentioned above, this approach was dropped in accordance with state policies when the goal became the production of cash crops for export. Even into the 1950s a variety of vegetables was still produced including onions, potatoes, melons, sugar beets, and corn fodder. Of these only potatoes remained in production by 1970 (see Table 11).

An examination of the development of the two main branches of the *pardess* and the banana plantation reveals several patterns within each branch. These include an emphasis on income production, especially for export; an increasing use of machinery; increasing job specialization; restrictions on hired labor; and interbranch competition.

---

[22] Interview with Z. Nichmod, treasurer of Har, 2 June 1975.

TABLE 11. HAR'S AGRICULTURAL LAND DISTRIBUTION,
1959 AND 1970.*

	1959	1970
Plantations:		
bananas	490	435
citrus	175	335
avocado	15	120
young avocado	—	190
carob	50	—
empty	—	5
Totals	730	1,085
Field Crops:		
vegetables	90	—
sugar beets	160	—
potatoes	60	100
wheat	460	300
field cover	300	—
fertilizer	120	—
cotton	—	835
Totals	1,190	1,235
Overall Totals	1,920	2,320

* In *dunams*; 1 *dunam* is approximately ¼ acre.

The banana branch is the highest income-producing branch
in Har aside from the factory.[23] Because of this it enjoys high
prestige in the community. Since work in the branch is physically demanding, members of the banana branch are considered to be the "real men" of the kibbutz. Volunteers who come
to Har are often tested out to see if they can meet the demands
of banana work.

The branch began at the initiative of the government when

[23] *Har Bulletin*, nos. 3 and 5 (1960), Har Archives. Kanovsky reports that
kibbutzim almost monopolized the bananas in Israel, having produced 87
percent of the market. *The Economy of the Kibbutz*, p. 83.

it sought to expand export crops. In 1953, the first experiment with bananas proved a success despite claims they would not grow near the sea. They did not severely deplete the soil, could be grown in winter and harvested in the early spring, grew rapidly, and provided quick returns on investment. The banana branch was the first agricultural success at Har.

Growing bananas demands specialized care, and one of Har's members has a national reputation in the field. He has travelled to South America to investigate new methods of growing that have helped to keep Har a leader in banana production.

The branch is one of the most labor-intensive in agriculture. Tractors never enter the field and men carry bunches often weighing over one hundred pounds from the field to the side of the road. In the beginning of the season, poorer plants are cut back to leave room for the better ones to grow; spraying occurs two to three times against weeds; and hedges are planted to cut the wind. Stakes two meters in height made of bamboo grown on the kibbutz provide support for the young plants. The jobs of staking and cutting are done by hand.

Between 1955 and 1963, the banana grove grew from 250 to 512 *dunams*. In the 1950s, the market for bananas exceeded the supply. However, by the 1960s, supply began to catch up with demand and the government restricted production to 440 *dunams*. In 1970, Har had 435. Income from bananas has almost doubled that of any other agricultural branch (see Table 12).

Har markets the bananas with Tnuva, the Histadrut market cooperative which exports 75 percent of the kibbutz's production. They are sent primarily to Greece, Yugoslavia, and Eastern Europe. Only the smaller bunches remain for internal national use.

Within the branch, the main problems have had to do with labor. The nationally famous branch manager who has been in

TABLE 12. INCOME OF KIBBUTZ HAR, 1971 AND 1972 (in thousands of lira).

	1971	1972
Bananas	900	850
Citrus	500	654
Avocados	215	171
Cotton	270	380
Potatoes	65	103
Wheat and Hay	39	36
Poultry	265	324
Guest House	750	800
Food Service	4	4
Outside Work	185	210
Factory	4,500	5,630
Totals	7,683	9,162
Other Income	45	50
Final Total	7,728	9,212

charge of the branch throughout the entire period of its success is an individualist rather than a team worker. His refusal to rotate his position has caused other members to leave the branch. In addition, the hard physical labor required continually discourages members from joining. Because of this, the branch relies heavily on volunteer labor sent to the kibbutz from national absorption centers and from kibbutz federation offices and, in season, on hired labor. Volunteers are welcomed at Har for periods from one to six months. They receive room, board, and "pocket money" in exchange for working eight hours a day, five days a week.

Although the nonmember laborer works as hard as any member, the elite attitude toward nonkibbutzniks is apparent in the fields. Volunteers and hired labor are usually put into their own working sections and members work only with each other except when joint work is required. At mealtimes, the segregation pattern is maintained. Arab hired laborers, some of whom have worked for years in the branch, eat in their separate shed. The sense of solidarity based upon shared agrarian work is absent. Members have commented that they do not wish to work in the banana plantation because of the necessity of working with "outsiders." Only the branch head and one other member have stayed in the branch for more than a few years.

The *pardess* also began in Har on the suggestion of the government. Yaakov Pari, who has headed the branch in recent years commented on its history during a fieldwork interview: "The government began to distribute the confiscated Arab lands to the kibbutzim in 1952. We knew this area would be good for orchards. . . . In this area a *pardess* was a new thing . . . we did not know what kind of trees to plant so we met with some people in Israel who knew a lot about *pardessim* and decided to make two plantings, the first in 1956 and if it went well another in 1960." In 1956 a wide variety of oranges and grapefruits were planted on 135 *dunams* to see what would grow best. Grapefruit grew very well and now constitute 70 percent of the *pardess* in its present 335 *dunams*. The trees live seventy to seventy-five years, a little longer than the varieties of orange trees at Har (Washington, Shamuti, Valencia) and much longer than the lemon trees, which only last fifteen years and are prone to disease.

A separate national bureaucracy controls the sale of citrus, which is Israel's largest agrarian export. Har sells its citrus to Tnuva, which takes charge of its cleaning, packing, and distribution. A Citrus Board National Council sets the export selling price. It does this in consultation with the Ministry of Agriculture. The national council also sells part of Har's citrus production for juice and other products to the regional Miluot system. Har thus does no direct selling outside of Tnuva. Annual prices vary according to market demand and crop quality.

Like the banana branch manager of Har, Yaakov, the *pardess* manager, is nationally known and has been the representative of the regional kibbutz *pardess* system to the Ministry of Agriculture and Citrus Board. This position is rotated among regional members every three to four years. The job of regional representative includes deciding on experiments with plants. Har's area is well-organized and does more experimentation than do most regions. It also involves scheduling a national picking season that allows for fair competition among the regions with their different harvest seasons. The job demands travelling outside of the kibbutz once or twice a week. This can be seen as a job-benefit as most members do not have the opportunity to travel regularly.

The *pardess* is much more mechanized than the banana plantation. Spraying and much of the picking is done by machine (the latter only since the 1970s). Mechanization, aside from cutting down on the physical labor, saves overall labor time spent on production. This in turn cuts down the need for volunteer labor that is still necessary during picking season.

Work on the *pardess* is more decentralized than the banana branch. One member is in charge of tree diseases, another in charge of tractors, another in charge of picking. The position of branch manager rotates among the five full-time workers. The members of the *pardess* have opposed hiring labor to help during the picking. The extra work is done by volunteers who are usually members of the *ulpan* work-study program and by a general call-up of members who work after their regular workday and on Saturday. Certain idealistic commitments still prevail in the *pardess* especially when reinforced by social pressure on the membership.

A major problem of the *pardess* is in the increasing disenchantment of the kibbutz youth with the branch. Picking lasts eight months out of the year and is considered boring work. One reason why Har chose to concentrate on grapefruit production is that grapefruits can be picked more quickly than oranges and lemons and thus demand less labor. In the very beginning, a few women worked in the branch, but since 1960 the only women doing so have been volunteers. Yaakov attributes this to the physically boring aspects of the work, although it is hard to imagine that ironing is more exciting. A major disadvantage to picking is, more likely, the distance from the kibbutz to the fields, which would separate mothers from children.

Branch pride exists among the agricultural workers. This is due to the shortage of certain equipment, water, and supplies, which puts each branch in competition with the others for efficient production. A certain amount of status comes to each branch and to each branch member depending on how well the production went for the year. A great deal of the internal status stratification in Har arises from a member's branch affiliation, at least in the case of men. During the early periods of economic development, much of one's self-esteem derived from individual output. Since the creation of the state and increased mechanization in the agrarian sector, stress is put on efficient use of machinery and other resources to aid production. Yaakov maintains that he would rather borrow an extra machine from the *pardess* branch of another kibbutz before asking for it from another branch in Har.

Among other agricultural projects that Har began developing successfully after 1948 are avocados, poultry, and small field crops. The poultry branch only held its own until after 1967 when a major modernization effort occurred.[24] Potatoes and cotton are all that is left of field crops. Avocado production began in 1957 and grew in importance to the kibbutz so by 1970 they occupied 120 *dunams*. Avocado production has been successful because avocados are scarce on the world market and are suitable for Har's terrain since they require less water than bananas and grow in poor soil. Because avocados are tall trees

[24] For history of poultry branch at Har see *Har Bulletin*, no. 5 (1960).

(11 meters) picking is done mostly by machines. The branch belongs to the National Avocado Society subsidized by the state. The society has subsidized Har's avocado branch and serves as the national center for branch planning.

As the various agricultural branches developed in Har from 1948-1967, economic stability began to be achieved for the community. The bananas and *pardess* in particular raised income to above subsistence levels. However, the agrarian prosperity was not sufficient to meet the growing population's needs or desires for a standard of living comparable to that of urban workers in Israel. The factory developed in Har as a response to these internal economic interests and, like the agrarian branches, in response to the needs of the state.

THE INDUSTRIAL SECTOR

Dan Karmon, Director of the Kibbutz Industrial Association, summed up the movement within the kibbutz economy from an agrarian to an industrial base in a fieldwork interview: "We are no longer the vanguard, so we are turning to industry." While the process of industrialization at Har substantiates his perception, what has remained consistent is the kibbutz's commitment to the needs of national development.

There were both external and internal pressures for industrialization. On the national scene, agricultural surpluses were achieved in the mid-1950s reducing overall market profits. Government aid to the agricultural sector was now mainly for dairy and vegetables in branches that were the specialty of the moshavim, or family cooperatives, rather than those of the kibbutz. In order to deal with the surpluses, the government also restricted production of branches in Har, including the bananas branch. Moreover, and most significantly, there was the continuing problem of limitations of land and water.

After 1948, the government was particularly interested in developing industry that would bring in high export profits and increase self-sufficiency, especially in the area of military security. During this period nearly one half of the Israeli gross national product was earmarked for military-security. The tax rate to help cover these huge military costs was the highest in the world. Kibbutzim, as were other sectors of the cooperative and private economy, were encouraged to industrialize in needed areas.

Har had already responded to the industrial needs of nation building during the Mandate years when it secretly produced arms for the Haganah in its small workshop. After 1948 the pressure for larger scale industrialization by the state met favorable internal response. Members realized that complete reliance on the agrarian branches was risky and would limit increases in the desired standard of living. The population was getting older and members felt industry would provide workplace opportunities for those no longer able to do agricultural labor. There was also some sentiment that women would enter the industrial workplace and thus expand their income-producing roles.

The decision to begin a small factory, which in the beginning was a large workshop, was not an easy one for Har. A number of members still felt strong ideological ties to the conception of the kibbutz as an agrarian community and did not want a factory. Others brought up the issue of hired labor, which was to become a main problem of kibbutz industry. After numerous General Assembly discussions, the members decided to take up the government's promised support for a new factory. Probably no other single decision has had as strong an effect on the community's economic and social life.

The decision to industrialize at Har indicated a new emphasis on economic considerations and a further lessening of Socialist-Zionist ideologies. Aside from diminishing the stress on agrarian labor, industrialization necessitated the employment of more hired laborers, whose very presence in the kibbutz economy was against its ideological tenets. In addition, industrialization meant job specialization that would further reduce job rotation possibilities and create an overall increase in the specialization in the kibbutz.[25] Kibbutz members increasingly saw themselves as owner-managers rather than *poalim*, or workers.

The movement of Har's industrial venture from a workshop size plant to an internationally linked, full-size factory occurred in three principal stages: 1953-1958, 1958-1965, and 1965 to the present.

At the end of 1948, the small clandestine arms workshop for the Haganah ended but a few members continued to make small parts for movable lamps, mechanical pencils, and switches for ovens. None of these products earned much income for the kibbutz, and it was generally felt that the workshop should close. In 1953, the government initiated a new, larger industrial effort at the kibbutz. The member who headed the workshop received a call from the Defense Department inquiring whether the kibbutz could supply the same kinds of precision tools that it had done for the Haganah. The government agreed to finance the necessary materials through grants and loans, and Har then began producing specialized cutting tools. The factory turned out high quality products but at a minimal profit. This was due, according to the present manager, to the fact that little attention at the time was directed to the economics of production.

The government financed the building of a factory at Har according to its grant and loan policies that took into account the strategic importance of the area. In an interview Mica Lebon identified the government financing policy for each area: "The country is zoned into three parts: near the borders is zone A; next to the border areas, zone B; and farthest away from important defense areas, zone C. Har is in zone A. This means

---

[25] Menechem Rosner, *Social Aspects of Industrialization in the Kibbutz* (Givat Haviva, Israel: Social Research Centre on the Kibbutz, 1969).

we receive one third of investments as gifts, one third as loans at 6 percent interest due in eight years. Zone B receives only 20 percent as gifts and 40 percent as loans. Zone C receives no gifts and receives 50 percent as loans. All zones pay only 25 percent of income tax for five years."[26] Zone A was considered to be the most strategic and included the regional area of Har. According to the policies zone A received one-third of its investment capital from loans and one-third from gifts. The rest comes from kibbutz profits.

The beginning of the factory not only strengthened the ties from the kibbutz to the state institutions but also initiated strong, direct economic links between Har and international markets. The factory director made two trips to Europe where he purchased factory machine tools from Switzerland and Germany with a 9,000 lira loan from the government. Several orders for Har's products were placed in Great Britain. The international framework in which the factory operated gave many of Har's members a chance to increase their awareness of international markets and to bring back to the community a more sophisticated understanding of the outside world. The outside visits were both appreciated and resented by the rest of the members, whose world remained quite parochial. The factory personnel were fulfilling the role the treasurer had served during the Mandate years when he brought back news of a movie to the kibbutz.

By the end of the fifties, the factory, which employed thirty-eight workers, was still on the scale of a large workshop and a decision was made in the kibbutz to develop it further under the new directorship of Rami Don, a nationally-known Haganah hero, who had become an engineer through correspondence courses. He began his term as factory director with a trip to Europe in order to develop plans for factory expansion. With approval of the kibbutz and a government loan of 55,000 lira,

[26] Interview with Mica Lebon, 24 April 1975.

machines were purchased at the cost of 500 to 10,000 lira in a number of countries. Thirty workers, including ten members and twenty hired laborers, produced milling cutters, borers, screw-tops with precision threading, and circular saws. Har was successful in cornering the Israeli market for such goods and began developing its export trade. In 1958 milling cutters were exported to Switzerland, and since 1970 trade has taken place with the United States, Canada, and Uruguay.

Rami Don is credited by kibbutz members for bringing concepts of automation and engineering sophistication to Har's factory. However, he had difficulty making his ideas work "because he was too in love with ideas and not enough with realization."[27] During this period, the factory was run without the team approach that characterized most agrarian branches. Like the head of the banana plantation, Rami Don was an individualist and was not able to foster a shared management pattern. Although the factory had sales of one million lira a year, it had still not reached a very profitable level.

By 1965 the kibbutz was confronted by a number of questions concerning its future. The number of people working in the factory had jumped to fifty-nine, including forty-one hired laborers (primarily Sephardic Jews from the nearby towns of Shlomi and Nahariya). The existence of hired laborers in the *meshek*, or economic organization, was a direct violation of kibbutz ideology, and the increasing number in the factory could not be ignored. The kibbutz also invested heavily through loans and grants in the continued development of industry. Each year the industrial sector was gaining in importance in the overall mix of the economy.

The larger Israeli economy during the beginning of this period was in the midst of a recession. There was a slowdown in production and export sales were decreasing. It was not an encouraging moment to expand industrially.

[27] Ibid.

For the second time, the factory became the focus of a critical event in Har; the major issue was whether the factory should expand, remain as it was, or disband. The latter choice was not really considered because the kibbutz clearly relied on it. Strong opinions developed on the two alternatives. The strongest objections to factory expansion were based on ideological concerns such as hired labor and increased individualism and on doubts concerning future economic returns. As Mica Lebon, the factory manager, notes, the original kibbutz settlers were especially attached to the kibbutz ideal as an agrarian community: "The kibbutz veterans do not like industry. They think it's something foreign coming and stealing from them their romanticism, their ideal. Second, they think that industry will change attitudes. . . . The kibbutz with industry is not the kibbutz with agriculture."[28] Those supporting factory expansion took a number of actions designed to educate and convince others of the industrial advantages for the kibbutz.

Mica Lebon, who succeeded Rami Don in the directorship of the factory, was a key person in insuring the continuation of Har's factory. He reorganized the management of the factory by establishing joint management with a four-person Management Committee. The committee consisted of a technical, a production, a sales, and a general manager. This democratized the leadership of the factory and promoted a decentralization of decision making (see Figure 2). However, since all managers were required to be kibbutz members, the basic dichotomy between hired laborers and members remained.

The new management presented two alternatives to the General Assembly: one was to reduce the factory to a thirty-five man workshop, the other was to expand the factory to its full economic potential. A central feature of the expansion plan was the concentration on the export trade. Mica argued that once the factory was expanded, production would increase reducing

[28] Interview with Mica Lebon, 1 May 1975.

cost per unit and thus allowing for more advantageous competition in the international markets. To confirm his point he decided to go to the United States to develop export contracts. His hope was that with an assured market the rest of the kibbutz membership would support Har's industrial development. His reception in the United States was really formidable;[29] Mica was able to secure ninety-thousand dollars worth of contracts. He then sought the approval of the General Assembly for his overall expansion plan.

Factory expansion was a new experience for the kibbutz in the 1965-1973 period. Many of the issues involved a technical knowledge possessed by only a few members. The membership usually considered economic issues a year in advance, but this

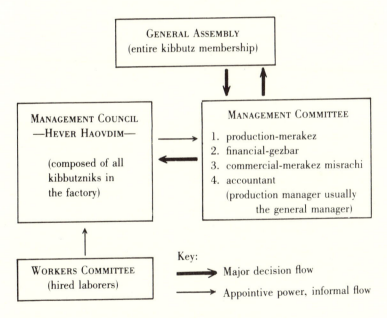

FIGURE 2. Decision Making for the Kibbutz Factory

[29] Ibid.

was one with long-range consequences. Expansion proponents conceded that "the way of kibbutz deomocracy" would change, but saw this as inevitable in the kibbutz's necessary transition from its romantic past to a commitment to modern realities.

It was the national military-political situation that again played a critical role in influencing internal events. The Six Day War came and was followed by a period of economic boom. Moreover, the products of the metal industry were in increasing demand. Mica Lebon notes that "all the papers, all the country was talking about the need to develop the metal industry. So we [the Management Committee] said that the country needs the factory, the Minister of Defense needs the factory. And the plan succeeded."[30] The General Assembly vote in favor of a two-million lira investment plan passed after a close debate. The announcement, though received "as a shock and blow," was cushioned with favorable reports from government representatives, Israeli economists, and outside engineers. The government gave the kibbutz a four-year investment schedule, which was increased by 10 percent when the Ichud Federation also accepted the plan.

After 1967 Israel's metal works industry prospered, and Har's factory began an unprecedented increase in profits. In four years its total sales were three million lira. The initial ties to international markets made through other national institutions and its own sales efforts became solidified. Internally, however, problems concerning hired laborers grew and accentuated the stratification of the community.

HIRED LABOR

The hiring of outside labor for Har's economy is a source of considerable tension in the community and reflects subordination of traditional socialist principles to new rationales of economic calculation. Dan Leon, a kibbutznik sociologist, has

---

[30] Ibid.

called the existence of hired labor in kibbutz life, "the Trojan horse of capitalism." For Har, the hired labor phenomenon provides evidence of a new middle-class orientation in the community and the acceptance of middle-class attitudes.

Hired labor first entered the kibbutz economy in the agrarian sector, but industrialization greatly enlarged the practice. Har's factory is one of the largest of any kibbutz; and, since its inception, it has primarily employed hired laborers. The transformation from a small workshop to a medium-scale factory was coupled with an increase in hired labor from twenty to over a hundred. In addition, the factory is located in the community's center and hired laborers cannot be kept out of sight as they can be in the valley fields twelve kilometers from Har's center.

Har's factory is divided between members and hired laborers. The stated aim of the factory organizational plan is to foster cooperation in decision making. A general monthly meeting of all factory workers is held to discuss issues within the authority of the Management Committee, listen to committee reports, and to comment on these reports. All essential factory decisions are made by the Management Committee, which is elected by the General Assembly from among kibbutz member nominees. The committee meets at least once a week to make operating decisions that are then ratified by the Management Council. The laborers are organized into workers' committees that are represented in the Management Council. So the position of hired laborers in Har's factory is similar to their position in Histadrut firms and in many private Israeli enterprises. The relationship between hired laborers and kibbutz members is one of employer and employee.

A hired laborer is prevented from assuming any top management role. Only members can hold these positions. The factory manager indicated that everyone working in the factory was aware that management jobs were reserved for kibbutz members: "We are lucky that those salaried workers near the top

know they can do no more. It could be that one of them could
be able to perform a management job. That would create problems because the kibbutz decided to have a factory to guarantee a special working place for its members."[31] This limit on
upward mobility is comparable to that in a capitalist economy
with respect toward disadvantaged minority groups and women.

While hired laborers do not take top management roles, kibbutz members have gradually removed themselves from production roles so that since 1965 no member has had a job in
primary production. Working on the machines became viewed
as beneath the status of a kibbutznik who had become a factory
owner-manager as noted by the factory's general manager:
"Many of the sons of the kibbutz who came to work in the
factory did not want to work with their hands. They do not want
to begin with the beginning. They are sons of the masters."[32]
The separation of kibbutzniks from the means of production
has been a significant departure from the Socialist-Zionist goals
of creating and maintaining a Jewish working class and prac-
ticing the religion of labor.

The presence of hired labor has had a deep effect on Har's
sense of ownership and work motivation. In the early years of
the community, kibbutzniks believed that the sense of ownership would motivate them to do necessary, but unpleasant
work. Instead, a distinction has been made between formal
ownership and participation. Needs for specialization and efficiency tended to differentiate participation in production from
ownership.[33] These have devalued the ideals of cooperation and
equality. Moreover, in the case of Har's factory, two levels of
differentiation have occurred: between members and hired la-

[31] Ibid.

[32] Ibid.

[33] Adolf Berle and Gardner Means, *The Modern Corporation and Private
Property*. In the agricultural sector, the kibbutzniks remain more connected
with means of production than in industrial sector.

borers and between the top management and unskilled labor, including members. The factory situation has, therefore, had a direct effect on the overall community solidarity of the kibbutz and changed the system from a consensual to a contractual one.

Work in the kibbutz is no longer viewed as a sacred task. In the factory the workrole is the property of the kibbutz in the sense that "a job or claim to the services of another may be a possession."[34] In Har as a whole, the existence of hired labor has been a mark of a growing alienation of the kibbutz member from primary production. This not only indicates a movement from agrarian socialism toward advanced capitalism, but also the ascendancy of an individual rather than a communitarian ethos.

The transformation from *poalim*, or workers, to *baal bayit*, or house owners, among Har's members raises the question of whether the kibbutz is becoming closer to stressing private, individual values or cooperative socialist values. It can also raise the question of whether its original socialist ideals are a model for the present. A member of a kibbutz near Har has suggested that since industrialization, the kibbutzim's interests are definitely closer to those held in the private, capitalist sector of the Israeli economy and of the international level as well.[35]

The managers of the factory enjoy status and other benefits not available to the rest of the community. With increased specialized knowledge, their occupational tenure increases, necessarily limiting job rotation. For instance, each of the general managers of the factory has held that position for nearly a decade. Managers who commute to outside markets enjoy travel benefits and special car allowances. In Har, where the demand

[34]Talcott Parsons, quoted in Bendix and Lipset's *Class, Status and Power* (New York: The Free Press, 1953), p. 92ff.

[35] A Knesset member who resides at Kibbutz Gesher Achziv.

for use of automobiles is greater than the supply, this is no small benefit. These status differentiations are a constant source of friction within the small community. They demonstrate that the kibbutz is a microcosm of the transition from an agricultural to an urban-industrial society.

The relationship between Har's members and the hired laborers has social as well as economic dimensions. Most of the hired laborers immigrated to Israel in the 1950s from the non-Western world and became a part of the country's nonskilled labor force. Ben-Gurion called upon the kibbutzim to train and hire Sephardic immigrants as part of their nationalist service.[36] Har's factory became a primary training and hiring center for Shlomi and Nahariya residents, who are now transported up and down the mountain to the factory for various shifts by a bus the kibbutz provides. The position of Shlomi at the base of the mountain with Har at the top symbolizes their social and economic relations. Har's members generally come from a higher-income class background than do the hired laborers from Shlomi. Even those members who do not, have become part of the kibbutz movement and thus have achieved a higher position within the Yishuv community.

The situation is ironic for Har since it has one of the largest Sephardic populations (20 percent) of any kibbutz. While there is stratification along cultural background lines within Har, the Sephardic population of the kibbutz identifies more strongly with fellow kibbutzniks than with Shlomi residents. Sephardic kibbutz members, as do other kibbutz members, consider themselves part of a national, pioneer elite. Only a few Har members of Sephardic background have attempted to close the gap between the community of Shlomi and Har. Mica Lebon, the factory director, commented on this during a fieldwork interview: "One of my fights is to do something for Shlomi, maybe

[36] David Ben-Gurion, *Israel: A Personal History* (New York: Funk and Wagnalls, Inc., 1971).

because I am a Sephardic Jew. I came in fact from Lebanon and this question preoccupies my mind more than others." The relative absence of similar concern among most Har residents can be partly attributed to the regional isolation persisting from the prestate period. However, the employment of hired laborers brings into Har the very people most affected by the isolation. Many members of Har respond to having to deal with hired laborers by making the victim of prejudice the villain.[37] Kibbutzniks at Har have resented the intrusion of hired laborers into their lives. Their comments reveal this. One member says, "It is like they are from another country," and another, "The kibbutz is a home, and a home cannot be invaded by strangers."[38]

The dining hall of Har, the symbol of kibbutz communalism, provides a final example of the growth of class and social differentiation vis-à-vis hired labor. At first, hired laborers ate in the regular dining hall, but as their numbers grew, a separate eating facility was constructed in the factory area. Members working in the factory continued to eat in the kibbutz dining hall. Occasionally, the separate eating pattern is broken; but even when in the kibbutz dining hall, hired laborers sit only with each other or with members from the factory who have come to eat with them.

STANDARD OF LIVING

The higher standard of living achieved by Har during the 1948-1967 period clearly moved the community away from its subsistence economy. The kibbutz not only improved its economic standing in comparison with its own history but also in comparison with the larger society. The movement toward affluence was achieved at the cost of a weakening of its ideological traditions as well as of an increase in internal stratifica-

[37] William Ryan, *Blaming the Victim* (New York: Vintage Books, 1971).
[38] Fieldwork interviews by author during 1975.

tion. The newly attained economic status needs to be considered both in relation to losses and to achievements.

Har's experience of a major improvement in its standard of living beginning in the 1950s was common to kibbutzim in general. A study of consumption expenditures between 1953 and 1957 showed an increase in income of about 20 percent, bringing the income level of the individual kibbutznik equal to that of the average skilled urban worker in Israel.[39] Taking into account the collective provision for its members that an urban family must individually purchase, the kibbutz budget for a family came to 3,263 lira annually compared to 3,583 for the urban family of the same average size (3.4 persons in 1958).

By 1962 the average kibbutz budget for a family unit came to between 4,200 and 4,300 lira.[40] The average urban family by 1960 was expending 5,143 lira, with immigrants from America averaging 6,151 lira. Even with adjustments for benefits only enjoyed by the kibbutz family, the consumption standards for most kibbutzim did not quite keep up with those of the urban Jewish worker in Israel; and it has been estimated to be approximately 25 percent below those of established American immigrants. To compensate for the discrepancy, kibbutzim have increasingly stressed consumption expenditures at the expense of their current level of profitability. This is due to the need to meet consumption standards of the larger Israeli society and thus reduce defections from the kibbutzim. Each kibbutz is under considerable pressure from its federation to maintain a balanced budget but at the same time members press to "keep up with the Ben-Ami's."

Economist Eliyahu Kanovsky explains that the pressure for the kibbutzim to compete with the larger Israeli society adversely affects their long-range viability. It pushes the kibbutzim to raise their labor costs in the income-producing branches.

---

[39] Kanovsky, *The Economy of the Kibbutz*, p. 69.

[40] Figures in this paragraph from Kanovsky, Ibid., p. 72.

In addition, the desire for an equal amount of leisure time as urban workers enjoy further increases the need for hired labor. The pressure for the kibbutzim to keep up with the 5 to 6.5 percent annual rise in consumption levels between 1955 and 1964 has encouraged the kibbutzim to live beyond their means.

Har's standard of living began to rise appreciably starting in 1955. The amount spent on consumption more than doubled between 1955 and 1960 and increased even more between 1960 and 1963. From 1963 to 1967 the amount leveled off, largely due to the influx of two new immigrant groups into the kibbutz. The increasing standard of living affected housing (both individual units and communal constructions), clothing, food, leisure-time activities, adult education, as well as the consumption for the individual in the kibbutz. The overall process is characterized by a significant movement away from the fulfillment of community-defined norms to the fulfillment of individually determined desires and needs.

The first construction program after the state's establishment was begun in 1950 with the aid of a government loan to replace the crude wooden huts and hastily built shacks that had served as individual units and communal buildings. Two thirds of the costs were to be paid back over a twenty- to twenty-five-year period.

The first individual units were built on the Geva along the eastern side of the highest hill in the kibbutz. Thirty-four units housed the original members of the kibbutz who received the new housing on the basis of seniority. The old individual quarters consisted of one room, twelve meters square with a small covered terrace. The new buildings were twenty meters square. Instead of terraces each unit had a hallway. A common shower and toilet serviced two family units.

In a second building program begun in 1955, two units were built on the Geva and a new housing section was started to the north. This new section was closer to the border and some members were reluctant to move into it. However, when a few members moved from the Geva to the Gai, there were enough new units to house all of the members who had been in Har in the early years. The Gai units were twenty-five square meters and included a large room, a small room, a terrace, and an individual toilet and shower room. After this construction in 1958, houses were built along similar plans with the addition of a seven-meter square room added on to each new unit. This housing was built along the central part of the kibbutz between the dining hall and the museum (see Map 2).

While the amount of floor space has increased slowly, most structural change has had to do with multiplying the number of rooms. The members preferred the intimacy of small rooms to having a single larger room (see Figure 3).

Outside each unit was a garden space that became the responsibility of the residents in the unit. The various flower gardens and fruit trees that were planted expressed the differences in interest and talent among members. Some members have expended considerable energy during their leisure hours on their small gardens.

An increase in the amount of and quality of furniture paralleled the increased size of the housing unit. In 1958 each unit had two large wall cabinets, basic furniture such as beds and tables, the infamous electric teapot, and a radio. At first, radios were only given to members who had been there at least five years, but by 1960 everyone, including candidates to membership, received a radio. Surplus furniture owned by the kibbutz was given out according to a point system permitting the member a choice among the available furniture. Points are collected over five-year periods, but if one does not marry, 50 percent of the points must be relinquished. The point system indicates the implementation of choice over standardization, and a bias in favor of marriage.

The communal buildings were also vastly improved in this

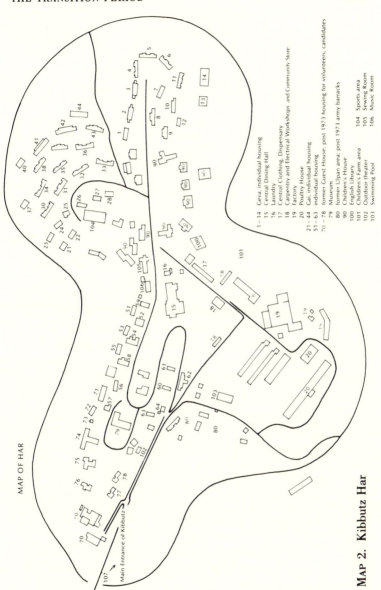

MAP OF HAR

MAP 2. **Kibbutz Har**

1 – 14 Geva, individual housing
15 Central Dining Hall
16 Laundry
17 Central Clothing, Dispensary
18 Carpentry and Electrical Workshops and Community Store
19 Factory
20 Poultry House
21 – 44 Gali, individual housing
51 – 63 individual housing
70 – 78 former Guest House; post 1973 housing for volunteers, candidates
79 Museum
80 former Ulpan area; post 1973 army barracks
90 Children's House
100 English Library
101 Children's Farm area
102 Outdoor theater
103 Swimming Pool
104 Sports area
105 Sewing Room
106 Music Room

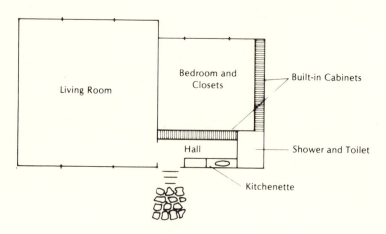

FIGURE 3. Individual Family Unit, 1962

time period. Har's November 1960 newsletter reported, "our landscape has had two transformations, a new hill and a new hole" that marked the foundation for a new dining hall. The ground floor of the new dining hall had rooms built for various administrative functions, bathrooms, and a common game room where members could read newspapers, play chess and dominos, and drink coffee. A television set was placed in the entrance hallway of the dining area.

In 1957 a large swimming pool was installed in the southwest corner of the kibbutz. It overlooked the valley below and the Mediterranean Sea on the west. The pool was landscaped with green lawns and trees, and locker rooms were built nearby. A lesser amount of money went to the building of a sports site for basketball and a general play area.

Like the trend in housing patterns and furniture there has been a trend toward greater individuality in dress. Standardization of clothes was characteristic of the early kibbutzniks, with men and women wearing baggy shorts and pants with workers' shirts. The informality of kibbutz apparel influenced the larger society so that Knesset members preferred shirt sleeves to ties and jackets. All members received numbers which they would sew on their clothes, insuring their return from the communal laundry to the individual owner. Each member received several pairs of pants and two sweaters a year in addition to work clothes. Women could chose material to design dresses. Every two years a member received a new pair of shoes and every three years, a new pair of slippers.

The clothing system underwent great change in the 1950s when a system of the norm replaced the old system of absolute standards. Under the new system each member not only received a given number of articles that were for exclusive use but from 1958 had a personal cash budget that could be used in any way a member chose; a certain amount of money was still allocated for clothes, children's gifts, extra food, etc. Within this amount, the member had a free choice of what to spend, although limited by the alternatives available in the small kibbutz store. This was quite a change from the days when the only distinctive personal belonging a member had was the toothbrush.

Women began wearing dresses more frequently after they no longer worked in the agrarian sector. Those unable to sew their own clothes were able to have dresses designed by women who worked in the sewing room. It was also possible to get yarn for crocheting and for knitting personal items. Make-up and hair styling also became more common as women in the kibbutz wanted to look more like their sisters in the urban areas. Looking like a kibbutznik was no longer a status symbol.

There also has been a trend toward greater individualization in eating patterns. The most significant aspect in the change of food was not what was eaten but where it was eaten. In the 1960s the General Assembly debates centered not on a teapot but on a refrigerator for every home. The decision to have refrigerators in each home would have a major impact not only on eating patterns but on the community as a whole. It meant members could take out food from the central dining hall and keep it in their own units. As more and more units were built with full kitchenettes, including stoves, ovens, and the refrigerators, many members began eating their evening meals in their separate homes. The main meal of the day at lunchtime in the midst of the work schedule continued to be eaten in the central dining hall.

Food rationing necessary in the early years now has disappeared. Upon awakening a member has a cup of coffee and some bread and butter. At about 8 A.M. members in the kibbutz go to the dining hall for a buffet breakfast of eggs, salad, yogurt, bread, coffee, sometimes fruit, and in the winter months, hot cereal. Members in the field have a heavier breakfast served to them, usually by kibbutz volunteers assigned to the dining hall.

The midday meal is the main meal and consists of vegetables, meat, fish or chicken, and fruit. Meals of Har tend to be fried and include overcooked vegetables reflecting the European background of many of the cooks. Special food needs are met, such as those caused by dietary restrictions or by illness. The midday meal is also served by people assigned to work in the dining hall. If one is especially friendly with a dining hall worker or one of the cooks, the opportunity for special helpings is increased.

Evening eating patterns have changed most. The food served is similar to that of breakfast except that hot rolls or soup may be added. It is served as a buffet and members carrying baskets can load up with food and carry it back to their homes where they dine. At home the members prepare the food in a variety of ways to escape the monotony of the dining hall cooking.

On Friday evening, the beginning of the Jewish Sabbath, most members still attend the short ceremonies in the dining hall and eat there. The best meal of the week is served together with wine. A similar pattern occurs on holidays.

In the 1950s the dispensary supplied each member with packages of coffee, sugar, and occasional cake. Extra items were available for parties. By 1960 these items became part of the personalized budget list allowing members to choose what they wanted. This included extra staples as well as sweets. Cigarettes are freely provided to members. This also includes pipe tobacco, although if members want a better brand than the one provided by the kibbutz it must come out of their personal budget.

The increased mechanization of the kibbutz economy and the overall rise in the standard of living also gave members more time for leisure activities. Members began new hobbies, educational study, and attended cultural performances. A personalized budget allowed members to purchase items necessary for the pursuit of particular interests. Music and photography became popular when cameras and stereos could be purchased. Most of these items were imported so they represented a substantial investment. A dark room was built and members shared the record collections that included classical, jazz, and popular Israeli music. A small library was also created with books in German, French, English, Hebrew, and Spanish.

During the initial years of the community, most cultural events were provided by the members themselves. In the 1950s, some members of the French *garin* group that immigrated to Har started a theater group in the kibbutz. It lasted a few years, although one of its members continues to direct theatrical events for the community. More recently movies have begun to appear regularly once a week, many are French and American films with subtitles or Hebrew dubbing. They are shown in the outdoor theater in summer months and in the central dining hall in the winter. Orchestras and locally popular entertainers appear frequently on Friday nights. Political speakers from the Knesset or from foreign countries also stop at the kibbutz to give lectures.

Travel outside of the kibbutz became more common between

1948-1967. A number of members joined singing groups, dancing troupes, and sports teams that travelled not only in Israel but also abroad. Adult education classes held at Har or at other kibbutzim attracted quite a few members. These included classes that complemented workroles such as courses in plant disease, new machines and business correspondence courses as well as English and sewing classes. Many of these classes have been sponsored by the Ichud Federation, Histadrut, or a particular government department. All are free to members although the kibbutz may pay the teacher or the entrance fee. A few members also maintain subscriptions to music performances in the cities and the kibbutz buys extra tickets that are allocated on a first-come-first-served basis.

Vacations also are now provided for each member. At first every member has one week off with a limited amount of money for travel. Vacation time later increases to two to three weeks with members allowed to accumulate travel allowances that permit them to vacation abroad as well as in Israel. Special funds are set aside to allow members to visit parents living in Israel and in foreign countries. Funds for this kind of travel are allocated according to budget possibilities and a seniority system. Camp outings and nature trips are regularly sponsored by national organizations and the Ichud Federation maintains a vacation home for members.

While members still work a six-day week and many remain active in extra-hour community affairs, the general tendency is toward an increase in leisure activity, much of which permits passive rather than active participation.[41] An increasing amount of leisure time is spent with one's family rather than with the community. Moreover, although all members benefit from the steadily increasing standard of living, certain individuals gain more than others from leniencies in applying the system of the

[41] Uri Merri, "Changes in Leisure Patterns in the Kibbutz" *Interdisciplinary Research Review* (July 1973).

norm. The rise in family-based activity and the growing differentiation in personal possessions indicates an expansion of internal community stratification, as well as individuation of consumption and personal styles.

Social Integration versus Social Stratification

The 1948-1967 period was characterized by the replacement of ideological concerns with technological considerations. The emphasis on economic development was both national and local. Lessening of ideological pressures occurred once the establishment of the Jewish state had been achieved. The push for socialist goals became less pronounced in kibbutz announcements and less realizable due to factors of industrialization and individuation. The reorganization of the kibbutz federation to which Har belonged from the Hever Hakvutzot to Ichud Hakvutzot V'Hakibbutzim, in addition to other splits in the national kibbutz movement, indicates the difficulties facing kibbutz adjustment to the era of statehood. Internally, Har undertook the integration of a number of new immigration groups and experienced increased differentiation along individual and group lines.

The two events on the national kibbutz front that chiefly affected Har during the 1950s were the split in the Hameuchad Federation, causing the formation of a new Ichud Federation and the growing disenchantment with the Soviet Union that reduced kibbutz association with state socialist countries.

During the Mandate years three principle kibbutz federations were formed: Hever Hakvutzot, representing the concept of a small commune; Kibbutz Artzi, the most ideological with its own party of Hashomer Hatzair; and Kibbutz Hameuchad, a by-product of the demise of Gdud Haavodah favoring the forming of the entire Jewish state from rural and urban kibbutzim. The Gdud Haavodah had been the rival to the Histadrut as the principle Socialist-Zionist institution. A number of kibbutzim rejected its approach and formed Meuchad that supported the Histadrut and the freedom for members of the Meuchad Federation to decide their own political affiliation. In the 1940s, the Hameuchad Federation became more political and abandoned its goal of political neutrality. A split grew between those wanting to move closer to the stricter ideological position of Hashomer Hatzair (Mapam party) and those wishing to remain with the less ideological Mapai. In June 1951, the final split occurred causing major break-ups in several kibbutzim, especially Kibbutz Ein Harod. Fierce struggles for power took place within the kibbutzim resulting in members expelling others from the community, and, in some cases, resulting in family members taking different sides. The Israeli press gave the split wide coverage and painted a very dark picture of kibbutz politics.

The kibbutzim with Mapam majorities stayed with the Meuchad Federation and those with Mapai majorities joined a new federation, Ichud Hakibbutzim. A few months later Hever Hakvutzot and Ichud Hakibbutzim merged to establish Ichud Hakvutzot V'Hakibbutzim.

The reorganization of its national federation had two effects on Har. First, the split and its aftershocks further reduced the prestige of the kibbutz movement after 1948, and the change affected Har as well. Secondly, the new, larger federation's affiliation with the Mapai, the national party established more power over kibbutz federation movements. The ties to Mapai, which Har had continually affirmed during elections, were strengthened.

The other national event profoundly affecting the entire kibbutz movement in the 1950s was the overwhelming disenchantment with the Soviet Union as a model for socialism. Kibbutz Artzi, in particular, had been strongly attached to the Soviet Union. As awareness of Stalin's labor camps and anti-Semitic purges began to spread, faith in the Soviet Union was shattered and the larger Israeli population became suspicious of the kibbutz movement's socialist ideology. The break in sympathy with the Soviet Union foreshadowed an overall withering away of kibbutz links to international socialist movements. At the same time, the push for economic development brought about closer affiliation with the Western capitalist world, especially the United States. Har's ideological commitments, as we have seen, were especially affected by the forces of national modernization, which were linked to capitalist world markets.

Ideological and economic factors were at play as a series of new *garin* groups increased the kibbutz's population from 210 in 1946 to 410 in 1963. The demographic change was not only quantitative, but it also signified the changing character of the community from that of a small, intimate, rather homogeneous community to a much larger, more formalized, more heterogeneous community. Ideological factors influenced which *garin* groups came to Har, and economic factors were crucial in determining patterns of absorption and stratification.

The adult population of candidates and members eighteen years and over numbered 92 in 1949, 127 in 1955, and 226 in 1963. The first child born in Har became a member in 1958, and there was a membership class of seventeen students a year later. Natural increase only accounted therefore, for eighteen new members: the remaining 116 came from outside the community. These came in four main *garin* groupings, although unattached families also joined. Since most of the newcomers were in their early twenties, in the words of a member: "the average age went down."

The first three *garin* groups, Har Aleph, Har Beth, and Betelem were well received by the membership despite their initial lack of Hebrew and French cultural origin. The fourth group, Garin Har, was less well received due to the primarily Sephardic cultural background and the economic condition in the community. Defections from the kibbutz varied from group to group, but those who stayed began to raise families. Rather than achieving the ideal of being one large family, the *kvutza*, or large family, underwent transition to a kibbutz based on separate nuclear families.

Immigration of Har Aleph and Har Beth into Har was the result of youth group activity in France by Habonim, which is the youth movement of Mapai and the Ichud Federation. The head, or *shaleah*, of the Habonim movement in Paris in the early 1950s was a member of Har.[42] He was very successful in attracting young people to the kibbutz.

In France, the youth movement was divided into various age brackets, with each group studying Zionist goals and history. Movement members were part of regional, national, and even international networks. During 1949, a group of French, Belgians, and North Africans gathered at a summer camp and, under the influence of the *shaleah*, decided to form a *garin* to immigrate to Har. By December 1949 the plans for Har Aleph were set. The young people underwent agricultural training before arriving at Har in August 1950.

The group consisted of fourteen middle-class youth (eight of whom remain in Har). Most of their families had only recently migrated to France from North Africa. Many had personally suffered losses of family and friends in World War II and felt more conscious of their Jewish heritage than of their bond with France. A few had a superficial knowledge of Hebrew and only one had a college degree.

Garin Har Beth came to Har two years later, also influenced by a *shaleah* who was sent to France by the Ichud movement. Of eleven original members, only one remained at Har and this

[42] Many of Har's members have served as *shaleah* or representatives of the kibbutz movement outside of Israel. Their stays were usually for one to two years and included the countries of France, Argentina, Morocco, Germany and England.

second *garin* is usually remembered as a part of the earlier French group. The two groups combined to push Har's population over the one hundred member level.

From 1959 to 1962 one hundred new members, inducted by the Ichud HaNoar HaHalutzim movement (or Unified Pioneer Youth), arrived in the two *garins*, Betelem and Har. The Betelem group consisted of youth from Paris, Anvers, Brussels, Tunisia, Morocco, and Algeria. All attended youth camp in France and trained for immigration to Israel. Arriving in three waves from late in 1959, to early in 1961, the Betelem group totaled about fifty people of which twenty still remain. Unlike the two previous *garins*, they came from working-class backgrounds and many had experienced family disruptions resulting from World War II. For them, emigration meant movement toward a new society.

The Garin Har originated in cities of Algeria. A youth movement network connected Algiers, Oran, and Constantine with metropolitan France. In March 1961 the Algerians arrived, shortly followed by a group of twenty-five Moroccans and a number of Europeans from France and Belgium. Of the total number of forty-five North Africans in this *garin* about thirty-five have remained at Har. Their backgrounds ranged from that of poverty to that of middle-class civil servants. Few had finished high school and none knew Hebrew.

Each of the four *garin* groups was faced with the same norms governing integration into the kibbutz but their experience was varied. According to the norm, each *garin* group had to go through a year of candidacy; then only after an affirmative vote in the General Assembly would the group become members. Full membership benefits were not accrued until five years of residency. According to the norm, a newly arriving *garin* would be housed in the least favorable units until, after seniority was achieved, they would move to better facilities.

Variation from the norm reflected the economic situation of

Har at the time of the *garin's* arrival and how well the new group fit in with the rest of the community. When Har Aleph and Har Beth arrived in the beginning of the 1950s, the kibbutz had started to feel the pressure of economic expansion, and it, therefore, needed added labor power. Both *garins* were immediately made members of the kibbutz without going through a candidacy period.[43] Socially, a strong connection between the new *garins* and the older *vattikim*, or original settlers, from Eastern Europe had been assured through the work of the youth movement representative in France who was a Har member. His wife, in fact, was a member of the group arriving from France. Ongoing housing construction allowed the newly arriving immigrants to move into better housing at a fast pace and quickly to feel a part of the community.

The Betelem *garin* received a similar warm welcome. Additional labor power to meet the increasing work demands was a top priority for the kibbutz. The *vattikim* expressed the view that additional labor power was urgently needed to further kibbutz economic development: "We find ourselves now in full economic expansion. . . . The necessity of developing all our lands and to make up as quickly as possible for lost time has led us to ask the authorities to designate a *garin* for us without delay."[44] Between March and May 1959 the Secretariat of Har negotiated with the Ichud Federation and the Betelem *garin* arriving that October. After four months they were made members and in March 1960 they hosted a thank-you dinner for the older residents.[45]

The Har Aleph, Har Beth, and Betelem *garins* were also

[43] *Har Bulletin*, vol. 2 (January 1960), Har Archives; see the article by Natan, "When You Become a Vattik."

[44] *Information Bulletin*, vol. 200, put out by the Ichud Hakvutzot V'Hakibbutzim Federation on the occasion of Har's twenty-fifth anniversary, Har Archives.

[45] *Har Bulletin*, vol. 3 (February 1960), Har Archives. Conversation with Yakkov Pari cited in the French Report.

welcomed as new faces in a small society. They filled a gap between the older members and their children who were just beginning to become members. Har Aleph and Har Beth members were later known as the French *vattikim* since they assimilated so well into the existing community.

Garin Har's experience was quite different. Separation between its members and the rest of the community still exists in the kibbutz today to some degree. At the time of their arrival the older members were growing tired of waves of new faces and the exuberances of new youth. The *garin* had to finish an entire year of candidacy before acceptance as members. Their immediate predecessors also did not warmly welcome them.

The economic situation was not much changed between the times of arrival of the Betelem group and the Har *garin*. Garin Har was kept physically segregated from the community for a much longer time: it lived much longer in the wooden barracks of the *atsmaout*, or freedom, section of the kibbutz reserved for newcomers. When housing became available, it was in a one-block area. Many Garin Har members were also grouped together in work branches, so contact with others through work was also not easy. The *garin* was in a paradoxical situation of being labeled as separatist while the larger kibbutz community was doing little to ease their assimilation.

During interviews, members of Garin Har explained that their poor welcome was the result of older member disapproval of their North African background. Har Aleph and Har Beth were French Europeans who quickly renounced the ties to their *garin* to become part of the kibbutz. North African members of the Betelem and Har *garins* were much slower in giving up *garin* affiliations. In fact, they consciously held onto their *garin* identification as a comment in the Har newsletter notes: "We decided to keep a semi-autonomous structure for the first three months of candidacy. There is a secretariat common to Har and Betelem composed of five havarim from the *garin* and two havarim from Har."[46] However, the Betelem group, unlike the Garin Har, was quickly moved to housing that was dispersed throughout the kibbutz and its members have worked in many of the branches. Most of them are European in origin and all were affiliated with youth groups in France. Garin Har is more completely of Sephardic origin.

There were wide cultural differences between the older members and the North African newcomers. Although the older members were a mixture of various European origins and Sabras, they projected a unified picture as a Hebraicized, Western-oriented group. Collectively they were named the "Roumanians." The first two French *garins*, Aleph and Beth, were eventually included into this group. The newer French-speaking *garins*, which included a large number of Sephardic Jews, brought with them a strong Zionist commitment and attachment to the Diaspora youth movement. For example, they insisted that the kibbutz newsletter should advocate strong ideological commitment. The newcomers still retained older idealistic notions of Israel and the kibbutz that they assimilated in the youth organizations prior to their arrival in Israel. They were, for instance, shocked at the large numbers of hired laborers at Har and some stated: "We should purify this root with which we want to identify, purge it by our presence of the salaried element."[47] They remained caught in a bind of wanting to be accepted as full members of the kibbutz and maintaining affiliations and ideas that were no longer emphasized by the older members. Their ideological fervor in their first years at Har was not appreciated by the older members who were already more interested in economic development.

Throughout this period and until the present time many of the Sephardic members of Har have continued to speak French in their own apartments and celebrate holidays such as Me-

[46] *Har Bulletin*, no. 2 (1960), Har Archives.
[47] *Har Bulletin*, nos. 6-7 (1960), Har Archives.

moona according to their own cultural tradition.[48] The clinging to cultural tradition has gone on in spite of increased integration over the years of the "French" into the "Roumanian" environment.

The gradual integration of the *garin* groups into the community has been marked by the learning of Hebrew, the founding of families, and the assumption of regular work and roles in community affairs. Night courses have been provided at the kibbutz in Hebrew, and those more inept at languages enroll in an intensive one-month course in Jerusalem. The kibbutz has been willing to lose labor days so that the newcomers may become "Hebraicized."

Establishing families further solidified the attachment of the newcomers to the community. Family formation has been viewed as rooting a member in the community and contributing to increased stability. Having children also encourages the parent to learn Hebrew. As the new groups begin to raise children the kibbutz loses some of its communal character and much more attention is focused on family affairs.

Status differentiation between groups in the kibbutz can be most clearly seen by examining of work and community roles. Although economic differentiation also increases in the community, differentiation of status still largely reflects these work and civic roles. In the early days of statehood leadership roles were primarily held by the prestate members and the French *vattikim* of Garins Har Aleph and Beth. Members from Betelem and Garin Har began to achieve important economic positions, but remained excluded from most significant social affairs. Significantly, as members of the "French-speaking" groups assumed leadership roles in the kibbutz, the "European" leadership assumed more key positions in outside institutions

[48] Memoona is a Sephardic celebration at the end of Passover. It is celebrated by the Sephardic members of Har with open houses and the serving of sweets, liquor, and delicacies.

related to Har such as in the Ichud Federation, the Regional High School, and the Milouot enterprise.

The members of Garins Har and Aleph and Beth were quickly given leadership roles in the kibbutz. Mica Lebon, later the general manager of the factory, became the *maskir*, or general secretary of the kibbutz, in 1956. In 1960 Noam became *maskir*, Gila became education secretary, Mica became factory manager, and Samuel became economic coordinator for the kibbutz. Later, Gila became *maskira* and Samuel, kibbutz treasurer. These members, with the addition of a few of the older members, have continued to occupy the principal leadership positions. Leadership positions in Har have often been held by both members of a married couple, and there has been a close friendship network between these leadership couples.

Beginning in 1960 a number of the members from the Betelem *garin* were assigned roles in various community committees: one in the *Maskiroot*, or Secretariat, two in the economic committee, two in the cultural committee, and three in the education committee. These were most often passive roles, but they assumed more of a leadership position through their own workroles, particularly in the factory. After 1967, they started to assume major roles in the kibbutz economy.

Members of the Har *garin* were the slowest to gain any major leadership role in the kibbutz. Before 1967, the major role they had was in the agricultural sector as head of the *pardess* and second-in-charge of the banana plantation. They began to assume leadership roles in the overall economic positions after this time, but not in the area of social affairs.

As of 1967, therefore, processes of integration and stratification have simultaneously occurred within the community. There is evidence of cultural antipathy between those of a French Sephardic background and those of a more Westernized background. However, identification with national interests and the kibbutz community have been sufficient to encourage integration of the new groups into Har through language acquisition, family establishment, and assumption of work and civic roles. The movement toward a Westernized approach to modernization has principally shaped the present ethos of the community. The new arrivals have often abandoned the ideologies of their youth groups.

A brief mention of the rate of departures is appropriate in the discussion of integration. Har as a kibbutz has always been a voluntary and selective community, and a departure rate of 50 percent for any *garin* is considered normal. However, the departure of a member, of one who has been accepted as a candidate, or of a youth born in the kibbutz, has always been taken very seriously and has been considered defection. Most of the blame has been usually put on the individual's inability to acclimate to the kibbutz environment. A member of Har indicates that those who leave are viewed as weak and implies that those who stay are the strong: "Those who wear out prematurely, throw up their arms and leave . . . should be considered with pity and nothing more, for we cannot blame the weak."[49] Many who leave return to their native lands, but, as Har has not kept exact records of all who have departed, it is impossible to determine the percentage remaining in Israel. Quite a few leave the kibbutz and Israel during their fourth year because this is when their new immigrant status ends under Israeli law and they are eligible for military service. The most frequently heard reasons for departure from Har are the inability to find a spouse and start a family, inability to find a regular position, or incompatibility with the general kibbutz style of life. The latter includes dislike of the repetitive routine in a small community, lack of personal opportunity, and an aversion to taking on community responsibilities.

The departure of a youth born in the kibbutz is especially difficult for the community. Youths at the age of eighteen are

[49] *Har Bulletin* (March 1960), Har Archives.

eligible for membership. Between 1946 and 1963, 117 children were born in Har, and most became members after their military service. A member of the Betelem *garin* stresses the significance of children of members returning after army service: "We must underscore the capital importance of the return of the children of the Meshek throughout the year [1961-1962]: a year ago practically all were in the army, the majority are now in Har."[50] For those who leave, their choice implies a rejection of their home and is painful for their parents.[51] No statistics have been kept for all the children of the kibbutz leaving Har since 1948, but members report that a majority of the first group of children born at Har have left the community. A number of social scientists have suggested that the success of the kibbutz education system in encouraging personal fulfillment has pushed the *bnai meshek*, or kibbutz children, to go out on their own to establish themselves. A child of Har who left the kibbutz writes: "If you consider the nation-building efforts of a pioneer-member as a revolutionary act, the child of the kibbutz continues along the path of his parents. . . . This natural continuity is the principal difficulty in the life of a youth with a revolutionary bent."[52] In order to be a revolutionary a kibbutz child may be pushed to break his or her commitment to the community to assert independence. Thus, success in socialization to ideals of revolutionary achievement may conflict with the success of the community. The question remains if a revolutionary spirit can still be given a home in the increasingly routinized kibbutz.

While the processes of *garin* integration combined with social and economic regimentation have continued among the

[50] *Garin Betelem Newsletter* (January 1962), Har Archives.

[51] See Melford Spiro, *Kibbutz: Venture in Utopia* (New York: Schocken Books, 1970); and Bruno Bettelheim, *Children of the Dream* (New York: Avon Books, 1971).

[52] *Har Bulletin* (August 1960), Har Archives.

various original groups in the community, differentiation at the individual level has increased. This has been partly due to the general subordination of socialist, ideological communication to economic concerns. During the prestate period, the principal factors of cohesion were the commitment to nation-building and the ethos of creating a community in a hostile region. After the state was achieved and as the national institutions pushed for economic development, Har began its successful economic expansion by bringing in hired workers and developing an industrial base. The population increases of the period were badly needed to fill labor requirements. The close-knit large communal family was replaced by a network of cooperating of family units. The family increasingly became the focus of everyday life with members spending more and more time in their own apartments. The rising standard of living allowed individual kitchenettes, and members no longer ate most meals at one large dining hall.

Social relations within the community became more subject to formal procedures. In the early days everyone had the opportunity to discuss each major decision facing the kibbutz. In the 1950s and '60s, the formal internal organization expanded by the creation of new committees and an increased hierarchy in decision making. There was less rotation of positions in both the work and civic sphere as technical knowledge replaced personal qualities and a reputation as a worker in the selection of leaders.

The average member of Har became less identified with the community. Even as new groups became integrated into the kibbutz, the formal participation was sustained; the "we" and "they" dichotomy between groups was not as completely abolished as in earlier days. Moreover, the members identified Har as "the kibbutz," an external agent, and did not express the earlier idea that they were the kibbutz. Home was no longer the entire community or the central dining hall, but the individual housing units in which members lived separately with their families.

The general economic improvement allowed a transition from strong communal identification to greater individuation. Personal choice in consumption items became feasible with the creation of an individual consumption account for each member. Har was no longer the "place where everyone is equally poor" but rather a place where all necessities were met but abundance was not yet secured.[53]

Personal consumption became an important force within the kibbutz. It was in this area, as well as the political-work leadership area, that individual differentiation became more pronounced and, in some cases, institutionalized, permitted, and encouraged. Policies of the community relating to gifts, inheritances, and other income reveal the leniency of the kibbutz toward individual consumption.[54]

Originally, all gifts received by members would automatically become the property of the community as a whole. In 1951-1952 after the arrival of the Garins Har Aleph and Beth, gifts started arriving for these new members from relatively prosperous families in France. An individual member was then allowed to keep such gifts if they were for himself or herself but would have to turn them over to the children's houses if they were sent to a member's child. From 1955 on gifts for children could be kept if enough were sent for each child in the class of the one receiving the gift. By the 1960s, each child was allowed a certain number of personal items. However, not all of the members of Har have well-off parents and families.

---

[53] Y. Shatil, *The Economy of the Communal Settlements in Israel*, p. 136. Also see the study of twelve Ichud Federation kibbutzim directed by Yonina Talmon, in Viteles, *Cooperative Movement*, pp. 363ff.

[54] While kibbutzim belonging to Kibbutz Artzi Federation are less lenient, the overall movement for kibbutzim is in this direction; see Spiro, *Kibbutz: Venture in Utopia*, epilogue, and Yonina Talmon, *The Family and Community in the Kibbutz* (Cambridge, Mass.: Harvard University Press, 1972).

Gift recipients often received items that others in the kibbutz could not obtain.

During this period the question of what to do with German reparation money arose.[55] A number of members received the reparations, and most kibbutzim followed the recommendations of the federation with which they were affiliated. Har followed the path laid out by Ichud allowing the receiving members to keep a portion of the total for their own use. One member contributed part of his money to the building of the swimming pool. Others put their money into a savings account for their future personal use.

It is difficult to gather information about individual inheritances since it is still not "kosher" for members to have private accounts outside of the kibbutz. But a number of Har members have them due to inheritances and other money gifts. By examining what various members have done on vacations, one can clearly see that some could only have afforded trips with private subsidies. A number of members sanction private accounts by arguing that if a member decided to leave the kibbutz, there would be little payment to make do until a new life could be found. The whole sense of keeping a private account, however, would have shocked the earlier Har community. Other changes in the norms of the kibbutz have increasingly provided for an economic allowance for members if they wish to depart.

The elaboration of the marriage ceremony at Har illustrates both the overall economic change in the community and the acceptance of increased individualized differentiation. In the early period, many couples did not even bother to get married, but simply lived together as a couple. After statehood there was more pressure to legalize the relationship, which in Israel meant having a religious, orthodox ceremony. In the first dec-

[55] German reparation money refers to payments made by the government of Germany to Jews who suffered losses during World War II.

ade or so after 1948 the community would celebrate a marriage in a simple manner. A few guests would be invited to join members in celebration, a large communal meal would be served, special cakes would be baked and wine would accompany the meal in small, limited amounts. Entertainment would be provided by classmates of the one getting married, and gifts would be mostly handmade. A rabbi would be brought in to officiate at the ceremony.

By the 1960s, the marriage ceremony resembled the middle-class affairs in the United States. The bride would wear a ready-made gown, the groom a suit. Printed invitations would be sent out to guests who would often number a hundred. The menu became more lavish, drinks more plentiful, and dance bands would be brought in for entertainment. Gifts would often be store-bought. The opulence of the event depended upon the wealth of the member's family rather than on what the community could afford. Amidst all these changes, the presence of the orthodox rabbi has been constant.

Throughout this period Har's members have viewed the economic expansion and increasing standard of living as signs of the community's success. They were serving the national interests, while achieving middle-class standards. Another major influence on Har's development during this period encouraging the transformation from pioneers to technical managers and landed gentry was the establishment of regional institutions, particularly the Milouot system. The regional organizations created patterns of bureaucratic formality that seriously affected the community's internal work environment and ideological commitment.

CHAPTER THREE

The Regional Cooperative Organizations

Since 1948, Har has become increasingly engaged in regional cooperative activities that are both economic and service oriented. The pattern of vertical linkage to the national institutions such as the kibbutz movement federation and the Histadrut enterprises had been established in the Mandate years when the military-political factor caused kibbutz settlements to be scattered and isolated from each other. After the foundation of the state, Har's military function lessened and economic developments became more prominent. Regional cooperation among kibbutz settlements began to be formed to overcome the economic constraints facing each of the separate communities.

Agricultural expansion was limited by land, water, and other environmental factors. Mechanization of the agrarian branches that eased labor needs and an aging population combined to produce the need for more nonagricultural work. The everpresent shortage of capital for investment made it attractive to pool resources in order to reduce operational costs, introduce new technology, and train personnel. The need to centralize education and cultural activity, municipal administration, and economic expansion resulted in Har's membership in three primary regional cooperative frameworks: the Regional High School, the Sulam Tsor Region Council, and the Milouot Regional Enterprises.[1]

---

[1] The term *framework* is utilized here to be consistent with present research conducted in Israel on rural regional cooperation. Erik Cohen and Elazer Leshem in *Survey of Regional Cooperation in Three Regions of Collective Settlement* (Jerusalem: Keter Publishing House Ltd., 1969), define framework as "a permanent complex of formal or informal social ties woven around any particular issue"; see p. 4.

Each of these three regional organizations has played a specific function in Har's development and has its own separate membership structure and its own geographic boundaries (see Tables 13 and 14). The Regional High School includes seven kibbutzim and one moshav and overlaps parts of two adjoining regional council areas. Sulam Tsor Regional Council is one of fifty-four national regional councils, has eight members (six kibbutzim and two moshavim) and serves a wide range of municipal functions. The Milouot framework has twenty-six members (twenty-three kibbutzim and three moshavim), serves four regional council areas with some of its services extended to additional regions, and has had a strong economic impact on Har's growth. The increase of horizontal, regional networks is an outcome of structural changes in the economic and service dimensions of the kibbutz as the community has undergone the process of modernization.

Internally, Har evinces a number of the signs of modernization. Formalization of internal administration has expanded in both the economic and social spheres. The sense of being an intimate community has been lost and has been replaced by the increased atomization of the individual and family unit. A close attachment to the natural environment has diminished especially among the younger generation.[2]

TABLE 13. THE REGIONAL AFFILIATIONS OF KIBBUTZ HAR, 1975.

Regional Organization	List of Members	Function	Type of Organization	Type of Labor-Power	Har's Labor-Input	Indicator of Change
High School	Bet Haemek Evron Gesher-Achziv Har Lochamei HaGetaot Matzuba	Education	Sub-regional	Member/ Hired	5	Preparation Course for Baghrot

[2] Daniel Katz and Naphtali Golumb, "The Kibbutzim as Open Social Systems," mimeo (Ann Arbor: University of Michigan, 1970).

ABLE 13. (*cont.*)

Regional Organi-zation	List of Members	Function	Type of Organi-zation	Type of Labor-Power	Har's Labor-Input	Indicator of Change
ulam sor	Rosh-Hanikra Regba Admit Beset Eilon Gesher-Achziv Har Lehman Matzuba	Municipal Functions	Regional	Member/ Hired	2	Plans for Psych-Center
Tilouot	Rosh-Hanikra Admit Eilon Gesher-Achziv Har Matzuba Rosh-Hanikra Lochamei HaGetaot Evron Shomrat Kabri Gaaton Ein Hamifratz Kfat Masark Yasur Bet Haemek Saar Yehiam Afek Usha Parod Ramat Yohanan Regba Bet Oren Hasolelim Kfar Hamaccabi Shavi Zion	Economic	Inter-regional	Member/ Hired	4-6	Expansion of Services

TABLE 14. MOVEMENT AFFILIATION OF KIBBUTZIM IN WESTERN GALILEE.

Ichud Federation (Hever Hakvuzot)	Meuchad	Artzi	Hanoar Hatzioni (religious)	Moshav
Bet Haemek	Afek	Admit	Hasolelim	Beset
Gesher-Achziv	Bet Oren	Eilon	Usha	Lehman
Har	Kabri	Ein Hamifratz		Parod
Kfar Hamaccabi	Lochamei HaGetaot	Evron		Regba
				Shavi
Matzuba		Gaaton		Zion
Ramat Yohanan		Kfar Masark		
Rosh-Hanikra		Saar		
		Shomrat		
		Yasur		
		Yehiam		

The rise in the standard of living and movement toward centralization that Har has experienced are usually associated with urbanization. Instead, the kibbutz has become a rural, industrial community. Har has been able to achieve this situation mainly because of its regional affiliations that are centered outside of the community and yet provide opportunities for internal agricultural and industrial expansion. The Milouot enterprises, in particular, have allowed the kibbutzim in the area to industrialize their economic sector without undergoing the urbanization process.

This pattern of development raises the crucial question of whether the community can retain existing patterns of social integration while meeting the demands for further economic development. The regional organizations clearly offer possibilities that otherwise would not be available for the kibbutz. At the same time, it is clear that the nature and scope of the organizations not only moves Har further away from fulfilling socialist-communitarian ideals, but they may threaten its long-range economic well-being.

The most significant limiting characteristic of the regional cooperatives to which Har belongs (and this holds true for other regional organizations) is the failure to include the entire population of the region. The expansion of production and services affected by the regional organizations is largely limited to the improvement of the member settlements, which are predominantly kibbutzim and include a small number of moshavim. The organizations do not focus on the development of the region as a whole and exclude the interests of local nonmember villages, development towns, and individual family units.

The principal reason for the regional organization's concentration on serving only the needs of the member cooperative settlements is the continuation of the historical tendencies shaping cooperative settlements during the Mandate period. These tendencies are evident in the regional organizations' pattern of institutionalizing segregation between the cooperative settlements and town and village dwellers. Israeli regional planner, Arthur Glickson, suggests that "The distinguishing feature of this mentality is the deliberate use of the terms 'them' and 'we': 'them,' being the town dwellers and 'we' those who live in agricultural settlements."[3] The distinction, as has been noted in previous chapters, originated in the Socialist-Zionist ideology of the kibbutz with such tenets as the self-labor meant to insure the building of a separate Jewish economy in Palestine that would not be dependent upon the Arab economy. The "we" and "they" attitude was, therefore, first applied to Jewish-Arab relations. Since 1948, the attitude has been extended to the separation between Westernized kibbutzniks and Sephardic

[3] Raanan Weitz reporting the thinking of Arthur Glickson, an expert on physical regional planning, in *Spatial Organization of Rural Development* (Tel Aviv: Rehovot Settlement Study Centre, 1968).

Jews who live mostly in urban development towns. It also extends to the Arab population in the region.

The regional organizations exacerbate the tendency for the kibbutz to deal with nonkibbutz residents in terms of an employer-employee relationship. The kibbutzim are geographically established in centers that are in uninhabited zones, thereby insuring only minimal contact between the town dwellers and the kibbutz community. This has definite impact on achieving the mutual aid and regional interdependency necessary for building a genuine socialist society.

In addition to the constraints the present regional system puts on meeting socialist-communitarian goals, it has significant implication for Har's future economic development. By keeping kibbutz economic and service expansions separate from a totally regional integration, two sectors of development, one kibbutz, the other urban-town oriented, are being established within the same area. This means national resources have to be divided in establishing two separate economic infrastructures that include communication, transportation, and utility facilities. This pattern of regional segregation presents three major problems. First, it does not make optimal use of national resources, which are already limited due to military-political factors. Second, it sets up a dichotomy between village and kibbutz-moshav sectors that are interdependent in the sharing of labor, capital, and other resources in development planning. Finally, the segregated pattern will, if continued, add fuel to problems stemming from class and cultural tensions. It places Har's members and other kibbutzniks in the role of managers, separating them from the workers', or *poalim*, class, the pattern prevalent in Har's metal works factory. This is in profound contradiction to the Socialist-Zionist ideological statements of the kibbutz that stressed the need to create and maintain a Jewish peasantry and proletariat controlling the means of production.

There has been little, if any, state regulation of the regional cooperatives. It remains to be seen if Har and the other member settlements of the regional organizations will initiate action to alter the present pattern of regional-cooperative development.

The Regional High School

The stress on education is an element of Jewish tradition that the kibbutz has strongly continued. Investment per child in education is higher among the kibbutzim than anywhere else in Israel. The average class size of eighteen is less than half of the national average. Research suggests that the 100,000 kibbutz population reads more books and newspapers than any other national grouping. These include two hundred regularly published periodicals and weekly newsletters published by various kibbutzim.

Prior to 1958 all children in Har were taught in the kibbutz by members who had little or no special training. Teaching in the primary school has been women's work. The kibbutz schools were an integral part of the independent workers' trend in education supported by the Histadrut. These schools served half of the children of the Yishuv population; the other half went to general and religious schools. The kibbutz schools emphasized the redeeming qualities of manual labor, the history of the Jewish people, and Socialist-Zionist principles. Education incorporated a work-study approach with children gradually increasing the time they spent working in the various economic branches. Sex differentiation tracked boys into the income-producing, agrarian branches and girls into the service branches. The classroom environment was informal with no marks or exams, so that passing was an automatic process. Children moved through the grades as a group from the toddler stage to each of the primary classes.[4]

[4] For material on kibbutz education refer to Dan Leon, *The Kibbutz: A New Way of Life* (London: Pergamon Press, 1969), ch. 8; and Melford Spiro, *Kibbutz: Venture in Utopia* (Cambridge, Mass.: Harvard University Press, 1970), ch. 5.

After the state was established, one of the first significant actions of the government was the closing of the Histadrut workers' schools. The act symbolized the ending of the Social- ist-Zionist pioneer era under the Mandate and the movement toward consolidating powers into the newly created state to meet the new political and economic goals. The 1953 State Education Law set up two categories of education—state and religious—that gave new power to government and clerical par- ties.[5] It ended the extension of a private school system that encouraged socialist ideals. The 1953 Law unified national ed- ucation by standardizing 75 percent of the curriculum and making education compulsory between the ages of five and fourteen. The curriculum made reference to the pre-1948 ide- ology of manual labor and pioneering, but added new stress on the value of the Jewish culture and achievements of science, on love of the homeland, and loyalty to the state and the Jewish people.

Ferdinand Zweig comments on the state system's two goals of religious identity and simplicity: "The Bible becomes a liv- ing thing, which he [the student] studies with reverence and an extreme and avid interest. The Bible comes to life and its he- roes become living figures on which he tries to mould himself. What happened 2,000 years ago is of greater interest to him than the immediate past. . . . He styles himself on a peasant's mentality, although he is not a peasant and far from simple. But he rejects complexity and intellectuality, and he likes to think of himself as a simple straightforward man without far- fetched ideas and claims."[6] These goals reflect the concentra- tion on the historical rationale for a Jewish state in Israel and

[5] Ferdinand Zweig, *Israel: The Sword and the Harp* (London: Heinemann Educational Books Ltd., 1969), p. 5. Dorothy Willner in *Nation-Building and Community in Israel* (Princeton: Princeton University Press, 1969), discusses how the division of the Israeli education system into religious and state cat- egories has divided new immigrant communities and slowed their integration into the national society.

[6] Zweig, *Israel*, p. 5.

the younger generation's attachment to pragmatism rather than idealism. They both run counter to more intellectual and secular aspects of kibbutz ideology. Specific problems are also raised concerning the issue of education for the non-Jewish residents of Israel.

Kibbutzim were permitted by the state to maintain their internal educational systems and to provide education for grades one through twelve. Notions of creating an agrarian proletarian society through voluntary cooperation were wed uncomfortably to Freudian psychology stressing the necessity of repressive elements in human civilization.[7] Moreover, the kibbutz primary and high-school grades were influenced by economic and political goals of the state:

> This Council [Third Council Meeting, December 1960 of Ichud Hakvutzot V'Hakibbutzim] should ask itself, what should be the goal of our education under conditions to which the kibbutz is now subjected. . . . they [kibbutz teachers] must be able to demonstrate that the kibbutzim can yet achieve all the goals for which the State was established. They must equip their youth to perform Zionist service. For example, the youth must be convinced that the basic purpose of obligatory one-year post-military service is not so much to help the young kibbutzim but to help to make productive for the State large areas of waste lands. To a greater degree than in the past, the emphasis of their education should be on the unique pattern and the *functional aspect* of the kvutza [original italics].[8]

The regional high school serving Har's children from grades seven through twelve is located at Kibbutz Gesher Achziv on the Mediterranean coast about fifteen kilometers from Har. It

[7] Ruth Sidel in *Women and Child Care in China* (Baltimore: Penguin Books, 1974), in a comparative section on Israel, China, and the Soviet Union relates that kibbutz children demonstrate more aggressive behavior than the other systems' children in day-care centers and that Israeli child care workers are more accepting of Freud's views of human behavior. See also, Sigmund Freud, *Civilization and Its Discontents* (New York: W.W. Norton and Co., Inc., 1962).

[8] Harry Viteles, *A History of the Cooperative Movement in Israel* (London: Vallentine, Mitchell & Co. Ltd., 1967), 2:214.

is similar to the other regional organization to which Har belongs as it encompasses both kibbutz and moshav settlements. Moreover, as other Har-affiliated regional organizations, it cuts across kibbutz federation lines and serves member settlements of Ichud Hakvutzot V'Hakibbutzim, Kibbutz Meuchad, and Kibbutz Artzi. In this respect it differs from most regional high schools that tend to serve kibbutzim belonging to only one or two of the national federations.

The geographic area served by the regional high school is larger than that of the Sulam Tsor regional council but smaller than that of the Milouot framework. Its focus is directed at the one issue of education, although this is broadly defined to include cultural and youth group activities, special training seminars, and the fostering of cooperation among member settlements. The high school's curriculum seeks to give its youth an attachment for kibbutz living and the desire to fulfill the needs of the larger Israeli society.

It was begun in 1958 by the three kibbutzim of Har, Gesher Achziv, and Matzuba for grades nine through eleven. Children were sent to the national Ichud Federation high school for the twelfth grade. The three founding settlements were members of the Ichud Federation, and the high school was formed in response to the difficulties of maintaining separate classes in each kibbutz for each of the higher grades. Ideally, each kibbutz wanted to have all the classes within its own community, but the number of students in each class was limited. It was decided that greater possibilities could be offered to the older students if a central school were established. The original goals of the consolidated school were to broaden the social life of the students and increase the possibility of individual development.

By the end of the 1960s, the regional high school was extended to include the additional kibbutz settlements of Rosh Hanikra, Lochamei Hagetaot, Bet Haemek, and Evron and the moshav settlement of Regba. Rosh Hanikra and Bet Haemek also belong to the Ichud Federation; Lochamei Hagetaot to Meuchad, and Evron to Artzi. Special classes are provided for children needing extra attention, and these service additional kibbutzim including Gaaton and Shomrat. Each federation also runs schools for the more severely emotionally disturbed, and Har sends these students to the Ichud school.

The high school is run by a board of directors that meets three to four times a year to arrange its general program, investments, and areas for change. In between these meetings smaller committees deal with everyday operational issues. The board is composed of three members from each member settlement; usually a kibbutz sends one teacher, one member from the economic committee, and one member from the education or social committee. The more significant problems facing the high school are first discussed in each settlement's General Assembly; their decisions are then taken by the representatives to the board.

Internally the school is headed by an educational director who consults with a school committee that meets weekly. The school committee is only made up of school personnel and its membership reflects different aspects of school life—the *metapelets*, the teachers, and special workers. Teachers are also organized into committees according to their disciplines.

During the 1970s, a member of Har has served as the educational director of the regional high school. He is responsible for both the organizational and instructional operation of the school and heads both the school's board of directors meetings and its internal committee. In addition, he has continued to teach social science courses. His national reputation as an educator increases the already forceful influence he has on the school's development.

The regional high school is connected to a number of national institutions, especially to the Ichud and Meuchad national educational systems. Although an Artzi kibbutz sends its students to Gesher Achziv, its federation usually separates itself from the other two when educational programming is involved.[9] The principals or educational directors from the regional high schools of Ichud and Meuchad settlements meet together regularly and occasionally include discussions with the Ministry of Education. The educational director of the Gesher Achziv regional high school is a representative on a smaller committee that meets more frequently with the government's Minister of Education. This gives him added prestige and influence not only in the local regional high school but throughout the kibbutz educational system.

Each member settlement contributes to the cost of the overall school budget. Costs include building and maintenance, school books and other equipment, teachers' salaries and extracurricular activities. Teacher cost allocations are based on the total budget divided by the number of children, with a ratio of ten students in principle allocated to one teacher. Hired teachers, coming from outside member settlements, receive about the same rate of pay, which is determined by the Ministry of Education. The hired teachers belong to the teachers' union of the Histadrut. Each member kibbutz is given a quota for the number of school personnel it must assign to the regional high school. If a member settlement fails to meet its quota of teachers, it must make up the difference monetarily. During 1975-1976 Har sent 35 to 40 students to the regional high school and had to send 7 school personnel.[10]

[9] See Erik Cohen and Elazer Leschem, *Regional Cooperation*, for a comparison of Jezreel, pp. 53-54; of Bet Sha'an, p. 41 and of Sha'ar Hanegev, p. 24, with the other regional frameworks.

[10] A number of Har members teach at the high school and one member provides psychological support services. It is interesting to note that at least two of the women working with high school students are married to men who hold important jobs at Har, the secretary of the Milouot and the general manager of the factory. The principal is married to the *maskira*, general secretary of Har. There is, thus, a type of specialized grouping among those holding leadership roles in the kibbutz with those working in the professional jobs outside of the kibbutz.

Many members at Har, especially among the women, consider the high school jobs attractive since they offer more intellectual stimulation than many other kinds of community work. Teaching also offers them an opportunity to leave the small area of the kibbutz, to travel to regional and national educational meetings, and to reap the prestige of being a professional. Kibbutz teachers are required to undertake special training in their teaching area. This limits job rotation. In prestate years, the teaching role did not fulfill the idealized norms, but today this is not considered to be a drawback.

The curriculum of the high school is divided between liberal arts subjects and vocational studies. Hebrew and Jewish history are required courses. Math and other language courses, including French and Arabic, are studied according to the student's ability. All students are expected to take English. History and science courses are also given, and there are science laboratories for chemistry, biology, earth science, and geology.

The vocational study courses reflect sex differentiation. Girls take courses in home economics, secretarial skills, and child care; and boys take shop, mechanics, and construction. When the educational director was questioned if girls could take shop, the reply was in the affirmative, but few girls do. By the time children reach high school age they are well aware of where they will probably work in the kibbutz. After their return from army service, the boys will work in the income-producing areas and girls in the service areas. No boy, for instance, that was interviewed showed any interest in child care.

New courses are instituted at the high school on the recommendations of the board of directors, school committee, teacher department committees, or upon request of at least eight students. In state and religious school systems the minimum number of students for a course is usually twenty. Most of the technical courses are taught by hired teachers rather than kibbutz teachers. Surprisingly this includes agricultural courses. The explanation offered by the educational director was that any kibbutznik knowledgeable about agriculture would rather be working in the fields than teaching.

Recent decisions at the high school concerning preparations for exams and higher educational training indicates the influence the larger Israeli society has had on the regional high school framework and ultimately on the individual member settlements. The changing attitude toward the *Baghrot*, or university entrance examination, provides an example of the incorporation of the larger society's values into kibbutz life. Originally the regional high school held to the kibbutz educational tenet that education was for the many and not for a special group. The kibbutzim tried to provide the best education it could afford with the expectation that after high school the adolescents would perform a year of service for the kibbutz movement, enter the army, and then return to the kibbutz adult labor force. Preparation for university matriculation was, therefore, not part of the high school curriculum for both ideological and economic reasons. Bettelheim points out that cash is always in short supply in the kibbutz, and after great expense to the community, many youngsters sent to the university never returned.[11]

The educational director of Har's regional high school still considers preparation for the *Baghrot* against the interest of the kibbutz. However, the high school now has a special course for *Baghrot* preparation and 40-45 percent of the students take the exam. This compares to a national average of 18 percent. The educational director reports a low rate of failure among those taking the exam at Gesher Achziv. He acknowledged that although he personally does not like the idea of the *Baghrot*, many youngsters and their parents want the kibbutz to give opportunities for university study. It indicates the increasing emphasis on individual development rather than community needs. It also indicates an increased acceptance of professional work in the place of manual labor.

[11] Bruno Bettelheim, *The Children of the Dream* (New York: Avon Books, 1971), p. 245.

During the 1970s, Har decided to send 6 to 7 percent of its adult population to higher educational training each year. The decision on each request is made in the General Assembly after a recommendation by the Educational Committee. Initially members were permitted to begin training if it led to skills that were needed by the community such as teaching, nursing, and technical knowledge. By 1975 members were also allowed to begin studies in filmmaking, anthropology, and even rabinnical studies. The latter was a particularly interesting decision by the community since the kibbutz is ideologically opposed to religious orthodoxy.

Consequently, the principal function played by the regional high school for Kibbutz Har is the expansion of educational school opportunities for its students. By cooperating with other kibbutz and moshav settlements in the area, different interests and needs of Har's students can be better met.

In addition to the educational function, the regional high school provides workroles for members not available within Har itself and thus gives some members a chance to fill jobs that are less physically demanding and more intellectually stimulating than most kibbutz jobs. The loss for the community is of labor power that might have been shifted to fill service area or income-producing branch slots.

The regional high school is one of the main avenues of furthering cooperation between the kibbutzim and, to a lesser extent, moshavim in the area. It allows the community a broader base for sharing experiences. The educational framework, however, is limited to units of the cooperative settlement movement and does not include residents of nearby towns or villages. The predominantly North African population of Shlomi, the residents of Nahariya, and the region's Palestinian-Arab population are excluded. The school thus maintains a homogeneous base.

Educational trends in the high school may have a large influence on Har's internal community life since the future of the kibbutz depends upon the attitudes of the second and third generations. Yet the pressure of parents and children to emphasize preparatory courses for the *Baghrot* and to teach English rather than Arabic or French as a second language indicates the acceptance by the kibbutz of the values of the national economic, political, and social order. Specifically, it strengthens the forces of individualization and professionalism at the expense of communalism and manual labor.

Sulam Tsor Regional Council

Sulam Tsor is one of fifty-five regional councils set up after the establishment of the state to perform municipal functions for the cooperative settlements within its geographical boundaries (see Map 3). The state defined a town as an area including at least 15,000 people; lesser populated areas are considered local municipalities. In consultation with government officials the central organization of cooperative settlements in Har's area decided to form a municipal agglomerate of eight separate members: Kibbutzim Har, Gesher Achziv, Rosh Hanikra, Admit, Matzuba, and Eilor, and Moshavim Beset and Lehman.

Sulam Tsor means "ladder of Tyre" and describes the rising of the chain of hills in the region toward Tyre, Lebanon.[12] The Sulam Tsor region covers 66,500 *dunams* that include 18,600 *dunams* for agricultural use, 3,100 *dunams* of beach cost, 1,-900 *dunams* for industrial use, and 42,900 *dunams* of forests, pastures, and rocky ground. All the land is held by National Land Authority that includes the Jewish National Fund, and over half of the land is leased to the member settlements on a ninety-nine-year basis. The Sulam Tsor Regional Council has jurisdiction over the remaining 30,000 *dunams*. The total pop-

---

[12] Tyre is mentioned in the Bible as a Phoenician city in Lebanon. The name was proposed by Moshe Dayan when he was a candidate for membership at Har. He never became a full member.

SULAM TSOR REGION

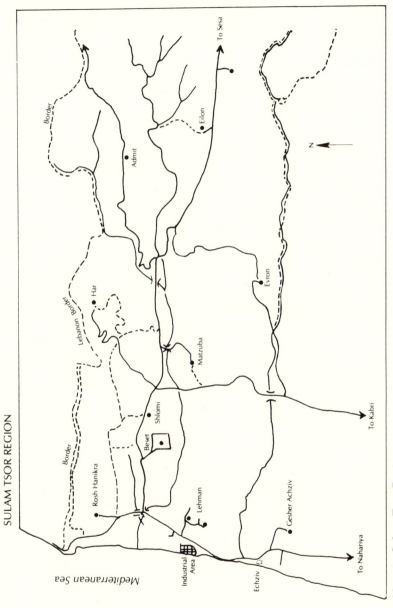

MAP 3. Sulam Tsor Region

ulation of the member settlements of the Sulam Tsor region is approximately three thousand.

Sulam Tsor Regional Council administers the district. There are eight cooperative settlement members of the council: six kibbutzim and two moshavim. The six kibbutzim belong to different kibbutz federations: Har, Rosh Hanikra, Gesher Achziv, and Matzuba belong to Ichud; Admit and Eilon belong to Artzi (see Table 15).

The council is divided into two operational parts. The Meleah (coming from the Hebrew word *maley*, meaning all) is composed of delegates from all member settlements. Each settlement initially had one representative to the Meleah, but in

TABLE 15. COMPARISON OF SULAM TSOR REGIONAL COUNCIL MEMBER SETTLEMENTS.

Name of Settlement	Type of Settlement and Federation Affiliation	Population	Date of Settlement	Economic Base
Admit	Kibbutz-Artzi	85*	1958	agrarian & industry
Beset	Moshav	70 families	1949	agrarian
Eilon	Kibbutz-Artzi	650	1938	agrarian & industry
Gesher-Achziv	Kibbutz-Ichud	435	1949	agrarian & tourism
Har	Kibbutz-Ichud	460	1938	agrarian & industry
Lehman	Moshav	60 families	1949	agrarian
Matzuba	Kibbutz-Ichud	386	1940	agrarian & industry
Rosh-Hanikra	Kibbutz-Ichud	365	1949	agrarian, industry & tourism

* Kibbutz populations refer to numbers of persons. The figures are as of 1973.

1975 it was decided that settlements with over 250 residents would get another representative. Har has two member representatives now, each with a vote. The Meleah is comparable to the General Assembly of the kibbutz. The second operational part is the Hanhala that is comparable to the *maskiroot*, or secretariat, of the kibbutz. The Hanhala has four members who are elected by the Meleah. Thus, while all member settlements are represented in the Meleah, only four are represented in the Hanhala. The Meleah is the principal legislative body for the region, and the Hanhala functions to undertake preliminary discussion, recommendations, and preparation of agenda.

A regional council president is chiefly responsible for the executive operation of the organization. The region has maintained a system of rotation of the role of president among the member kibbutzim, although rotation is not automatic. During this study's fieldwork, the president of the council was a member of Har, who had also served as president during the 1960s. The term is from three to four years. The fact that no moshav resident has ever held the office reflects the kibbutz orientation of the council.

The creation and development of the Sulam Tsor Regional Council was not easily achieved because of economic constraints of the pre-1948 years and early 1950s, in addition to resistance from separate settlements. The regional council president, who has been a member of Har, comments on early obstacles to regionalism: "When we came to Har our life was hard. . . . Eilon was on the left and across the road was Matzuba . . . but we had no time to cooperate, because we were busy . . . with our problems and no time to think of our neighbors."[13] As the subsistence era ended and the military and political situation in the region became relatively calmer, each kibbutz found it easier to enter discussion with its neighbors over such specific areas for cooperation as sharing agricultural machinery.

[13] Fieldwork interview with Eric Natol, 15 June 1975.

Har, however, and the other kibbutzim first viewed the regional council as a threat to their integrity. The regional council president has noted that in the beginning of the development of the regional council, it was seen as in conflict with the kibbutz. The kibbutz thought it could remain autonomous. The president continues, "The kibbutznik took all of it on his shoulders and said, 'Don't touch me. It's my business, I don't want your help.' "[14] Har and the other settlements gradually adopted the attitude that regional cooperation would be beneficial for the individual kibbutz as long as control of its administration was in their collective hands. Har has retained the right to cooperate or reject activities it does not wish to join, such as garbage disposal. (It disposes its own garbage separately despite a regional garbage unit.)

The Sulam Tsor Regional Council is an integral part of the national regional council system that is administered by the government's Ministry of Internal Affairs. The presidents of the four regional councils in the Western Galilee area meet once a month to discuss mutual problems. Every three weeks a formal committee meeting is held in Tel Aviv with all fifty-five regions represented. This committee votes for its own Hanhala that represents the concerns of the regional councils to the Minister of Internal Affairs.

Financial support for the regional council functions comes from the state and from public and private enterprise as well as from the member settlements. The cost to each settlement is based on a formula that takes into account such factors as population, land, industry, income, and buildings. For example, Har has 300 apartments and each apartment is assessed to pay 100 lira, so Har pays 30,000 lira. Har also pays 20 to 30 lira for each of its *dunams*. Every square meter of its factory costs 20 lira, and when Har had a guest house it paid 6 percent of its income to the regional council.

The income from member settlements, however, is only a

[14] Ibid.

small percentage of the regional council's total budget. The state contributes a major portion for most of the administration functions including education, road building, street lighting, and security needs. Additional money comes from public and private enterprises. Any business in the region pays taxes to the regional council. Government agencies such as the Mekorot Water Company pay taxes as does anyone building in the region. One interesting example of tax collection by the regional council occurred when a film company from the United States came to make a film in the region starring Sophia Loren. The regional council president acted quickly to insure that the filming would benefit the region: "I learned from our rules and from rules in the States, that if somebody is going to make a movie in a region, he must pay a tax. I decided to charge 4000 lira. The producer came up and asked if I was crazy. I replied, 'you are using our region. . . . We paid for the roads you are using, and the water, etc. I am permitted to take your money.' "[15]

The goals of the regional council are to administer its various functions for member settlements and to foster cooperation intraregionally and interregionally. The regional council acts in the context of rules laid down by the state; local rulings must, of course, be consistent with national law, and the municipal budget and functions of the regional council are continually subject to review by the government.

The functions of the regional council fall into ten main areas: security, construction, agriculture, industry, education, culture, health, legal services, tourism, and general services. Some of these functions are directed at the entire region, some to only a number of the member settlements, and some are part of an interregional framework. Within the areas the council administers a broad range of activities. A few examples follow.

(1) *Security*: The council is in charge of guarding all property in the area including fields of the settlements, busi-

[15] Ibid.

ness enterprises and sea shore. Fire protection is provided by an interregional framework that includes the city of Akko and Nahariva where the equipment is kept. It is responsible for the upkeep of bomb shelters in the region. Each settlement receives 800 lira for each of its shelters by the state through the Regional Council. The council has a special committee that conducts weekly inspection tours of the shelters in coordination with other regional councils. It can withhold money from the settlement for shelters if all is not in order. The council is not responsible for the overall military security of the area which is administered by the state.

(2) *Education*: The council is a conduit for state money that goes to pay the teachers of the elementary grades in the settlements. Since all the settlements pay state taxes the government gives them educational funding. It is easier for the state to funnel its funds through the central regional councils than to each settlement individually. It pays for both member teachers and hired teachers. The council is also the conduit for high school funds. As for university education, the council provides 50 percent of the cost for each member of a settlement that goes to university (50 percent of tuition; room and board is paid by the individual settlement). Since there are no universities in the region the Council sees tuition subsidy as a municipal function. Together with three other regions the council supports a conservatory and classes for children and adults in the arts. Seven buses are owned by the council to transport members to various educational and cultural activities.

(3) *Health*: Together with Akko, Nahariya, and two other regions, the council has developed a health care framework; Igud Arim is a cooperative effort to begin a good hospital system in the region which is being done in consultation with the state Ministry of Health that is re-

sponsible for a good system in each region; recently the council was critical of the emergency room services in the region and is working to improve the service. A special committee is organized to take care of emergency needs during wartime. Each of the kibbutz settlements has its own resident health care team (Har has its own ambulance) but war needs such as gas masks and maintenance of emergency electrical and water service are supplied on a regional level.

(4) Agriculture: Since the council is a regional organization of member settlements that primarily have an agricultural economic base, it has created supportive services for agrarian activity. The president of the council suggests that "this is a special contribution of the kibbutz movement to the development of what is the regional council system." In coordination with Akko and the national government, through the Ministry of Agriculture, the Sulam Tsor Regional Council has established an experimental agricultural center. The center offers planning for the agrarian development of the area. Its activities include land planning, irrigation improvement, disease control, and plant experiments. Decisions of the center are made by regional council representatives, government officials, and agrarian experts. A member of Har is the representative to the center for four regional councils in the Western Galilee area. The work consumes one half of his workrole (the other half-time job is his work as head of Har's internal security-defense).

(5) Tourism: The council has created a separate corporation, Yishuvei Sulam Tsor L'Pituach HaAzor, or Sulam Tsor Settlements for Development of the Region, to be in charge of tourism. There is a guest house at Kibbutz Gesher Achziv (until 1973 there was also one at Har, but, because of military conditions, it had to close); a camping site near the beach coast; a restaurant, and tour-

ist area on the cliffs of Rosh Hanikra; and plans to build a park, with an open air theater, near Achziv. The area is one of the loveliest in Israel and despite increased political-military tension in the region since 1967 tourists continue to come to the beaches and cliffs in large numbers.

Additional services of the council for member settlements include street lighting within the settlements and on public roads in the region, establishing libraries for the moshavim, and granting licenses for zoning changes and building permits.

All regional councils operate under the authority of the state's Ministry of Interior. However, differences exist among regions regarding the scope of membership and services. In some of the regional councils only kibbutzim of a single federation are represented, others do not include moshavim. In no cases do the councils include development towns or Arab villages. A number of the regional councils supervise the regional economy. In the Sulam Tsor region the economy is supervised by the Milouot enterprises. The Sulam Tsor Regional Council deals with the Milouot in ways similar to the ways it deals with any private or public business enterprise in the region, including tax collection and providing security services.

Har was a founding member of the regional council. Initially, as noted the membership of Har was cautious about the extent of its involvement in regional cooperation reflecting the community's history of regional isolation, its attachment to the norm of self-reliance, and its attitude toward other settlements in the area. This attitude of caution especially held true toward the moshavim and even more so with noncooperative settlements.

Economic considerations and the personal involvement of individual members altered the extent of Har's attitude toward regional cooperation. The kibbutz has paid state taxes since 1948 and the state in turn helped to create the regional council system as a way to transmit financial and other aid to the settlements. The membership of Har gradually realized that it could benefit from the services provided by the regional council, especially in the areas of agrarian development, educational aid, property protection, and emergency support. Har thus began to participate actively in more of the services provided by the council.

The increased participation and acceptance within the regional council system was greatly furthered when one of Har's members became council president. He had already served in leadership positions within Har, as had his wife, and both of them were well respected in the community. As president one of his roles was to encourage support for the council in all of the member settlements. No doubt his message to his own kibbutz was particularly strong. His resumption of the presidency for a second term in the mid-1970s after his first term which had begun in 1963, indicated that Har supported his work, for the assignment of labor is critical in the community.

In addition to having a member serving as president of the council, other Har members also have been assigned to the Sulam Tsor regional structure. One member is the council's representative to the center for agricultural experimentation. Another works in an automotive repair shop run by the council. Since labor shortages have always been a crucial factor in Har's economic development, the assignment of some of its members to regional activities is an indication that the community believes the benefits outweigh the costs.

In exchange, Har receives many services from the council that are characteristically the services a neighborhood would receive from a municipal government: street lighting, security, educational aid, and building services. Har pays taxes to the council and is subject to the jurisdiction of the rulings passed at the regional level such as zoning and building regulations. Har, in 1975, still resisted acceptance of regional garbage disposal because of lingering "I can do it better myself" sentiment.

Har's relations with the Regional Council of Sulam Tsor are also significant in furthering cooperative activity among regional settlements. This has social, as well as economic and political implications. In its first fifteen years, Har remained quite isolated from other regional cooperation, although its dependency on the national institutions was great. Its first regional cooperative ventures occurred with other kibbutzim in the Ichud Federation and then with kibbutzim in its region of other federations. The Sulam Tsor Regional Council also includes the moshavim. It is important, however, to note that the regional council has not extended membership to all inhabitants of the region. Its membership remains narrowly focused on eight cooperative settlements. Within the council the kibbutzim maintain control. Shlomi, a development town, and Palestinian-Arab residents of the region, including those in a settlement near Kibbutz Admit and a family grouping near Rosh Hanikra, are not included in the regional cooperative structure. The president of the council comments on the absence of Palestinian-Arabs from council activities. His statement reflects how local Arabs are excluded from regional municipal services and are not considered citizens of the area: "The Arab village near Admit is a special case. We are now transferring them to new land. They build huts without permission on soil that they do not own. . . . The government decided to transfer them 3 kilometers from Admit . . . and I am responsible for transferring them. They will pay taxes and I must build schools for them . . . but now I have no responsibilities because they are living without a passport, so to speak. They are not an integral part of our region."[16] The relationship between Har and non-cooperative settlements and Palestinian-Arabs in its region remains largely an economic one between employer and employee and occurs also at the regional level in the Milouot enterprise.

[16] Ibid.

The Milouot

The Milouot is essentially an economic interregional cooperative based on the economic interests of the area's kibbutz settlements. It was founded in 1960 by twenty-three kibbutzim,
representing the three major national kibbutz federations from
four regional districts in Western Galilee. In 1975 it had
twenty-six shareholding members (twenty-three kibbutzim and
three moshavim) with eight plant operations, two of which are
legally separate companies. One of the latter, the Miloubar
Central Feed Mill is jointly owned by two other regional areas
of Israel and serves over ninety cooperative settlements in the
northern part of the country. The divisions of the Milouot are
Miloumoz (the banana-packing and ripening plant) established
in 1960, Milousiv (the cotton mill) established in 1960, Milouof (the chicken slaughterhouse) established in 1963, Miloupri (the fruit-grading and cold storage plant) established in
1963, Milouad (the data-processing service) established in
1970, and Milouda (the research and development laboratories)
also established in 1970. The separate companies of Milos (the
citrus and fruit products plant) and Miloubar (the feed mill)
were set up in 1965 and 1961, respectively.

The Milouot enterprise serves settlements of four regional
council districts—Sulam Tsor, Gaaton, Naaman, and Zevu-
lon—in the Western Galilee and Haifa Bay Area. The area
extends from the Lebanese border on the north to the city of
Haifa on the south; from the Mediterranean on the west to the
central Galilee mountain range on the east. Kibbutzim com-
prise twenty-two out of forty Jewish farming settlements in this
region.[17] The member settlements of the Milouot farm 126,000
dunams or 64 percent of the total arable land in this area.

[17] "Milouot and Its Enterprises," published by the Milouot in 1971 and
"Milouot" an abridged version of a paper presented at the March 1971
F.A.O. Symposium on the Economic Organization of Agricultural Enterprises
in Paris, by the Milouot Enterprise (referred to from now on as the F.A.O.
Report).

The Milouot facilitates communication between the member settlements and national markets. An information bulletin is sent monthly to the main agricultural branches of each settlement and regular contact is maintained between the branches and the various Milouot plants. The communication network provides communication of the agricultural needs of the settlements and the Milouot. The main goals of the Milouot can be summarized as follows:

(1) the development of intersettlement cooperation on a broad and solid basis;
(2) the development of a regional agricultural industry for the settlements' agricultural produce;
(3) the development of modern industrial plants serving the settlements' agricultural branches;
(4) the reduction of production costs of the agricultural produce;
(5) joint endeavors to increase technological knowledge in the fields of industry, agricultural industry and of the settlements' agricultural branches.

The enterprise is set up at two industrial centers separate from any inhabited area. The northern center is located between Gesher-Achziv and Rosh Hanikra in the Sulam Tsor region between the Nahariya-Rosh Hanikra railroad and the highway. The southern center is located between Haifa and Akko in the Naaman region and has also been set up between a main highway and the railroad. Miloumoz, the banana plant, and the Milos fruit plant are at the northern center while the southern center houses the Miloubar (the feed mill), Milousiv (the cotton gin), Milouof (the chicken slaughterhouse), Miloupri (the noncitrus fruit plant), Miloudar (the research laboratories), Milouad (the data-processing service), the central Milouot administration, a petrol station, a store for sale of Milouot products, and a refreshment stand. Both centers have direct rail link-ups with the main lines.

Har's ties to the Milouot are principally economic: the Milouot serves Har as a marketing cooperative and labor exchange. In recent years, the economic activity of the Milouot has been enlared to include educational functions such as job-training programs and nutrition seminars.

Specifically, Har benefits from the Milouot organization in three ways:

(1) As an original shareholder, Har receives profit returns in the form of rebates or discounts on service costs and of interest on capital shares.

(2) Har's agrarian sector is expanded through the various divisions of the Milouot including the feed mill, cotton mill, the banana-packing and ripening station, chicken slaughterhouse, the fruit grading and cold storage plant, the research and development laboratory, the data-processing service, and a citrus and fruit products company of which the Milouot enterprise is the chief shareholder.

(3) By serving as a labor market for Har's members, the Milouot provides job possibilities that are not available within the internal economy, or *meshek*. There are three categories of kibbutz members who work in the Milouot enterprises: people that the Milouot requests because of their known skills and talents; people who request to work in the Milouot to expand their job horizons; and people who have a hard time finding a workrole in the kibbutz who the kibbutz asks the Milouot to help place.

This three-pronged relationship to the Milouot has helped Har raise its standard of living, to bring new technology to its agricultural sector, and generally to increase the material development of the community.

The membership of Har, especially those in leadership positions or involved in the Milouot enterprises, have realized the Milouot has had a strong impact on the individual member settlements. The Milouot has reflected and reinforced the movement away from the ideological emphasis on labor intensity toward mechanization, and capital intensity. An example of this trend is that the increased importance of the Milouot to the member settlements is occurring at the same time that attachment to the separate kibbutz federations promoting ideological concerns is decreasing.[18] The general secretary of the Milouot, a member of Har, comments on this transition:

> In the past, the movement [federation] used to have all the activities, all the functions, that we needed inside the kibbutz—education, culture, economy, work problems, etc. It made sense for the movement to have all these activities especially when you think of 30 years ago when the kibbutzim were weak and had to have support in the government and high-level institutions like the Jewish Agency, the Dept. of Settlement. But as the economic side improves, the kibbutz can get along better. . . . the branches became stronger and we became ready for better organization of the branches. . . . the Milouot was the result of the need for this type of organization. . . . there is little difference in the economic branches among the settlements in this area. . . . we have more in common than with settlements . . . in our federation. . . . the branches are different, the distances great. It doesn't make sense to work together. . . .
>
> Within Har I would say there is a switchover from more idealistic life to materialist life. . . . We used to work together, go to meetings together, elect representatives. . . . Today, who cares who goes to a council meeting of the [federation] movement? We just had the elections last month and I don't even remember who were the candidates. . . . nobody knows and nobody cares. . . . People are much more materialist-minded. I think this is why the place of the Milouot is much greater than ever.[19]

[18] An important and insightful study of the relationship between the regional economic systems and the national movement federations has been written by Daniel Rosilio, secretary of the Meuchad Federation and member of Kibbutz Kabri in the Western Galilee, entitled *The Regional Structure in the Kibbutz Movement* (Tel Aviv: Van Leer Institute, 1975), which is only in Hebrew at present. He suggests that as the regional structures grow more powerful they take away influence from the national movements.

[19] Fieldwork interview with Ben-Hazak, 2 May 1975.

It is revealing that many kibbutz members express the attitude that the Milouot "has the kibbutzim" just as industrialization of the kibbutz has caused the "factory to have a kibbutz" rather than a kibbutz having a factory. This expression indicates a realization that Har is now dependent upon the Milouot for its economic stability. Shalom Peled, head of the Miloubar Feed Mill, notes that "the dependency of the kibbutz on the regional enterprises grows every day. . . . it is feasible that the Milouot secretary knows more about the economic situation of a kibbutz than the economic manager of the kibbutz. . . . tomorrow the standard of living in the kibbutz would drop catastrophically if we [Milouot] closed up shop today."[20] The kibbutz is tied to the labor and production policies of the Milouot that are creating an economic definition of regional cooperation and reducing the individual community's degree of autonomy.

LABOR

As of 1974, the Milouot employed a total of 982 workers, of which 550 were hired regular workers, 270 hired seasonal laborers and 162 were kibbutz members.[21] The May 1975 Milouot figures, according to Milouot subdivisions, are outlined in Table 16. Akiva Nir, Head of the Kibbutz Member Milouot Labor Power, is in charge of meeting needs for member labor. Each member kibbutz is responsible for sending a specific number of its members to work in the Milouot every year. The exact number to be sent by each kibbutz is determined according to the extent the kibbutz utilizes Milouot services; the extent of purchases in the Milouot central purchasing organization, the Mishkai Hamifratz; and the population of the kibbutz. For 1974-1975, it was determined that a total of 200 kibbutz members were needed to work in the Milouot, 175 in its plants, and 25 in related regional activities. The latter includes such

[20] Fieldwork interview with Shalom Peled, head of the Miloubar Feed Mill, 6 May 1975.

[21] Figures from *1974 Annual Financial Milouot Report*.

TABLE 16. Milouot Labor Power Division, 1975.

Milouot Division	No. of Member Laborers	No. of Hired Laborers	No. of Seasonal-Hired Laborers
Miloumoz (bananas)	3	13	52
Milouof (chickens)	22	190	38
Miloupri (fruit)	10	52	—
Milousiv (cotton)	5	25	—
Miloubar (feed mill)	45	27	—
Milos (citrus fruit)	22	207	98
Miloumor* (cottonseed oil)	7	22	—
Milouot Central Administration	37	38	—

* New experimental division to develop ways of extracting oil from cottonseed for new products, as of 1975.

jobs as liaison to the regional research station run by the Ministry of Agriculture.

The northern and southern centers of the Milouot are located ten minutes and thirty-five minutes respectively by car from Har. Public transportation to both is infrequent, and direct transportation to the southern center does not exist. Members from Har working at the main southern center use car pools. The automobiles are provided to members holding important positions in the Milouot system and serve as "company cars."

Because of their location it is difficult for a great number of Har's members to work in the Milouot. Most of the kibbutz members working for the Milouot come from settlements that are near the centers. It is especially hard for any woman from Har who is breast-feeding to work in the Milouot, as she would be separated from her child for the workday.[22]

Har in the time period under study was expected to send a total of eight members, seven for the plants, and one for regional work. In fact, Har sent six members, four working directly in the Milouot and two in the region. Pressure can be placed on kibbutzim not fulfilling their quota, but, as Akiva Nir stated "we are very liberal in our pressures. We know sometimes kibbutzim are in trouble." Kibbutz Admit, a relatively new settlement on the Lebanese border, for instance, has the smallest quota of three but could not send even one. Kibbutz Ein Mifratz, with the largest quota of fourteen, sent twelve.

Pressure on the individual kibbutz could include cutting back on allowed services necessary to its economy. Instead most pressure is verbal, with the head of labor power going to the kibbutz to negotiate an understanding. This contrasts with the policy of the kibbutz movement federation that fines members for not filling their labor quotas.[23]

Nir is aware that the relationship between the individual kibbutz and the Milouot rests on mutual understanding and that member settlements realize they must send workers to maintain their control of the system: "the Milouot is an important part of the kibbutz. The kibbutzim understand that if they do not give people to Milouot they will lose the possibilities of managing the plants. You can manage plants only with your own people. Otherwise there are problems."[24] Kibbutzniks, therefore, fill all

[22] Work hours vary but the average is a long day, from 6:30 A.M. until 3 to 4 P.M., and members often have meetings in the evening or other times. No day care is provided at the Milouot itself for members or hired workers.

[23] The Ichud Federation demands that 4 percent of the kibbutz membership be assigned to work for the national federation. In 1975, Har had five full-time, one two-thirds-time and one half-time members working at the Ichud Federation or about 2.3 percent.

[24] Fieldwork interview with Akiva Nir, 15 May 1975.

of the top managerial positions and many of the skilled work-roles. Almost none is in a semiskilled, blue-collar worker position. The work term is determined in consultation with the kibbutz economic manager and is usually for four years, which allows the member enough time to learn the job, produce optimum work, and then to train a new member. Not infrequently, however, members stay on after four years and a few have been at the Milouot for almost its full fourteen-year history. Three Har members are among those who have worked in the Milouot longer than four-year terms.

The relationship of the kibbutz members working in the Milouot to hired laborers is not merely one of management and the manual laborer. The Milouot managers are members of the kibbutzim that own the plants. Thus, kibbutznik Milouot workers are representatives of "self-employed" business firms while hired laborers are employees. The Milouot enterprises are controlled by only a selected group of communities in the region. Workers who are not residents of the cooperative member settlements do not enjoy the same benefits as do kibbutznik and some moshav workers.

The ideological dilemma posed for the kibbutz is well recognized by both labor power division heads. Akiva Nir, head of member labor, commented in a fieldwork interview that "it's not easy to be the manager and believe in the equality of people. . . . it's one of the big problems we face here." Shoshanah Sagay, head of hired labor, continued: "It's hard to be one of the bosses. That's something that has to be learned. . . . I always try to keep in mind that here [in the Milouot] I am regarded as a boss. . . . They [hired workers] receive salaries from us, we fix the working conditions. The management of the Milouot is not like the management of private industry for kibbutz members not even working here make decisions. . . . the task of the Milouot is to serve the farm [kibbutz] settlements." Gila Resh, the *maskira*, or general secretary of Har, remarked that the placement of kibbutzniks into managerial positions was one of the most significant influences of the Milouot system on the life of the kibbutz. She believed that the more members assumed the task of managers, the more they would assume managerial attitudes toward others.

Hired Arab laborers constitute 20 percent of the permanent hired labor force and are an overwhelming majority of the seasonal work force. Sagay reported that "we [the Milouot] are very careful about problems with Arab workers." During the 1973 War, 90 percent of the Arabs showed up for work and were instrumental in maintaining factory output. Hired laborers working in the northern center come principally from Nahariya, Shlomi, and local Arab villages. They come from Akko, Kiryot, Tuv Shalom, and Arab villages to the south center. Most of the seasonal, temporary hired workers are Arabs and school students on summer vacations. The permanent hired workers consist of both Sephardic Jews and Arab laborers.

Wages for hired laborers are determined according to fixed scales set by the Histadrut. Time and a half is paid for overtime and night work. Average wage rates vary from division to division. In the slaughterhouse, for example, wages are set according to the food-worker scale that is the lowest in Israel and metal workers in the Milousiv, or cotton gin, earn the highest wage rate.

Hired female laborers fill the majority of jobs in the Milouof, or slaughterhouse, the Miloupri and Milouz, or fruit-packing plants. Their wage levels, reflecting the nature of their jobs, average considerably lower than that paid to men.

At first, all labor needs for the Milouot were determined independently by the director of each factory or division. Now, a centralized labor-power division is in charge of filling all labor requirements. Shoshanah Sagay reported that she hires workers through her connections with absorption centers for new immigrants and with the Ministry of Labor and through the newspapers. In replying to a question concerning how new immigrants respond to working for an enterprise run by kibbutzim, she stated it makes little difference to most of them. However, a number of immigrants from the Soviet Union want nothing to do with "socialist" systems.

During interviews kibbutznik Milouot managers suggested that the Milouot treats hired laborers better than do other enterprises. In stating that the Milouot had a distinctive relationship with its hired workers, they cited the ways kibbutzniks try to improve the workers' lot directly. These included efforts to consult with the hired workers about "social rights" as well as wages, and to allow representatives of the hired labor force to participate in lower-level decision-making processes. By "social rights" they meant benefits other than wages provided by the Milouot such as good insurance coverage, scholarships for the workers' children, bundles for workers during wartime, and special privileges at the Milouot "company store." Sagay, however, added that any kibbutznik who takes pride in the way the Milouot handles things is not familiar with the workings of most modern capitalist enterprises.

There are not many alternative work possibilities for the hired laborers of the Milouot, and most nonseasonal workers work for long terms with little turnover. After ten years the Milouot gives a worker a watch. Very few, according to Sagay, receive training because "the workers in our enterprise are very simple workers" and for the most part "are people without any education." When a hired woman worker was sent to an inventory course since she "wrote so nicely" it was considered a major achievement. Sagay maintained the managers want to send workers for special study programs but they do not want to go.

This can be contrasted to the increasing numbers of training programs available to the kibbutzniks working at the Milouot. According to Nir, about twenty kibbutzniks in 1974-1975 took short courses on engineering, computers, and laboratory research work at the Technion in Haifa. Many of the kibbutzniks sent for such study are women working in the Milouot's laboratories and its data-processing center. The lesser skilled jobs in these plants, like key-punching, are left to hired women workers. In addition, a number of kibbutzniks have been able to get college degrees while working within the Milouot.

A final comparison involves decision-making opportunities for hired workers and kibbutzniks. The principal decision-making structure resembles that of an individual kibbutz, with a General Assembly, called Asefot Meshakim, to which all member settlements are invited; a secretariat, which meets each week and is composed of the central Milouot management and plant managers; and workers' committees in each division. In addition, there is a board of directors that meets twenty to twenty-five times a year and is composed of fifteen kibbutzniks. It includes five kibbutz members who work in the Milouot, including the general secretary and four division heads, and ten members elected at large by member settlements. The director's term is two years and is rotated among the member settlements, with federation affiliation as one criteria. Each settlement has an equal opportunity for representation as another on the board. Aside from the formal decision-making structures, kibbutzniks have an informal structure of maintaining contact and working out problems. During a fieldwork interview the general secretary of the Milouot reflected on how rather informal, intimate networks contribute to decision making: "We are not a mass but only 166 or so people. We know each other. When we eat lunch together we can settle problems. There is a committee of kibbutz workers in the Miloubar [feed mill]. If they have problems, the manager of the branch can tell me since we drink coffee together every morning at 6 A.M." A sense of camaraderie and unity of purpose guides the kibbutzniks in the Milouot in making decisions. They are all members of the same club.

Hired laborers belong to various Histadrut labor union groups depending on their work. If there is a dispute, they can first turn to the workers' committee within their division, and minor issues are settled there. Larger disputes come to the workers' committee that represents all of the workers in the Milouot and consists of five people. If it is a personal dispute, the committee often will be bypassed and the matter taken directly to the head of hired labor manpower. One man is the single representative of all of the hired workers in the Milouot and he organized the slaughterhouse workers in the only strike to ever hit the Milouot. He was described by the general secretary of the Milouot during a fieldwork interview, as "a man from Morocco, who you think is primitive, but when you get used to him you see he has natural intelligence." He is the only link between the hired workers and the management structure of the Milouot. During the strike and other Milouot disputes outside arbitrators have been called in from Histadrut offices in Akko or Tel Aviv.

A period of difficult negotiations between the management of the Milouot and the hired laborers was in process in the mid-1970s due to the skyrocketing cost of living in Israel. The hired workers wanted increments as percentages of their salaries while the management wanted to tie raises to production.

The hired laborers have not battled for inclusion in decision making but rather have concentrated on wage issues. As Sagay stated during an interview: "It's hard to live in Israel. Taxes are high, everything is expensive and little remains for the worker. They fight and we do not give." The workers have not been enthusiastic about the idea of a joint kibbutznik and hired labor cooperative plan that some kibbutzniks have put forth as a solution to the exclusion of hired laborers from decision-making control. This reflects the hired workers' rejection of "socialist schemes" and their understanding that the final control of the Milouot would ultimately remain with the kibbutzim. Maintaining control of the management of the Milouot is perceived by many kibbutzniks as significant for insuring profitability:

One thing is the actual management of the factory, the second is the profits. They are different things. In the future, proposed plan the kibbutzim must be assured that we will have the right to decide things for our agricultural branches. If people at the Milouot decided to close down something, we would have to close our branch and it doesn't make sense. It must be decided in advance that the members of the kibbutz have rights to manage the factory even if they are a minority. They [hired labor] have to understand that and they do.[25]

It is fundamental to the labor structure of the Milouot that management is not simply in the hands of the 162 kibbutznik workers but in the hands of the 26 member settlements. The Milouot management thus represents the 6,000 person population of these settlements. Only lower-level decision making, within the separate plants, is thus open to nonmember input.

CAPITAL

Just as the labor division in the Milouot indicates kibbutz managerial control, a look at capital investment reveals kibbutz capital control. However, the Milouot kibbutzim have been dependent on governmental and private financial support. The Milouot, also known as the Haifa Bay Settlement Development Company Ltd., was established in 1960 as a private holding company by 23 kibbutzim associated with the Mishkai Hamifratz purchasing organization. Mishkai Hamifratz had been founded by the kibbutzim in 1948 as a central purchasing agent for kibbutz supplies. In addition to providing this service for individual kibbutzim, Mishkai Hamifratz also provides purchasing services, collection services, and the administration of other financial services for the Milouot organization. In 1968 Mishkai Hamifratz made purchases of 40 million lira and had a currency turnover at the banks of 130 million lira.[26]

Within ten years after its establishment in 1960, the Milouot enterprise consisted of six main divisions, became the chief

[25] Ibid.
[26] "Milouot and Its Enterprises."

shareholder in the Milos Citrus and Fruit Products Company, and was a joint shareholder in the Miloubar Feed Mill. It had a total investment cost of 32 million lira. By the end of 1971 the Milouot accounted for 23 percent of the agricultural regional investment in Israel. The kibbutzim of Western Galilee, including Har, hold capital shares of 13.5 million lira, a major part of the total national net worth of 16 million lira. Total revenue has gone from 30 million lira in 1965 to 87 million in 1974.[27]

Fifty-one percent of the founder shares of the Milouot are owned by the Mishkai Hamifratz Purchasing organization, and 49 percent by the twenty-three original members united in Mishkai Hamifratz. Ordinary shares are held by these twenty-three kibbutzim and three additional cooperative moshavim. The three main sources of investment capital are:

(1) *Government Development Loans.* Since the Milouot plants are accorded the status of approved enterprises, the Milouot plants are given rights to special development loans and tax exempt status.

(2) *Bank Loans.* These provide about one-third of the investment of regular banking rates.

(3) *Members' Shares.* An initial assessment is made of the capital need of each Milouot project and members' share capital is fixed at 20-30 percent. Settlements wishing to use the plant's services are asked to participate according to their share of estimated use in the first four- to five-year period. The capital is received by the Milouot from the settlements over a four-year period. Any future increases in share capital comes from other settlements wanting to use a plant's services as full participants; additional capital from members for new projects; and retained profits of the plant that may be converted into share capital as member settlements decide.

[27] *1974 Milouot Financial Report.*

The principle of user participation is the guideline for redistribution of share capital every four years, based upon the previous four-year utilization. A settlement that has used a plant's services more than the average would be required to purchase more shares while one using a plant less would be eligible for a rebate.[28]

The member settlements also receive discounts from the Mishkai Hamifratz. The cost of the purchasing organization represents from about 1.3 to 2 percent of total purchases. Rebates have increased from a 22 percent return on members' investment in 1967 to 70 percent in 1971. This indicates a relatively low share of capital in relation to total liabilities and is a feature of the intermediary function of the regional enterprises.

Har has approximately 4 percent of the total shares in Mishkai Hamifratz. Its share varies according to how much the kibbutz purchases in a given year. The same holds true for the Milouot. Har utilizes the Milouz, the banana plant, more than the Milousiv, the cotton gin and its shares reflect this pattern of use. In 1970 the revenue collected on the settlement's behalf by Mishkai Hamifratz was over 34 million lira; according to Har's 4 percent shares this would translate into 1.3 million lira for the kibbutz.

Yet, it is impossible to describe benefits to member settlements strictly in terms of profit since the kibbutzim both use the services of the Milouot and are the suppliers of the services. Kibbutz members speak of "achievements" rather than profit. In a fieldwork interview a Milouot manager described the difference between the Milouot system and normal capital enterprise: "In a normal private factory you can see the difference between the input and output and know the profit. Here you buy chickens from the kibbutz and give a low or high price

---

[28] The F.A.O. Report reports that the problem of a plant suffering from a fallen demand by the settlements is solved by a guarantee for its continued operation until a limit for its operation is reached by all members.

which depends on what is best for the kibbutz. You determine
the price margin according to what would be best overall for
the kibbutz interest." What is "best overall" for the kibbutz is
usually judged in terms of overall economic profitability for
kibbutz member settlements. The same holds true for the Miloubar, the feed mill, which can charge higher or lower rates
for its animal food supplies. A regular capital enterprise would
naturally take the higher price but this may not happen in the
Milouot. The "profit" there is determined by the difference between the estimated cost of preparing the food compared to the
actual cost. If the actual cost is lower, a "profit" had been
made.

Although the exact workings of the Milouot regarding fi-
nances is not the same as in capitalist enterprises, it maintains
a pattern of returning the profits from hired labor into assets for
its member settlements.

THE MILOUBAR FEED MILL

A close examination of the Miloubar reveals how the Milouot
plants serve the kibbutzim and how they are linked to national
and international organizations. The Miloubar Feed Mill is
unique among the Milouot enterprises. It is an interregional
venture of the Milouot settlement members including cooperative settlements in the Jezreel Valley and Upper Galilee, and
it is the only Milouot enterprise where kibbutz members constitute the majority of plant workers with forty-two kibbutzniks
out of sixty-four workers. The feed mill is crucial for the run-
ning of all the livestock and poultry branches of the member
settlements since they would be in serious trouble if it were
shut down or if foul-ups occurred. Its labor force composition
is based on the recognition of the differences between *poalim*,
or hired workers, and kibbutz members working in the Milouot.
The former, as employees, could call a strike that could per-
manently cripple the member settlements' economy while the

latter would not act against their own interests. Hired Miloubar laborers work primarily in the servicing and repair jobs, while kibbutzniks fill the production jobs (see Table 17).

Har's link to the Miloubar is through its poultry branch. In 1974 Har modernized its poultry branch by replacing a faltering nonmechanized set-up. Its original purchase was of 20,000 chickens from Kibbutz Beit Haemek for 42,000 lira and it started raising them for slaughter at the Milouof plant.

The main criteria used to determine the economic viability of the poultry branch are the length of the growth cycle of the chickens and the relationship between the amount and cost of feed used to the weight of the chickens. The greatest profit is made when chickens reach optimal weight within a specific time period and can be sent immediately for slaughter. The cost of meat per kilo food rises when full-grown chickens cannot be sent to market quickly. They must then continue to

TABLE 17. MILOUBAR OCCUPATIONAL DISTRIBUTION (hired labor and kibbutz members).

Sector of Miloubar	Workrole	No. of Hired Laborers	No. of Kibbutzniks
Management (Total)		3	6
	Head Manager	—	1
	Top Managers	1	1
	Office	—	2
	Marketing	—	1
	Accounting	2	1
Services (Total)		19	6
	Maintenance		
	Labs and Warehouse		
Production (Total)		—	30
Total No. of Workers (64)		22	42

SOURCE: Daniel Rosilio, *The Regional Structure in the Kibbutz Movement* (Israel: Van Leer Institute, 1976), p. 128.

be fed after their weight has reached its full limit. Because food costs are so high, it may become more profitable to slaughter chickens even if the market is oversupplied and prices are low.

As a member shareholder of the Miloubar, Har both purchases its chicken feed from the plant and receives a rebate from the plant after "profits" have been determined. An outlay of 123,000 lira was originally made for feed purchases from the Miloubar for Har's poultry. Annual rebates to member settlements have averaged from 3 to 3.5 percent or over 11 lira per ton of produced feed (estimated at 175,000 tons in 1975). During a fieldwork interview Ishai Tov, head of Har's poultry branch noted that "Har is a seller of chickens and an owner of the firm that buys the chickens." Thus the cost of the poultry branch and its final income each year take into account the Milouot shares held by Har.

In the first years of Har's poultry branch, the kibbutz was responsible for purchasing its own feed and producing the best mixture, an often hit-or-miss process. Today, the Miloubar offers a wide range of feeds produced with advanced technological knowledge and equipment. The advantages of the Miloubar to Har's poultry branch include better storage of feed raw materials and cheaper costs due to bulk buying; quality control with a high standard of raw materials and final feed product; optimal feed composition using computers; greater efficiency in producing feeds in pellet form that reduces labor needs. Transport of the feed is also supplied by the Miloubar, and it also offers scientific advisory services to meet the special needs of the branch.

Har is linked through the Miloubar to a wide network of national and international organizations. Together with five other feed mills in Israel, the Miloubar has formed an association with a technical bureau, active in poultry branch and other livestock feed experimentation. The association maintains an experimental dairy herd and fish feed station. Through its technical bureau, the Miloubar cooperates with the cattle and poultry divisions of the Volcani Research Center, the Technion's Food Technology Faculty and the Fisheries Research Station. There are also a great many direct ties to the Ministry of Agriculture. Its international links include not only import and those through export trade, but also education centers. The major equipment for the Miloubar has been provided by the Swiss Buehler Brothers Company. One percent of the Milouot production is exported to European countries. Educational contact is maintained with Centre de Recherches International de Nutrition et Alimentation (CRINA) in France, affiliated with Miloubar since 1965, and Forschungsinstitut Futtermitteltechnik der I.F.F. Braunschqeig (I.F.F.), a German research center for food production technology. Contact with the United States Department of Agriculture and private feed production companies is also kept up by Miloubar.

Har's agrarian branches also use other Milouot plants: Milousiv, the cotton mill; Miloupri, the fruit processing plant; Milos, the citrus fruit plant; Milouof, the chicken slaughterhouse; and Miloumoz, the banana plant. The latter is headed by a member of Har. Other members who work in the Milouot from Har are the Milouot general secretary, who formerly headed the cotton mill, the head of the Milouda, or the research laboratories, and a member working in the Milouad, the data-processing plant.

POLITICAL AND MILITARY DIMENSIONS OF THE MILOUOT

The Milouot framework provides Har and other member settlements with a structure for maintaining agrarian production during security emergencies and war. The organization for support during emergencies was instituted after 1967 and became particularly important during the 1973 War. It reflects the strengthening of the maintenance of a national emergency network called the Meliah, Meshek Lishat Cherum (Organization for Emergency Economy). The chairman of the Meliah is the Minister of Defense whose ministry supervises all of the needs of the nation during military crisis. The general secretary of the Milouot, a member of Har, is also the head of the Meliah in the Western Galilee region.

Since the majority of Israel's army consists of its citizens, when a crisis or war erupts and troops are called up, most of the country's labor force is called away from work. It is crucial that there be arrangements to maintain production and essential services. Each Milouot plant has a list of people available in the region who can be substitutes for workers if they are called into the army. For instance, the cotton mill has issued a questionnaire to all member settlements requesting information on which members have experience with cotton picking and gin operation so they can be called if needed. The 1967 War came in the middle of the cotton planting season and the 1973 War at the end of that season. Cotton production suffered during the 1967 War, but with a better organized emergency plan in 1973, more produce was saved. The head of the mill commented in a fieldwork interview on how emergency plans were put into operation in 1973:

> During the last war my unit was by chance stationed here in the region. . . . the war caught us just at the beginning of the picking season and it was very difficult. . . . I knew which kibbutz needed people and which had extra people to help us. Once picking was finished in one place we moved on to the next kibbutz. Our gin was the only one in the country kept running. . . . Our Arab workers also all came to work and others called to see if we needed help. We got in over half the crop and that is how the gin kept running.

There were substantial losses to Milouot members, particularly due to the first days of the call-up in the 1973 War. However, the emergency preparations organized in the Milouot protected, as much as possible, the economies of member settlements during the crisis. This scale of protection would not have been available without the Milouot organization. This kind of economic security is not available to the region's urban and development town residents.

CHAPTER FOUR

The Recent Years

For Kibbutz Har the years since 1967 have marked a period characterized by strong social reaction to two major Israeli-Arab wars, an increase in military tension along the Lebanese border, and the further development of its industrial economy. The community faced the challenge of adapting to the changing political and economic conditions while maintaining a viable internal social organization. Its response to these challenges largely depended upon the community's ongoing relationships to regional, national, and international institutions.

The specific problems the kibbutz struggled with during the period reflected cultural changes in the general Israeli society and the difficulties of maintaining communal forms of social relations in the midst of an increasingly complex, capitalist environment. Would the kibbutz be able to deal with the growing tension along its border? How would community life be affected by the need for more internal security? In what way would Har attempt to overcome the contradictions to its ideological position on hired labor and job rotation? How would the growing sense of individualism in place of a collectivist orientation be translated into the community's organization?

The 1967 and 1973 Wars each had a pronounced effect on the life of Har. Originally the 1967 Israeli victory created a sense of elation and pride in conquest. However, the general national euphoria was tempered by war casualties and by an unusual questioning of the purpose of the war. Kibbutzniks in particular were engaged in the retrospection documented in the book *The Seventh Day*: "Can we go on holding the sword in one hand only? There's something here that contradicts the basic tenet of kibbutz life which says that every man has his own world and the right to fashion it. The question is whether this really applies to every man as a man, or whether it holds good only for the man who's a kibbutznik and a Jew and an Israeli?"[1]

Two of Har's members never returned from the 1967 war-front, and many of those who did were left with difficult memories. Varied emotional responses to the war are still evident in the community. During interviews with second generation members, for instance, one recalled the exhaltation of reaching the Western Wall in Jerusalem, while another recounted the pain of being a medic in the army hospital outpost.

The 1973 War did not bring such extreme poles of reaction. The lingering elation from the 1967 victory was ended by an effectively waged battle by the Arabs. By not clearly winning the contest, Israel lost the war. The myth that Israel was invincible and the Arab soldier incompetent was destroyed. Har's members experienced the national feelings of shock, dismay and concern. By 1973 Har was also experiencing the increase in military incidents along the Lebanese border that were a result of general Arab opposition to Israel's occupation of conquered territory and the growing activism of Palestinian nationalists. The Lebanese-Israeli border, which had been relatively quiet since 1948, now became the scene of guerrilla raids by Palestinians based in the southern Lebanese refugee camps. Har became a target of these attacks that started in 1971 and that increased after 1973 and in the fieldwork period of spring and summer 1975.

The national economy, of course, reflects the effects of a war posture on the Israeli society. While the 1967 War ended the worst recession in Israeli history, it escalated the crisis of meeting both military and civilian needs. Military-defense requirements absorbed over one-quarter of the national gross na-

---

[1] *The Seventh Day*, ed. Andre Deutsch (Tel Aviv: Steimatsky's Agency, Ltd., 1970), p. 135.

tional product. There was additional strain on the public sector of the economy to provide for the influx of 210,000 immigrants during 1967-1972. Not much was left over for basic social welfare requirements.

After 1967 Israel's dependency on foreign capital and imports increased. To support the greatly expanded military budget, campaigns to raise funds from the Diaspora Jewish community were organized. Israeli Minister of the Treasury Pinchas Sapir reported in September 1970 on the importance of raising funds from private sources in the United States:

> We set ourselves the aim of raising $1000 million from world Jewry in the coming year, by means of the United Jewish Appeal and the Israel Development Bonds campaign sponsored by the Jewish Agency. This sum is $400 million higher than that raised in the record year of 1967. . . . During the recent trip to Israel of the U.S. financial research team we explained that even if we succeeded in raising all that we expect from the United Jewish Appeal and the Israel Development Bonds campaign we shall still be millions of dollars short of our requirements. After summing up our arms requirements, we informed the U.S. we shall need $400-$500 million per year.[2]

At the same time Israel's price index of imported goods rose by 75 percent and exports increased by only 45.4 percent. By 1975 imports were equal to 60 percent of the gross national product. Even if defense production imports were subtracted, Israeli dependency on foreign trade was the greatest of any world nation. From 1972-1975, there was a 113 percent growth in the national trade deficit.[3]

During this period Israel, like the majority of Western coun-

---

[2] *Yediot Ahronot*, 30 September 1970. Out of a total of $1,034 million of United States military aid to foreign countries excluding Vietnam in 1970, Israel received $500 million.

[3] Uzi Nedivi (foreign trade officer in the Israeli Ministry of Commerce) in "The Fight to Close the Gap," *Jerusalem Post*, 23 April 1975.

tries, suffered from huge inflationary rates. Between 1972-1974 the prices of fuel, raw materials, and basic food commodities more than doubled. On 15 March 1975 *Forbes* magazine reported that in the previous twenty-four months prices in Israel had risen 80 percent. In this report Chaim Bar Lev, Minister of Commerce, states: "In effect, we are asking our people to accept a lower standard of living." Meanwhile Israel's tax rate remained among the highest in the world, especially in the middle-income brackets. An additional defense levy of 15 percent of paid income tax was imposed following the 1967 War.

Two new war-related factors were prominent in the labor force: the inclusion of a new labor force from the occupied territories and the proliferation of unemployment and strikes. Over 30,000 Palestinian workers from occupied territories joined the Israeli labor market, chiefly as unskilled and semi-iskilled workers in the construction trade. From 1967 onward the Israeli industrial sector became increasingly reliant on this new, inexpensive source of labor.

Although large numbers of soldiers remained in uniform following the 1967 War, the unemployment rate in 1968 was relatively high, with 5.71 percent of the labor force out of work.[4] In reaction to the growing burden of taxes, inflation, and unemployment, strikes became more commonplace with the number of strikers increasing from 25,000 in 1967 to almost double that in 1968.[5] Despite calls for national unity, a serious wave of strikes broke out in 1969 among postal workers and Ashdod port workers. In order to repress the strike effort the government, in alliance with the Histadrut leadership, issued army mobilization orders to the militant strike organizers. These pro-

[4] Israeli Government, *Bank of Israel Annual Report* (Jerusalem, 1968), p. 211.

[5] Israeli Government, *Israel: Statistical Yearbook* (Jerusalem: 1967 and 1968).

tests marked unprecedented internal dissent on economic issues.

In the midst of the military tension and economic difficulties of the 1967-1975 period, Kibbutz Har celebrated its thirty-fifth anniversary. From 1938 to 1973 the community had grown from 49 original settlers to a population of over 400, including 257 members, 150 children, parents of members, volunteers, and *ulpan* students. The cultivated area had increased from 340 *dunams* to over 2,900. In place of tents and make-shift huts were concrete apartment buildings, a large central dining hall, service buildings, and a modern swimming pool overlooking the valley. The factory complex stood nearby. During the anniversary year plans were begun to enlarge the dining hall and build a new, highly automated chicken house. Two-story apartment structures began to appear to accommodate the increasing population and to expand in spite of the limitation of space on top of the mountain.

Clearly, the community had vastly improved its standard of living. Its continued economic, political, historical, and symbolic importance to larger Israeli society had helped to guarantee favorable financial considerations. Its cooperative internal structure eased the individual family burden that most households in Israel were suffering from the worsening economic situation. Har was able to offer its members a degree of economic security and freedom from fears of poverty and unemployment not available to the majority of Israeli citizens.

The amelioration of material conditions, however, was not obtained without a cost to Har's communal organization. As the economic conditions supported a more individualized pattern of living, a noticeable "withering away" of communal structures occurred. Participation in the General Assembly greatly decreased, and fewer and fewer people ate the evening meal in the central dining hall. Leisure time was now spent "at home," and a decision was made to have children sleep with their parents rather than in the communal children's houses. The feeling of the solidarity of communal life was replaced by the expectation of growing military and political unrest. After 1967 Har was hit by bazooka fire, which just missed hitting a children's house. A new border road extending from the Mediterranean Sea to the Syrian border was only yards from the kibbutz, and the sound of patrol tanks going back and forth could easily be heard. After the 1973 War and the guerrilla raids on the nearby towns of Ma'alot and Kiryat Shmona, tension in the community became more evident. Some members began locking their doors. Travelling up and down the mountain and along the road to Nahariya-Akko came under military surveillance. Members began carrying guns at all times.

The situation was especially tense during the fieldwork period of the spring and summer of 1975. The military, in cooperation with the kibbutz, practiced war games in order to strengthen internal security in the face of an increasing number of attacks in the area. Bomb shelters were used, particularly for the children. A new community solidarity coming from outside danger became apparent in Har. It differed from the kibbutz's early pioneering days, however, in that much of the romanticism seemed absent, and a stubborn, worried concern took its place.

National economic, political, and military events and policies have, therefore, continued to play a crucial role in kibbutz community life.

Economic Transition

The major economic trends evident in the kibbutz since 1948 continued through 1975, including a rise in the standard of living, an increased division of labor and a movement from an agricultural to an industrial base. In spite of the increased local military tensions, the steady growth continued in both agricultural and industrial production. Agricultural production became more mechanized while the factory expanded its internal and international markets, with the aid of the emerging Kibbutz Industries' Association (K.I.A.) and Unico, a Har-affiliated export company.

With industrial expansion, the numbers of hired laborers within the internal economy increased in absolute and percentage terms. Har's members became more engaged in work outside the kibbutz, particularly in regional organizations. The community labor force remained largely divided according to sex roles with women predominantly in the service sector and men in the income-producing sector.

THE AGRARIAN SECTOR

Major questions concerning land use in the community have focused on the restrictions of further expansion and the limitations of water supply. Within the present national borders there is no possibility of Har expanding its farm holdings. Agricultural productivity also reflects the water supply. As noted by the economic manager of Kibbutz Har: "In the last few years we have planted only cotton, wheat, and potatoes for field-crops. For cotton we had to decide how many times we could afford irrigation. The quantity of water depends upon how much a particular planting takes and how much we can afford to pay in taxes for using more land."[6]

Major changes in agricultural production since 1967 included shifts in the types of oranges produced to adjust to price differentials, increased mechanization for planting and harvesting, and the expansion of the chicken house to include 20,000 chickens in a new, automated building. The breakdown of land use at Har during these years is reported in Table 18.

The military situation affected one section of land use very

[6] Fieldwork interview with Moshe Kadima, economic manager of Har, 22 June 1975.

TABLE 18. LAND USE AT HAR DURING RECENT YEARS.

Field crops	1,272 *dunams*
Plantation crops	998 *dunams*
Fallow	5 *dunams*
Woods and Forests	150 *dunams*
Empty land	65 *dunams*
Settlement Area	200 *dunams*
Open land	230 *dunams*
Total	2,920 *dunams*

directly—the guest house of the kibbutz. Because of Har's mountaintop location with its beautiful view of the Mediterranean Sea and coastal valley, it had been a favorite retreat for Israelis on vacation and for foreign tourists wishing to visit a kibbutz. In 1972 it had brought in over a million lira for the kibbutz economy and was a significant element in the overall budget. However, following the 1973 War when guerrilla attacks on the kibbutz increased, the area was no longer a vacation spot. The road leading to Har became dotted with military check points and a military watch guarded the main entrance at all times. Since 1973 the guest house has been converted to housing for *ulpan* students, volunteers, army personnel, and the older children of the kibbutz.

The location of the kibbutz has also affected the type of building construction. Houses are now two-storied to conserve space. Moreover, walls are built with greater thickness and window areas are smaller and appear on only two sides of a structure.

Future land-use plans take into account restrictions on land and water. A member working in the avocado branch is experimenting with new types of plants that would be more suitable to the local conditions. A new, more efficient system of irrigation is being built. A long-range plan calls for the use of industrial water from the development town of Shlomi in Har's nearby fields. This could be an important step in coordinating the economies of Har and Shlomi.

LABOR

Changes in the community's utilization of labor, which had begun thirty years earlier, became even more accentuated after 1977. These subdivisions indicate the contradiction between the traditional kibbutz ideology and existent reality. By 1975 the continuation of hired laborers in the kibbutz economy violated the ideal of a classless society; division of labor according to sex in the service and income-producing sectors violated the ideal of equality of work status; and the increasing specialization of workroles violated the ideal of job rotation. The general membership's emerging self-definition as owner-managers stands in contrast to the original ideological goal of creating a Jewish peasant class that would join a revolutionary international workers' movement.

The existence of hired laborers in both the agricultural and industrial sectors of Har's economy remains a critical problem for the kibbutz. When Moshe Kadima became economic manager of Har in 1973, he felt his two main tasks were to reduce the number of salaried laborers and transform the service sector into more productive units. He has met only limited success in both endeavors.

The factory is the chief employer of hired laborers in Har, with only 29 kibbutz members in a total labor force of 142. In the agricultural sectors hired laborers are employed in some branches but not in others. This reflects differences in the branches in the strength of opposition to hiring laborers. For instance, no hired laborers are employed in the *pardess*, or citrus plantation, but there are a number of regularly employed workers in the banana branch. Members working in the *pardess* maintain a stricter adherence to traditional ideological positions. The members who work in the agrarian sector are among those most committed to the Socialist-Zionist principals of the kibbutz and argue for them in General Assembly debates. Their opposition is consistent with their attachment to the land and to the agricultural base of the kibbutz. In harvest seasons, however, even the most ideological of branches employed hired laborers as temporary workers to supplement the limited membership labor force.

A situation rarely mentioned in kibbutz studies is the existence of hired laborers in the service sector of the kibbutz. In Har salaried laborers work as shoemaker, barber, schoolteachers, and carpenters. The economic manager explained some of the reasons for their employment in the service sector:

> It is much cheaper to do carpentry in Har than buy it from outside. So we save money by hiring the two salaried workers for carpentry, one of whom has a license. For the same reason we hire someone in the garage. . . . We asked the shoemaker to open his shop in Shlomi and we would take our work to him there but he prefers to have his shop here because he doesn't like to work with the people of Shlomi. . . . We have a woman who used to repair the sheets for the guest house who doesn't want to leave and is still here.

The problem regarding schoolteachers for the elementary school is the shortage of female labor in the kibbutz. Elementary school teaching is defined as a woman's role. Since there are not enough qualified female members in Har for the job, women from outside the kibbutz are hired to teach. They usually live in the kibbutz for the teaching term, but do not have the full benefits of membership. Most hired teachers refuse offers of membership.

A major difference between the hired laborers in the service branches and those in the product branches is that the former are all Jewish. In the factory almost all hired laborers are also Sephardic Jews and those in the agricultural sector are Palestinian-Arabs.

As the kibbutz increasingly becomes economically dependent on the industrial sector, it has relied more on a hired worker labor force. This has produced a mixed response among Har members. While almost no one publicly applauds the need for hired laborers, there is a growing acceptance of their role in the economy. A significant number of members, especially those working in the factory, outside of the kibbutz, or among the second generation, think a small number of hired laborers in Har's economy is both acceptable and an economic necessity to achieve and maintain desired standards of living. However, there is a significant group in Har who still believes there is no room for any hired laborers in the kibbutz. It is a community issue that pits ideological considerations against goals for economic modernization.

Saadia Gelb, a leader in the Ichud Federation to which Har belongs, discussed in a fieldwork interview the issue of hired labor as an example of a direct conflict between state priorities and the ideals of the kibbutz:

> A direct conflict which was at our expense occurred when the kibbutzim were asked to take in masses of hired laborers shortly after the birth of the State. It was Ben-Gurion who asked us to take them and we yielded. We've been paying ever since. It made us look like bosses, it made workers hate the kibbutz, because who likes a boss? The subsidies we received were actually a form of bribe. It was bad to take the bribe and it was a big blow internally. As it is, we reaped some benefits and for those improvements we are now paying a heavy price.

In Har the issue continues to be debated and the choice among alternatives remains undecided.

The sexual division of labor in the service and income-producing sectors is another example of stratification that has become more firmly established in the kibbutz economy. Table 19 presents a membership labor force breakdown according to work branch, sex, and age. Out of 256 members in 1975, 50 were not in the labor force (e.g., in the army, attending school)

TABLE 19. LABOR FORCE PLACEMENT OF MEMBERS IN KIBBUTZ HAR, 1975.

Work Branch	No. of Men under 50	No. of Men over 50	No. of Women under 50	No. of Women over 50	Total
Inside Kibbutz:					
Factory	15½	8½	4	1	29
Accounting Services	1	2	2	½	6
Kitchen-Dining Room	2	1	11	1	15
Clothing Services	—	—	12	6½	
Taylor Center	—	—	4	3	7
Baby Houses	—	—	22	4½	18½
Children's Houses	1	—	7½	—	8½
Internal Education	1	—	3	—	4
Outside Education Work	2	3	2	—	7
Outside Work (i.e., Milouot)	4	6½	2⅓	2	14⁵/₆
Garage-Locksmith	3	1	—	—	4
Carpentry	2	2	—	—	4
Repairs	2	1	—	—	3
Kibbutz Administration	5	4	1	1½	11½
Electricians	1	1	—	—	2
Transport-Landscape Gardener	4	1½	—	—	5½
Agriculture					
Bananas	8	1	—	—	9
Avocado	4	1	—	—	5
Citrus	5	—	—	—	5
Field crops	5	1	—	—	6
Ulpan Work	1	1	1	—	3
Chicken House	½	½	—	—	1
Home Service Cosmetic/Store	1	1	2	2	6
Outside Kibbutz:					
Army Service	14	—	6	—	20
Travelling	—	1½	2	1	4½
Studying	3½	1	12¹/₁₆	—	16⅔
No Job Assignment	4	—	2	1	7
Totals	95	40	97	24	256

SOURCE: *1975 Annual Economic Report* (Economic Manager's Office, Kibbutz Har, 1975).

and this figure includes 26 women. Of the 206 members in the kibbutz labor force 95 were women. The workroles of the 95 women included 5 in the kibbutz factory, 0 in the agrarian branches, 6 in other income-producing branches, and 84 in the service branches. Women members who work in the factory performed such service as secretarial work. Six women in "other income-producing branches" included 2 in the Regional High School and 4 women working outside Har for the Ichud Federation or the Milouot. Those in the high school or working for the Ichud Federation were doing service type of work, even though it was income-producing for the kibbutz.

Women have usually done almost all service jobs. In the prestate period, they also worked in the agricultural sector. Men have continued to predominate in the income-producing jobs and perform few service roles. The service sector positions they do hold include carpentry, garage repair, building maintenance, and landscape gardening. These have traditionally been defined as male jobs. Occasionally, there have been male cooks, and the present head of the kitchen administration is a male. The rest of the male population serves in the kitchen-dining room only when their obligatory *toronut*, or service term, comes up in rotation.

While the agricultural sector and the factory have increasingly benefited from technological improvements, the service areas in which the majority of women work have been slow to receive budget allocations for new equipment. Through 1975 dishes were washed by hand, even for meals serving four hundred people.[7] The laundry was modernized only after 1972. Women, therefore, have worked in branches that have least benefited from the general rise in mechanization in the kibbutz. That rise has been largely confined to income-producing branches which are predominantly staffed by men.

[7] Since 1975, automatic dishwashers have been installed. The introduction of machines in the kitchen has reduced but not eliminated *toronut* work.

Efforts by the economic manager to make the service branches more efficient have not been very successful. He had proposed in 1974 that the service units redefine themselves as production units and start to keep income and output calculations. The women resisted this suggestion since they felt this would lessen their control of their work and place them under stricter supervision by the central economic management. While women working in the service branches do not accrue status for working in an income-producing branch, they still experience a sense of autonomy by controlling the service branches. The efforts to make them more "efficient" will no doubt continue to meet resistance. This is true despite the fact that mechanization could release women for the production branches, where women are greatly underrepresented.

In discussions concerning job satisfaction, women in Har expressed a general acceptance of service role assignments. Only one woman expressed any strong desire to work in agriculture. Quite a few younger women have indicated feeling restless and bored, however, at work. An early 1970 study, done by a member of Har, regarding job preference of members, concluded that a majority of Har's younger women wanted to work in the industrial sector or outside of the kibbutz.[8] Reasons for such preference included the chance to acquire more skills, meet other people, face new challenges, and become more professional. This, however, would further weaken agrarian communal socialization. Yonina Talmon, in her study of twelve Ichud Federation kibbutzim, also documented the overall discontent of women with kibbutz work. She concluded that kibbutz women are increasingly turning to the nuclear family setting in order to gain self-affirmation. This pattern became evident in Har as women led the successful movement to have children sleep in their parents' houses rather than in communal

[8] Study on Har's labor force by a member sociologist, Ben-Yarad, in the kibbutz library.

centers, and, of course, women are cooking more meals for their families in their separate apartment kitchens.

The separation of women from most of the income-producing jobs keeps them in the lower-status workroles and removes them from access to the basic means of market production. The separation from the income-producing sector of the economy has made the majority of women feel removed from the management of the kibbutz economy. Women thus rarely participate in General Assembly discussions of community economic affairs. This also reflects the fact that women were not equal to men in number and in status from the very beginning of the kibbutz.

Job rotation in the 1970s has been diminished not only by the increasing use of hired laborers and the segregation of women, but also by the growing significance of work specialization. In the agrarian sector only a few of the members have studied irrigation, the use of certain farm machinery, and plant science. No longer can each farm worker assume each other's job. As farming has become more mechanized and engaged in technological experiments, many of the members working in the fields have had to attend specialized courses sponsored by the Ministry of Agriculture or kibbutz federations. This has resulted in a tendency for each farm worker to remain in one branch, although within the branch he may be able to learn and share multiple roles.

The greatest push toward job specialization has been in the industrial sector. The management committee of Har's factory have held their jobs for a decade. While rotation takes place in the factory for certain jobs held by members (in 1975 no members worked directly on the production floor—these jobs were held by hired laborers), the rotation occurs among the same few male kibbutz members. These are the six to ten men who are considered to be the community's professional economic experts. They rotate among the positions of factory manager, Milouot leader, and head of the central economic offices of the kibbutz. They have become the elite professionals of the kibbutz. Three or four women who have undergone specialized training in kibbutz management are included in the elite group.

Job specialization in Har is viewed as a necessary element of modernization. The equation of specialization with progress appears to be unquestioned in the kibbutz and job rotation is still practiced when feasible. Within the factory, and to a lesser extent in the fields, it is determined by efficiency rather than by ideological factors.

CAPITAL

The sources for kibbutz capitalization, including its expanding export base, moved the community away from local self-reliance toward an international dependency. The principal sources of capital for Har have been the profits from the agricultural and industrial sectors. The latter contributes over 50 percent of the total kibbutz profit. Government loans and investments along with capital investments by other national and international institutions are other sources of capital. The 1975 Economic Report outlined the income and expense figures for the fiscal year ending 1974 as in Table 20.[9] Tables 21 and 22 provide a more detailed account of the income and expense categories.

TABLE 20. ECONOMIC REPORT OF 1975: INCOME AND EXPENSES (figures in thousands of lira according to devaluation rates of fiscal year 1974).

Income	21,479
Expenses	20,620
Profit	859
Income Tax	400
Profit for Investment	459

[9] *Har 1975 Annual Economic Report* (Har Economic Management Office).

TABLE 21. 1973-1974 Income Sheet Totals.

Branches	Income Total (after devaluation)	
Cotton	980	thousands of lira
Grain	125	"
Potatoes	303	"
Total Field crops	1,408	"
Bananas	2,352	"
Citrus	882	"
Avocados	864	"
Total Plantation	4,098	"
Chicken House	583	"
Factory	14,000	"
Outside Work	1,100	"
Other	290	"
Total	21,479	"

SOURCE: Economic Management Office of Kibbutz Har.

TABLE 22. 1973-1974 Expense Sheet Totals.

Items	Expense Total (after devaluation)	
Agricultural Expenses	2,222	thousands of lira
Salaries Outside Factory	364	"
Work Tax	290	"
Factory Expenses	4,925	"
Salaries in Factory	4,500	"
Expenses from Outside Work	30	"
General Expenses	4,889	"
Individual Subsistence Expenses	3,400	"
Total	20,620	"

SOURCE: Economic Management Office of Kibbutz Har.

The factory's profits accounted for over half of the total kibbutz net income from the early 1970s on. This is another significant indicator of the transition from an agrarian to an in-

dustrial economy. By 1974 the factory's income was more than double the combined income from the plantation, field crop, and poultry branches. The *yom avodah*, or workday, figures for the factory show a prorated income for kibbutz members averaging 165 lira per day and for hired workers 140 lira.

The average *yom avodah* figure is 112 lira per day for kibbutz members. However, there is great variance among the income-producing branches as is shown in Table 23. For instance, the banana plantation was more productive for prorated daily income than the factory.[10] Using these figures, the economic manager of Har estimated that in addition to the factory's hired labor force thirty nonmembers were needed to fill work positions to maintain kibbutz optimal economic viability.

After 1967 Har continued to receive special government financial support due to its strategic location. The factory received long-range, low-interest loans and the Ministry of Agriculture provided agricultural credit. The kibbutz also received government funds for security needs. A major form of government aid in this period was a gift-loan program from the gov-

TABLE 23. AGRARIAN BRANCHES: INCOME AND WORKDAYS.

1973 Report	Average Lira Income Per Day	Total Workdays (for kibbutz members)
Cotton	162	1,350
Field crops	169	2,100
Bananas	347	2,656
Citrus	63	3,720
Avocados	284	1,576
Poultry	38	337
Factory	215	7,323
Members Working Outside	64	6,995

[10] Figures from Economic Management Office.

ernment that was meant to finance the construction of a new *ulpan* center. Since the 1973 War forced the closing of the guest house, the kibbutz decided to use the tourist facilities as *ulpan* buildings. The government forwarded a 715,000 lira grant to the kibbutz to help offset community financial problems due to the spiraling national inflation. In addition, in 1974-1975 the treasurer of Har reported a moratorium of interest payments on government loans.

The Ichud Kibbutz Federation has established an old age fund. The fund is a guaranteed mutual fund under the supervision of Keren HaIchud. Each member kibbutz of the Ichud Federation pays into the fund according to a system of "shares" based on consumption rates, depreciation, and profit figures for each kibbutz. Har's shares came to 30,000 lira in 1972.[11] When kibbutz members no longer can work, they will receive a tax-free income from the fund. The establishment of the fund is another indicator of the transition from a communal ethos to a more individualistic community. It reflects the needs of a growing older population in the kibbutz. The younger members may view these elders as parasites so the fund is necessary to protect them. The individualism of youth in combination with that of the national culture results in a decline in communal responsibility.

Keren HaIchud also serves as an important financial agency for Har during periods of recession and inflation. When it was difficult to secure commercial bank loans, Keren HaIchud helped to fill the gap. In the 1950s, Keren HaIchud was the prime money source of member kibbutzim. Since 1960 each kibbutz has been affiliated with one major commercial bank but has used the resources of Keren HaIchud for management planning and future economic evaluation. Har helps to pay the

---

[11] Fieldwork interview with Haim Yulish, director of Keren HaIchud, 13 May 1975.

costs for Keren Halchud through allocating 6 percent of its member force to work on an annual basis for the federation.

On the international level Har has become increasingly financially involved with foreign companies through the activities of its metal works factory. Har's factory is one of the founding members of Unico Tool Corporation of New York that represents Israeli tool manufacturers in North America.[12] The corporation employs sales people to sell Har's industrial products directly in the United States, Canada, and Mexico to firms such as General Electric, Pratt and Whitney, Sikorsky Aircraft, United Aircraft, McDonnell Douglas, and Westinghouse. The majority shareholder of Unico is Solcoor Incorporated, which was established in 1952 as a subsidiary of Solel Boneh, Israel's largest construction company. Solel Boneh is part of Histadrut.

The increasing complexity of Solel Boneh's economic activity led to a reorganization in 1958 and resulted in Solcoor becoming a subsidiary of Koor Industries, Israel's largest industrial organization (see Figure 4). *Fortune* magazine in August 1975 ranked Koor Industries Ltd. 223rd of the 300 largest industrial companies outside of the United States. Its sales volume in 1974 was $903,000,000. Solcoor also represents the Kibbutz Industries Association, a cooperative venture of the kibbutz federations organized to promote the industrial economy of the kibbutzim.

Aside from the international economic relations of its industrial sector, Har has continually relied on contributions and capital investments made to Israel by the Diaspora Jewish community and foreign governments. In 1975 the international Jewish community contributed $750 million to the Israeli economy, the United States granted a $2.3 billion military and economic aid package, and German reparations provided another $340 million. Har relies on Israeli governmental and other institu-

---

[12] *Solcoor Publication* (New York: Solcoor Inc., 1976).

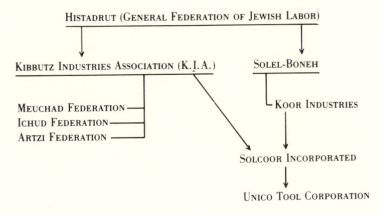

FIGURE 4. Organization of Solcoor Incorporated

tional support for financing that, in turn, is the product of this international support system.

The expenditures of the kibbutz include production costs, consumption expenses, payment of debts, interest, and taxes. For 1973-1974, loan repayments and interest came to 850,000 lira.[13] Individual consumption expenses as outlined in Table 24 are 2,500,000 lira. Production costs for the same time period for both agriculture and industry came to 11,647 thousand of lira.

Taxes paid by the kibbutzim have been the subject of a debate between kibbutz supporters and critics in Israeli society. Kibbutz supporters maintain the kibbutzim pay their full share of taxes while critics state that the kibbutzim receive tax advantages not available to other citizens. During a fieldwork interview, Dan Karmon, the Director of Kibbutz Industrial Association, commented, "kibbutzim have a greater flexibility when it comes to paying taxes but they are more above board in paying what they owe." He implies they pay what they owe. Israel's tax structure is progressive. The kibbutz tax rate is

[13] *Har 1974 Annual Economic Report* (Har Economic Management Office).

TABLE 24. Individual Consumption Expense Account, Har 1973-1974.

Item	Amount (in thousands of lira)	Item	Amount (in thousands of lira)
Basic Economy	885	Books	3
Clothes	23	Pamphlets	4
Shoes	10	Medical Aid	78
Laundry	29	Aid to Relatives	23
Furnishings-Supplies	91	Gifts	2
Paint-Repairs	57	Car Travel	48
Electricity	25	Reserve Provisions	1
Solar Heat	80	Insurances	100
Recreation	33	Water	14
Fuel	79	Health Education	40
Smoking	40	Vacations	14
Small Provisions	32	Personal Budget	373
Weddings	9	Parents	18
Gifts for Friends	10	Soldiers	28
Short Seminars	6	Volunteers	22
Driving School	15	Ulpan	41
Cultural Newspapers	24	Children's Education	215
General Culture	22	Other	1
Holiday Culture	4	Total	2,501
Social Club	12		

based on the total income of the kibbutz divided by the number of members. The average Israeli family in 1974-1975 paid from 55 to 65 percent of their income as taxes to the Israeli government. In Har the tax rate averaged from 45 to 50 percent of total income. The high costs of services on the kibbutz and lower income of certain production sectors result in lower average taxes for kibbutz total income. For 1974-1975 Har paid 400 thousand lira in taxes.

THE INDUSTRIAL SECTOR

The growth of Har's metal works factory has been the single most important factor in changing the community's economic and social patterns in recent years. We have noted that since the 1970s, the factory has contributed over 50 percent of the kibbutz's income base and its incorporation of hired laborers and management specialization has set the trend of increasing internal stratification.

Although the factory management is subordinate to the Central Economic Committee of the kibbutz with respect to decisions, few members outside of the factory have the necessary expertise to undertake an independent review of factory policies. During a fieldwork interview the economic manager of Har pointed out in 1975 that no one working as the manager of the kibbutz has ever held the post of kibbutz factory manager. Whoever has been economic manager has had to rely on information and interpretations set forth by the factory management concerning industrial decisions. Some kibbutz members believe that the "factory would rule the kibbutz" rather than the other way around.

The continued push for kibbutz industrialization has come from both internal and external pressures. Internally the kibbutz has reached its limit in terms of land expansion and water resources. Agricultural development is thus limited. Moreover, many of the younger generation do not wish to enter the agrarian branches but prefer the job specialization in the factory and the opportunities it offers for management, travel, and higher education. They are not, however, interested in working on production lines with its routine work and lack of opportunity for personal growth. Moreover, as the kibbutz population gets progressively older, a larger proportion of its older population is unable to do manual field labor and increasingly looks to the factory for job possibilities.

The external factors are considerable. Israel's balance of payments deficit for 1975 was over $4 billion, with imports at $8 billion and exports at $3.9 billion. The government is utilizing every means it can find to promote industrialization and increase exports. The Israeli lira has been devalued six times, and low interest loans and tax advantages are being made available to export industries. To reduce imports and force local industry to concentrate on exports, personal taxes have increased and import curbs imposed. As a result of these policies, Koor Ltd. doubled its export of chemicals, electronic instruments, and metal products in 1975 to about $200 million.

Israel has also been successful in opening up international markets for Israeli products. In January 1975 the United States eliminated custom duties on 2,700 Israeli-made products. A few months earlier a treaty with the United States was signed that ended double taxation of profits earned by American companies on investments in Israel. An agreement reached with Common Market countries in July 1974 allowed exported Israeli goods to be 80 percent duty-free and, as of 1 July 1977, they became completely duty-free.

Har's metal works factory, one of the largest kibbutz-based industries, has responded very favorably to the encouragement to expand. Following the factory general manager's successful bid in the General Assembly to approve a major expansion plan in 1967, the factory was enlarged and underwent modernization. In 1969-1970 all the machines in the factory were replaced by new semiautomatic and automatic machines. Two shifts keep the machines going at top efficiency. Output is checked by a sophisticated system of quality control. Security conditions, among other considerations, do not allow for a night shift.

The factory produces sophisticated precision metal tools, including high speed steel cutters, end mills, and taps. Har's factory products are well known throughout the country. It enjoys the highest rate of profit on end mills and in most areas of production has little domestic competition. Because of its near monopoly of certain products, the factory is regulated by the Ministry of Industry that establishes prices and output policy.

Some products are only produced for export trade, while

others are for local markets. Of the three main products, 70 percent of end mills are exported as well as 60 percent of cutters, but 50 percent of its taps remain in Israel.

During 1973-1974, the factory's total sales were 8,268,000 lira, about evenly divided between export and local market sales. Har conducts its export trade both through Unico, which is tied to Koor-Solcoor, and through its own sales people who represent the factory abroad. Unico was originally established in 1969 by three cutting tool factories in the north coastal area: Har, Vargos in Nahariya, and ETM in Herziliya. Since Unico did not do well in its sales to the United States, it was taken over by Koor. Generally, Har relies upon Koor for sales in Japan but deals with Western Europe, most of the United States, Latin America, and Iran through its own travelling sales representatives who are kibbutz members. Trade with African countries has been cut off except for South Africa.

The agreement Har signed with the government during the kibbutz's major factory expansion in 1967 called for 50 percent of production to be exported. Har has been able to fulfill the agreement. In 1973-1974 just under 50 percent of total production went to exports; in the seven months from October 1974 to April 1975 $572,000 were export sales and the prediction for the end of 1975 was for export sales to go over the $1 million mark.[14]

The export sales manager of Har metal works explained how the government supports kibbutz industrialization export efforts: "The Israeli government is very interested in export. The moment I prove to the authorities that I arranged an export of $20,000 I get a $20,000 loan at 6 percent interest. In Israel 6 percent is very little since the normal rate is 25 percent." In addition, Har's sales representative can use the export advan-

[14] Fieldwork interview with Har metal works export manager, 20 and 22 May 1975.

tages won by the government in international markets during their discussion with foreign companies.

Table 25 presents a listing of Har's export market, including a specific accounting of companies in the United States; it is apparent from the table that over half of the exports go to the United States. While exports to Canada, England, Holland, and Latin America are expected to decrease, the loss is expected to be more than compensated for by increases in exports to Germany, Iran, France, the Far East, and especially to the United States.

During the fieldwork period two representatives from the factory's management committee went to the United States and Western Europe to promote export sales. In informal conversations they both stated the great importance of maintaining close personal contacts with officials of foreign companies. The factory's general manager is particularly well noted for his ability to win the confidence of international corporation personnel. The opportunity to promote exports of the factory's output is enhanced by the ability of many factory managers to speak several foreign languages fluently.

Just as the export market largely is dominated by military-defense industries or related production, the internal market covers the same areas. Internal sales reflect the factory's policy of fulfilling national needs through production for domestic as well as international markets. For 1973-1974 the internal market sales totaled 4,309,000 lira and were distributed as recorded in Table 26.[15] Of the total domestic sales, 35 percent went to defense-related industries, 40 percent to stores, and 25 percent to private factories and schools.

One member of the factory's management committee is in charge of internal sales. Regular meetings are set up with Defense Department officials, and the Defense Department receives a 20 to 25 percent reduction from regular prices. In

[15] List provided by economic manager of Har metal works during fieldwork.

TABLE 25. HAR METAL WORKS EXPORT SALES, 1973-1974.

Country and Corporation	1973-1974 Sales (in U.S. dollars)	1974-1975 Estimated Sales (in U.S. dollars)
Canada-Osborn		
Manis	4,766	2,000
Uruguay	3,336	3,000
Switzerland	15,795	18,000
Sweden	682	—
England	790	—
Greece	23,890	25,000
Cyprus	1,569	800
Iran	15,616	22,000
France		
-Soveco	22,882	30,000
-Memors	31,067	40,000
-Le Profil	82	—
-Dechets	16,500	18,000
Total France	70,531	88,000
Germany		
-Zensen	7,924	—
-Hoffman	6,102	2,500
-Neumo	190	—
-Hurth	660	—
-Imatec	25,714	50,000
Total Germany	40,590	52,500
Holland		
-Van Ommen	20,307	20,000
-Van Krannenburg	3,148	3,000
Total Holland	23,455	23,000
Belgium		
-Boomsche	4,359	2,000
-Benedictus	3,431	1,000
Total Belgium	7,790	3,000

TABLE 25. *(cont.)*

Country and Corporation		1973-1974 Sales *(in U.S. dollars)*	1974-1975 Estimated Sales *(in U.S. dollars)*
Italy			
-Gaffuri		1,030	1,000
-CICMU		20,497	19,000
Total Italy		21,527	20,000
Philippines		6,057	20,000
Japan		895	—
Taiwan		8,150	—
Singapore		3,283	—
Hong Kong		6,023	10,000
New Zealand		9,093	12,000
United States			
(Direct Sales)			
-Dewitt Bros.	N.Y.	27,394	30,000
-Dewitt Tools	N.J.	5,612	10,000
-Travers Tool	N.Y.	20,922	30,000
-Sid Tool	N.Y.	47,597	80,000
-Victor	N.Y.	1,038	—
-Chase	Boston	8,610	5,000
-Liberty	Mass.	2,734	—
-Dewitt	Los Angeles	65,005	100,000
-Rutland	Calif.	32,140	50,000
-I.P.S.	Calif.	36,503	75,000
-Ash Mail	Detroit	10,537	15,000
-Dessil	Ohio	525	—
-Production	Warren	13,490	40,000
-Wholesale	Warren	17,726	12,000
-Kabaco	Detroit	14,170	18,000
-Pohl Tool	Mich.	831	—
-Ditco	Chicago	15,477	12,000
-Mid Cont.	Chicago	4,530	5,000
-ABA Ind.	Florida	758	—
-Empire	Colo.	1,897	2,000
-Big Joe	Texas	2,355	—

TABLE 25. (*cont.*)

Country and Corporation		1973-1974 Sales (in U.S. dollars)	1974-1975 Estimated Sales (in U.S. dollars)
-Sol Tool	N.Y.	17,196	30,000
-Detroit Auto		158	—
-Marin	N.Y.	204	—
-American Tool		—	—
-Warner Tool	Calif.	6,400	14,000
-Vermont Louisville		—	—
-Teledyne		253	—
Total Direct Sales		354,000	528,000
Total UNICO U.S. Sales		128,000	178,000
Total United States		482,000	701,000

TABLE 26. Har Metal Works Sales in Israel, 1973-1974.

Buyers	Sales in lira
Defense industries	282,000
Military of Defense Department (directly to armed services)	737,000
Aviation industry	452,000
Private factories	828,000
Plywood factories	116,000
Public/Technical schools	54,000
Wholesalers	1,840,000

addition, exhibitions are set up in trade fairs held all over Israel and mail orders are invited. Limited advertising appears in technical journals.

Supportive government policies also affect the factory's import needs. Machinery is principally imported from corporations in the United States and Western Europe. Major suppliers are: Hertlein in the United States, Reishauer in Switzerland, Richaud in France, Matrix-Coventry in England, and Bohle,

Travex, and Auerbach in Germany. High-grade, high-speed steel is imported from the multinational Vasco Corporation. Because Har is located in the most essential strategic zone (Zone A) in Israel, it does not have to pay an import tax. The government provides 30 percent in grants and 40 percent in six-year loans at 8.5 percent with no interest the first year for the cost of machinery.

While in 1975 the factory paid for imports in dollars at the exchange rate of 7.23 lira to the dollar, the government allows an export exchange rate of 7.64 lira to the dollar; this is another way that the state encourages kibbutz industry.

The expansion of Har's industrial base in response to national and community pressures has continuously influenced the community's social life. It is the largest kibbutz factory and its large number of hired workers are a major problem considering the ideology of the kibbutz. Although its internal organization retains a number of cooperative features—such as team management and workers' councils—it is essentially modeled after private, large-scale companies. In many important ways it is a microcosm of Koor Industries, which is owned by the Histadrut and is an umbrella organization for Har metal works and other kibbutz factories.[16] A former director of Israeli intelligence, Meir Admit, heads Koor and states that the primary aim of the company is "to make money." His attitude is summed up as follows: "The transition that Koor has made is the same transition that all of Israeli industry has to make: from the utopian-socialism of the Zionist pioneers to the hard-headed efficiency

---

[16] Kibbutz Industries Association Ltd. represents the three major kibbutz federations on industrial issues in Koor. K.I.A. represents kibbutz industry in its dealings with the government, the Histadrut, and other public institutions. Among its other functions are fostering cooperation between kibbutz factories, organizing each manufacturing branch, setting up investment funds, undertaking research and development projects, offering vocational training and acting as a public relations firm about kibbutz industries to the public.

needed to compete in the modern world—sad in a way, but
necesary for a modern state."[17] The kibbutz, while largely
agreeing with the analysis that pits ideology against progress,
is not yet ready to admit complete defeat of its socialist aspirations. Within Har, small battles have still been waged in the
1970s in an attempt to save kibbutz socialism while simultaneously gaining the benefits of a modernized economy.

The New Factory Plan constitutes one important experiment
in the battle. In 1969 the General Assembly voted to allow the
factory to expand to an upper limit of 130 workers. Although
the factory management was given the flexibility to expand to
142, it responded to the directive by exploring the possibility
of selling part of the factory's production to a company that
would erect a satellite plant in Shlomi. The general manager of
the factory outlined some of the ideas of the plan that was
accepted by the entire community in 1976:

> Our first idea was to put the taps production in Shlomi and keep
> cutter production in Har. . . . We wanted to keep the cutter pro-
> duction because we developed them especially for export and to
> get the government aid we have to keep our agreement to keep on
> exporting. . . . However, Har [the membership] thinks that even
> with only the cutters we will not be able to be without salaried
> workers. So now we are looking for a product to replace our whole
> plant eventually.

Har's search for a viable alternative is similar to that of many
developing nations.

The General Assembly elected a committee, made up of the
factory general manager, the kibbutz economic secretary, and
three at large members to come up with a new industrial project. A number of problematic issues face the committee. First,
it is difficult to replace its present, economically successful
factory with a much smaller one that would rely only on membership labor. The kibbutz has already become accustomed to

---

[17] *Forbes* magazine, March 15, 1975.

its standard of living; in spite of the desire of some members to uphold traditional ideology, most members would not opt for reducing material gains.

In addition, the town of Shlomi cannot afford to buy the taps plants from Har, and an attempt at selling it to an American plant that would base the operation in Shlomi has failed. Har now hopes that Koor Industries will develop the taps plant in Shlomi. However, Koor is primarily interested in export production and in large-scale development and is only interested in Har's plans if arrangements appropriate to these interests can be reached. One possibility is for Har to release ownership of the Shlomi-based plant gradually after it is more fully developed.

Thirdly, there is the problem of the labor force. Since the tap plant would be located in Zone A, as is Har, it could attract government investment incentives. However, the labor force of Shlomi is primarily unskilled and most firms would prefer locating near a major city. Har has trained 90 percent of its factory labor force: but a new owner may not be willing to undertake a similar commitment.

Finally, Har's relationship with the largely Sephardic population of Shlomi has been one of employer-employee rather than one of equity. This situation has existed in spite of the fact that 20 percent of Har's population is Sephardic. The overwhelming majority of Har members still resists entering into a more interdependent relationship with Shlomi reflecting their own strong attachment to Western culture and their sense of distance from those at the bottom of the mountain.

The general manager of the factory, who originally comes from Lebanon, offered several insightful points concerning the issue of the New Factory Plan during a fieldwork interview:

A cooperative may be the worst capitalist in the world. In the kibbutz, you cannot make socialism [by] only including the kibbutz. . . . Three months ago kibbutz leaders met with the Prime

Minister. . . . I said if the government had extra funds to give them to Shlomi before Har. I was looked at like a stranger. The other kibbutzim in this region do not think their life has to touch the people of Shlomi. But you cannot live in a villa in an area that has slums if you are building socialism. If the kibbutzim do not find a way to help, to be more involved in the area, they will not stand.

The fact that his opinion represents only a small minority in the kibbutz is not encouraging in terms of movement toward interdependency. However, it is significant that he is still a prestigious leader in the community and his ideas demand attention. Much will depend upon the outcome of other changes in the kibbutz reality that tend to support the transition from communal to capitalist relationships.

Social and Political Transitions

The transition of social and political organizations Har has experienced demonstrates the expansion of individualism at the expense of communalism. While participation in the communal centered activities has lessened, family and personal activity has increased. Along with this principal transformational pattern, Har's leadership group has become more firmly established and the general internal organizational structures have become more formalized. In the economic area this formalization is in the direction of controlled agreements rather than informal, consensual understanding. In particular, industrialization, the related increasing division of labor, and the *ba'al bayit*, or property owner-manager, attitude have discouraged the communitarianism processes.

Two primary indicators of this continuing transition are the changes in political participation, including leadership patterns, and changes in social organization. At the same time that attendance at General Assembly meetings has decreased, individual time spent at home and with the nuclear family has, as previously noted, increased. The fact that members now call their separate apartments "home" is itself symbolic of social change in the kibbutz.

THE GENERAL ASSEMBLY

General Assembly attendance records are presented in Table 27 covering the period of fieldwork for a total of seven months. Fieldwork notes also recorded the topics of discussion, the form of discussion, differences in male-female participation, and the final decisions.[18]

The adult membership population of Har as of 1975 was 260. Table 27 shows that during twenty-seven consecutive weekly General Assembly meetings the highest attendance was 143 or 55 percent of the membership and the lowest, 36 or 14 percent. The average rate of attendance was 63 or 24 percent.

The one week when over 50 percent of the members attended the General Assembly reflected a time when the kibbutz was on a military-security alert and a report was given at the meeting regarding the community's defense. Three weeks after the last recorded session on 28 June 1975, the scheduled General Assembly meeting had to be cancelled due to another security alert.

Table 27 also presents differences in male-female attendance. Of the 260 members, 122 were women and 138 were men. For most meetings women constituted approximately between one-third to one-half of those present. Only on the last recorded week did women outnumber men. Perhaps of more significance are the rates of male and female nonattenders. Twenty-six percent of Har's female members never attended a session during the study's seven-month period, while only 9 percent of the male members never came.

[18] For a fine comparative study of political participation patterns in kibbutz see Erik Cohen's "A Comparative Study of the Political Institutions of Collective Settlements in Israel" (Jerusalem: Hebrew University, 1968).

TABLE 27. Har General Assembly Attendance Record, November 1974-June 1975.*

Week Number	Total of Attendance	No. of Males	No. of Females
1	96	61	35
2	67	42	25
3	62	35	27
4	72	44	28
5	89	50	39
6	80	48	32
7	91	56	35
8	143	80	63
9	65	35	30
10	69	41	28
11	61	37	24
12	75	48	27
13	82	49	33
14	55	35	20
15	49	28	21
16	58	34	24
17	79	47	32
18	55	31	24
19	36	21	15
20	68	43	25
21	68	35	33
22	58	38	20
23	75	43	32
24	55	31	24
25	57	33	24
26	91	50	41
27	47	22	25

* SOURCE: Records kept by Ben-Hazak, Kibbutz Har member.

The difference between male and female political participation in the community's central decision-making structure is also apparent during General Assembly discussion. Although the chairperson for the week was often a woman (the job was rotated), the rest of the women present would rarely express their opinion during public discussion. Even when almost half of the attenders were women, men completely dominated the floor. It made little difference what topic was under discussion. When issues directly affecting the service work areas where most women work came up, men continued to predominate. On April 12, discussion centered on the need to build more children's buildings. After a brief presentation by the woman who headed the relevant study committee, not one woman who had children entered the discussion.

Women who attend the meetings appear to view the meetings as Saturday evening social gatherings. They usually bring their knitting or sewing projects, sit near their husbands, and partake of the tea and cookies that are served. The exceptions to this are the women who hold central community leadership positions. During the fieldwork period these included the general secretary and the heads of the Social Committee, the Education Committee, and the Health Committee.

When women were interviewed concerning their nonattendance or nonparticipation in General Assembly discussion, they responded that for the most part they were not familiar with kibbutz economic issues. They preferred spending time at home; if they went to the meetings, it was usually only to accompany their husbands.

There was little in the actual process of the meetings that discouraged women from participating. Discussion took place after a brief report of the issue at hand. The main points to be discussed at each meeting were posted on the public bulletin board before each meeting. Everyone in the kibbutz could attend meetings except on certain issues such as the vote on a new member. At that time only members could participate. Voting was by majority rule, but great effort was made to reach consensus. On May 10 only thirty-seven people were present at the beginning of the session, so a vote was taken to see if members felt attendance was sufficient for a quorum. They decided to go ahead, and by the end of the meeting the numbers swelled. This was a common occurrence.

Although the process of General Assembly discussion is open and informal, the same members continually dominate. Some of these members represent those still strongly attached to socialist ethics and keep reminding others of the kibbutz's deviations from the correct ideological path. Others seem mostly interested in hearing their own voices and are ignored when their predictable turn in the debate occurs.

It is clear from observation of Har's General Assembly meetings that the opinions of some members far outweigh the voices of others: quiet prevails when they speak and more considered discussion develops after their remarks. These members are primarily men, though two to three women enjoy the same status. These are recognized leaders in the community, and they are able to articulate the major issues under review. They often focus the discussion and frame the key question for a vote. Few women feel comfortable with public speaking in the General Assembly and have a clear grasp of the workings of the total community and this limits the scope and depth of their participation.

There is a strong positive relationship between those playing a central role in the General Assembly's decision-making process and those already holding key work positions. An established leadership group has emerged in Har that expresses the growing stratification patterns within the kibbutz.

As in many collective movements in history, leadership roles in the early days were assumed by those strongly adhering to the idealist pioneering roles.[19] As economic conditions became more favorable, leadership roles were increasingly filled with

[19] Rosabeth Kanter, *Commitment and Community* (Cambridge, Mass.: Harvard University Press, 1972) and Charles Nordhoff, *Communistic Societies of the United States* (New York: Schocken Books, 1971).

those with the greatest economic expertise. In Har the leadership establishment in recent years indicates a balance between personal charisma and administrative and technical expertise.

Table 28 outlines the principal kibbutz committees and their membership. Social and educational committees tend to be headed by women and economic and political committees by men. Because of the increasing emphasis on economic matters, the latter have more weight in the overall community organizational development.

Of twenty committees listed, five (general Secretariat, edu-

TABLE 28. HAR COMMITTEE ORGANIZATION AND MEMBERSHIP, SPRING 1975.

Committee	Chairperson	No. of Members on Committee
Central Management	Female	8
Economy	Male	8
Labor Force	Male	6
Education	Female	8
Social Relations	Female	8
Absorption	Male	3
Communications	Male	3
Security	Male	5
Programming	Male	5
Newsletter	Male	3
Health	Female	3
General Assembly	Joint-Appointment	4
Culture	Male	8
Sports	Male	3
Archives	Male	3
Daily Labor Assignments	Male	5
Parents	Female	3
Preservation & Upkeep	Male	3
Daily Coordinators		
Women	Joint-Appointment	5
Men	Joint-Appointment	2

cation, social relations, health, parents) are headed by women,
twelve (economic, labor force, absorption, communications, security, programming, newsletter, culture, sports, archives,
daily labor assignments, preservation and upkeep) by men, and
three are joint appointments. Although only five committees are
headed by women, this is more than in most kibbutzim. Har's
members often cite this in support of the existence of sexual
equality.

In addition to committee heads, the established leadership
is drawn from those heading the factory, the Milouot enterprise,
the Regional High School, and the Sulam Tsor Regional Council. In 1975 these four positions were held by men, three of
whom came from Eastern Europe and one from Lebanon.

From the early 1950s through 1975, the principal leadership
roles have been rotated among a small percentage of kibbutz
members. Gila Rosh, the general secretary of Har in 1975,
commented on the social distinction of a leadership group:

> I found that I was at a certain distance from a part of the members
> of the kibbutz because they saw me always as part of the estab-
> lishment. . . . I realized they were right because you've got influ-
> ential people in a kibbutz. So what happens is that whether I am
> on a certain committee or not I know what is going on since people
> come and talk over things with me. I've got my own group of friends
> and they're probably as involved as I am (in the kibbutz) and that's
> part of our subculture—to be involved.

At first, the placement of the French-speaking group into the
leadership positions was merely a token. However, in recent
years the original kibbutz leaders are increasingly assuming
key posts in external institutions linked to the kibbutz such as
in the Ichud Federation, the Ministry of Education, and the
Milouot system. Members of the later-arriving French *garins*
are replacing them in the important internal kibbutz positions.

The two groups tend to socialize separately. Many members
of the French-speaking group continue to speak French with

each other, especially within their individual apartments. In terms of kibbutz spatial distribution, the members of each group live in neighborhood sections close to one another. In daily socializing such as at teatime, members of each group usually visit one another rather than members of the other group. But these social divisions are not rigid; during large community celebrations everyone joins together.

As has been pointed out previously the rewards for holding leadership roles take the form of increased opportunity for travel, meeting outsiders and having the use of a car. Those holding leadership roles also have the opportunity to translate their ideas into action and, therefore, have a greater sense of participation and control in the community than does the average member.

There are, however, personal costs of assuming such roles. Thus, when certain committee heads have been needed, no members have volunteered for the job. On 3 May 1975 three members were nominated to head the Transport Committee and all preferred remaining at their previous work. The majority of Har's members, particularly in the last decade, do not wish to take on the additional problems that community leadership entails and, thus, leave these roles to the rather small group that is already committed to similar service. Most members prefer spending as much time as possible following individual pursuits or family activities.

Those assuming leadership roles usually put extraordinary amounts of time into their work since there is no way of completely separating time at such work from the rest of their lives. Everyone lives in close proximity and after work hours members can easily walk over to each others' residences to follow up on ideas and questions. The general secretary commented on the tension between public and private life for those taking on leadership roles in the kibbutz:

I think I have a right as a member to bring up my own ideas. But

I know that this is part of the problem of being in a responsible position within a small community. Because no matter how much I say it's my idea as "Gila" and not as secretary they will feel the influence of the position. . . . Life on a kibbutz is difficult for a person like me and a family like mine. . . . I found people weren't talking to me but always requesting things from me. . . . I'm involved with people all day long. . . . I don't go to lunch on Saturday because it is my only time I can use for myself. . . . My husband has always been involved too. . . . It has been especially harsh on the children. . . . the children had to go to high school while he was director and others could say "Your father, the director"—and they had no way of protecting themselves.

After her long terms as a community leader, Gila was considering some sort of manual work as her next job in order to give herself more of a chance to enjoy a private existence. However, she and other members of Har's leadership group no doubt receive satisfaction from the chance to influence overall community development and to be involved socially. Relinquishment of this type of power may not come easily.

The trend away from communal activity is evident in decisions made in the General Assembly since 1967. The decisions to allow children to sleep in their parents' homes and to increase personal property items were among critical events listed by the members for the last five-year period. Other decisions made during the fieldwork period, such as planning the dining hall seating arrangements and allocating study leaves reflect a new definition of self-actualization in the kibbutz. The new definition contributes to a growing tension between a new individualism and older communalism. The traditional ideological perspective was that individuals are primarily social beings—that individual creativity only flourishes in a social context; this is now deemphasized and increasingly ignored in favor of an increased emphasis on enhancing individual interests.

The previously cited responses to the critical events questionnaire distributed during fieldwork revealed that the most significant decisions of the General Assembly in 1967-1976 were to approve industrial expansion, to close the guest house, and to allow children to sleep overnight at the parents' home.[20] The first two have already been discussed, and this section will concentrate on the latter. It was the only decision that everyone responding to the questionnaire mentioned. In addition, a majority of respondents made reference to how the improving standard of living permitted positive decisions to be made regarding acquisition of more personal property.

The decision to allow children to sleep at the parents' home, known as *lena mishpatit*, or sleeping with family, was not a sudden act by the membership. It was the culmination of discussion that had been going on in the kibbutz since its foundation but that drew increased attention in the seventies.

The collective approach to child rearing and education had been a central feature of kibbutz organization and had always raised controversy in psychological and academic circles.[21] Kibbutz adherents have stressed that "educational and psychological precepts are inseparable from the theory and practice of kibbutz life."[22] Since the pronounced values of kibbutz society included collectivism, equality and labor, collective child rearing seemed a consistent and natural outgrowth of kibbutz life. It allowed mothers to be free to work during the day, gave

[20] A critical events questionnaire (in Hebrew) was distributed to all kibbutz members; it asked them to identify the events of each decade of Har's existence that had the most impact on kibbutz development. This section is based upon questionnaire responses. There was a 38 percent return rate.

[21] For instance, Melford Spiro, *Children of the Kibbutz* (Cambridge, Mass.: Harvard University Press, 1958), and Bruno Bettelheim, *Children of the Dream* (New York: Avon Books, 1970). Joseph Shepher of the Sociology Department of Haifa University has also done extensive research on this issue.

[22] Dan Leon, *The Kibbutz: A New Way of Life* (London: Pergamon Press, 1969), p. 97.

children equal access to resources, encouraged the development of cooperative behavior, and, perhaps most significantly, placed emphasis on the community rather than the nuclear family as a social unit.

Critics of this system have noted that although collective child rearing has fulfilled certain stated goals, it has produced children that are hostile to those outside their group and who find it difficult to express emotion. Recent Israeli sociological research suggests that although women were free to work a regular workday, they have not achieved equal status.[23]

In Har there has always been a minority of members, predominantly women, who favored children sleeping at home. During interviews, quite a few women mentioned the difficulty of putting a child to bed in the children's house and then leaving for the night. However, it was only after Har achieved economic stability that it became financially feasible to allow children to sleep at home. The cost of building additional bedrooms in existing apartments would have greatly taxed the community's budget.

The economic transformation also had a deep emotional and intellectual effect on women members. Working for the good of the community did not have the same value as it once did. It no longer seemed a labor of love to wash dishes for four hundred instead of four. With each apartment now having its own kitchen area, women began to undertake more housemaker chores in their own homes as well as having to perform them in the community. The ability to be free to work a full day, free from the children, increasingly meant taking on a double work burden. There had never been a fundamental change in

[23] Menachem Rosner, "Women in the Kibbutz: Changing Status and Concepts," *Asian and African Studies Journal* 3 (1967), 35-68; Yonina Talmon, *The Family and Community in the Kibbutz* (Cambridge, Mass.: Harvard University Press, 1972). Lionel Tiger and Joseph Shepher in their controversial book, *Women in the Kibbutz* (New York: Harcourt, Brace and Jovanovich, 1975), argue that women are tied to certain roles for biological reasons.

sex-role definition so that men shared domestic chores on an equal scale.

The younger mothers on the kibbutz were among those especially anxious to have the children sleep at home. They had never experienced the earlier romantic, pioneering days of the first women settlers. A focus on pragmatism became as strong as a commitment to ideology. After coming back from the army and seeing the world outside of the kibbutz, many younger mothers were attracted to the way of life prevalent in the larger Israeli society. They increasingly expressed a desire to fulfill the mother role in the more traditional nuclear family manner.

By the late 1960s a number of other kibbutzim in the Ichud Federation had already made a change over to *lena mishpatit*, and in the first kibbutz, Degania, children have always slept at home. In Har the combination of a favorable economic climate and growing pressure for the change resulted in members bringing the issue to the General Assembly.

The debate in the General Assembly went on over a number of months. Argument centered on the financial costs, the ideological ramifications, the educational benefits and limitations, and the effect on overall community life. Even during the period of debate, deviations from the regularized pattern of putting children to bed in the communal houses were already taking place. Some mothers began allowing their children to sleep at home with the justification that the children were afraid or felt ill and wanted to be near their parents. With kitchens in the apartments children began eating at home with their parents rather than returning after late afternoon playtime to the children's houses. The situation became very difficult for those parents who wished to continue the regular pattern because their children felt that those breaking the norm were getting more attention.

At the same time, the military situation intensified the level of tension in the community. Parents became more worried about their children's safety at night. A system of walkie-talkies between the children's house and the parents' apartments was installed. The system was viewed as necessary, but was felt to be insufficient. Parents slept in the children's houses on a rotating basis. It became more and more apparent that a majority of members were ready to vote for *lena mishpatit*. In 1974, a final decision was made and a committee was set up to begin working out the technical problems, including the financial costs of building additions to members' homes. A number of subsequent General Assembly meetings concerned themselves with this problem.

In May 1975 the head of the Building Committee reported on plans approved by the Ichud Federation for the construction of 60 meter apartments to allow the space for children to sleep at home. The question arose of what would happen if only sixteen apartments were built and the demand was greater than the supply. Members discussed alternative possibilities. These included setting up a priorities list, disregarding the need for additional space, and meeting the needs of the largest number of families. One member raised the point that in order to build additional units other areas of the community's standard of living might have to be lowered. There was almost uniform resistance to this suggestion. The final plan for applying *lena mishpatit* incorporated a step-by-step approach, extending over a three-year period.

PRIVATE PROPERTY

Within the General Assembly a series of decisions has also been made concerning the greater accumulation of private property. Before 1948 any deviation from the ethic of communal ownership of property was severely denounced. Even such items as clothing were communally shared, given out as needed, and then communally laundered. The decision to allow each house unit to have its own teapot had been debated in a lively manner. With the rising standard of living and a turn toward a more individualist attitude, the existence of personal property in the kibbutz has steadily increased.

During 1975 there were three separate decisions in the General Assembly that dealt with personal property: the distribution of televisions, repayment for the purchase of bicycles for individuals, and approval of a higher personal budget allowance. In 1974 the membership decided to permit each household to have its own television set. Until then there was one television set up in the communal dining hall building, and a few elder parents of members living in their own apartments had their own sets. Members, however, wanted to watch television in their own homes. After the decision was made for individual television sets, the community planned to buy them a few at a time over a three-year period, distributing them on the basis of kibbutz seniority. In April 1975, the economic manager reported that the economic situation at Har was better than anticipated and the community would be able to buy fifty television sets at one time. The General Assembly decided to allow them to be distributed immediately. This meant that some members would have their own sets while others could visit with them to watch television or watch the communal television set in the clubhouse. This unequal distribution of a major property item follows the distribution pattern of stoves, refrigerators, and radios.

The existence of individual television sets both reflects a movement away from communal activity and encourages individual consumption patterns. Members now spent much more of their leisure time watching television and inviting friends who do not yet have sets of their own to join them. A number of women members commented during interviews that they watch the daily soap operas to forget about work problems or community tensions. Men enjoy watching televised sport programs.

Television has also extended foreign cultural influence, particularly from the United States. Programs such as *Ironsides* and *Kojak* are dubbed in Hebrew and are among the favorites. Har residents can also occasionally pick up broadcasts from neighboring Arab countries. Following a week of considerable military unrest, members had the opportunity to watch a series of old, romantic Arab films broadcast from across the border.

In 1974 a decision was also made to allow children to have bicycles. At the time, some parents were already purchasing bicycles for their own children from personal savings. Personal savings were accumulated from setting aside money from yearly individual consumption allowances, as well as, in some cases, from small private gifts and inheritances or reparation money. The Education Committee decided it would be better for all the children to have them. However, the kibbutz could not afford to buy enough bicycles for everyone at the same time, so again the situation was whether some could have while others could not. The question of taxes on new consumer goods, which already had affected the purchase of television sets and other major property items, came up. Members considered whether people should pay taxes from their individual budgets or whether the community should pay as a whole. In May 1975 the General Assembly decided to leave the final decision to the Education Committee.

The question of increasing personal budgets came up in April 1975. The Ichud Federation recommended that its member kibbutzim raise their personal budget allowances by 5 percent to meet the cost of living increases. Some Har members argued in the General Assembly that the kibbutz already had a higher allowance than most other kibbutzim and that all other costs had also gone up, decreasing the community's surplus. However, the majority of members supported the increase, and it passed by a vote of sixty for and seven against.

A number of other decisions that furthered "privatization"

occurred in the mid-1970s. A decision was made to allow the son of a member to study for three years in a Yeshiva, or religious school. This occurred although the kibbutz did not favor religious education and the boy's attendance would result in a loss of needed labor power. The kibbutz was still reluctant to fill its 6 percent study-leave quota with those not choosing an area that would be directly beneficial to the community. However, in April 1975, by a unanimous vote, the members attending the General Assembly agreed with the statement that "if he feels it is important for his own education he should have kibbutz support."

The decision by the general secretary to formalize a Shabbat dinner seating arrangement for the central dining hall reflected the fact that most members wanted to sit with their own family and friends. People had started to come one hour early on Friday nights to save seats at tables. This meant that others found themselves without seats. The plan, based on a questionnaire, indicates a formalization of procedures in the kibbutz in order to recognize the existence of separate groupings.

Finally, the changing pattern of cultural celebrations also demonstrates both a growing formalism and family-centeredness. One example is the bar-mitzvah ceremony. Until the mid-seventies, the occasion of bar-mitzvah, a religious ceremony marking the coming of age, was celebrated communally. All members of the thirteen-year-old class would jointly have a bar-mitzvah ceremony with the entire kibbutz present. In the spring of 1975, though, one family decided to hold a private ceremony inviting parents, other relatives, and only a small number of kibbutz members and friends. The invitations were selectively sent, and only those specifically asked to come were expected to attend. After the ceremony, held in a small meeting hall in the kibbutz museum, a reception was held. The parents had bought foods and wines with money from their personal budgets while other guests baked cakes and cookies. Other parents in Har held similar bar-mitzvahs later on during the same year.

The movement toward individualism, formalization, and private personal property increasingly permitted by the kibbutz mirrors policies adopted by kibbutzim on the national level. The Ministry of Labor's Department of Cooperation proposed in the late 1960s a model *Statutes of the Kibbutz*. The statutes were devised as an ideal constitution for a kibbutz setting out the format for its structure, activities and responsibilities and delineating the rights and duties of individual members. They have been revised a number of times when the Knesset reviewed their incorporation into an established codification of law. Among the significant features of the statutes is the section spelling out the rights of members to personal property and financial settlement in cases when kibbutz members leave the community. While the kibbutz remains a voluntary community, the establishment of statutes formalizes organizational procedures and reduces autonomy of each settlement. It protects the individual's rights against the collective authority of the kibbutz.

Har's Present Reality

Since 1967 Kibbutz Har has experienced a transition to a higher living standard and a social drift from a communal focus toward that of the nuclear family. This has occurred even within the context of an increasingly tense military atmosphere when collective morale might be expected. The current prominence of the military situation in the life of the kibbutz is similar to the situation the community faced in the prestate era. Therefore, there has been a closing of the circle in at least one dimension. Yet, the center of concern seems to be the state and Israeli society rather than the kibbutz.

From the creation of the Israeli state until 1967, the Lebanese border had been relatively quiet. After the 1967 War

Palestinian-Arab nationalists, based in southern Lebanon, escalated guerrilla border raids. At first, Har was not the direct target of attacks. However, the worsening border situation after 1973 resulted in attacks on Har and intermitted bombardment. Major efforts were made to step up the community's military security.

The security efforts specifically affected the kibbutz's physical environment, its economic development, and its social and psychological atmosphere. At night the sounds of Israeli tanks searching for infiltrators can be heard and their lights shine in the darkness as they turn back and forth. A new electrified border fence that runs very close to the edge of Har is the major physical change in Har's environment. Whenever anything touches the fence, an alarm goes off creating a military alert. One such occasion occurred in June 1975 during my fieldwork. At 9 P.M. a loud boom was heard. The General Assembly was about to meet so many members were already congregated in the central dining hall area. Men quickly rushed to their security posts. Women members went to their children's house assignments. *Ulpan* students, volunteers, and parents of members were directed to the shelter area in the Club Room. One-half hour later all was declared safe. Border guards thought they had seen something, the fence alarm sounded, and the guards responded by firing a rocket through the fence adding to the commotion. Upon investigation, it was discovered that a wild boar had set off the alarms. The false alarm ignited fears and tension in the community and did not help to ease the general mental and physical exhaustion from alerts that had occurred earlier in the week.

In addition to the border fence, there are other physical evidences of more stringent military security in the area. Before 1973 members could walk up and down the mountain to reach public transport or to take an exercise hike. Since 1973 movement up and down the mountain is strictly regulated. A soldier guards the kibbutz's main entrance. After sundown until dawn no one can leave or enter the kibbutz without special permission. The new regulations have resulted in creating a more isolated, self-contained community.

Perhaps the most subtle, yet powerful new physical reality, are the guns male members carry at all times—to work, to the central dining hall, to sports events, and even when carrying their children to the children's quarters. Before 1973 guns were stored communally and made available only at moments of security alerts. Women of all ages are being trained to use guns and carry them into the dining hall after a training exercise. Although they have been accepted as a necessary feature of community life, guns are a constant physical reminder of war.

The military situation has been a factor in economic development. The costs of being on the border limit the benefits derived from special financial support benefits. In recent years the factory and agricultural work have been forced to stop operation during particularly serious alerts. During a fieldwork interview the economic manager reported on the effects of the military situation on Har's economy: "Because of security conditions we had expenditures. We lost money and income because of the 1973 War and afterwards. One day in December 1973 the factory was shut. Also we didn't go to the field before 8 a.m. in May 1974. There were terrorists in the area for several days. The factory did not work a second shift. We also had problems transporting salaried laborers to Har." On many occasions labor force energies have been diverted into fulfilling security needs of the community. Members stand night guard duty on a rotating basis—men in the border guard houses, women in the children's houses. Time is taken out for training sessions and in military preparedness exercises. During one week in April 1975 much effort was put into simulated war games at the kibbutz. Women, especially those living in houses closest to the border, practiced shooting, as they felt it was important to know how to use guns in case they were left alone and the kibbutz was invaded. The new head of Har's security organized the war game with cooperation from the Israeli military in order to see if the kibbutz could repel an attack by terrorists. One member was chosen to "play" terrorist and other men successfully "repelled" the raid. From 5:30 P.M. to 6:15 P.M. the games, which everyone had been told about ahead of time, progressed with real machine guns firing, mortars falling and bullets whizzing in the air. At 9:30 P.M. another simulation was made but this time the "terrorists" succeeded in capturing a house and holding "hostages." Kibbutz members rescued the "hostages" and "killed the terrorists." The next night in the central dining hall a map was hung showing the route of the "attack" and how it was repelled. People talked about the real attack the previous December. The games in a way were an extension of daily life at Har with a bit more drama. All of the local security jobs are in addition to the roles Har members fill in the national Israeli Defense Forces, which also affect the community disposition of labor.

The labor needs of the kibbutz have similarly been affected by the decrease in immigration and growing rate of emigration that are at least partly explained by the continued military tensions. The *Jewish Daily World* on 31 July 1975, reported that only six thousand immigrants arrived in Israel during the first five months of the year compared with 56,000 in 1972 and 32,000 in 1974. During fieldwork Uzi Narkiss, head of the Jewish Agency's immigration department, blamed the drop on fears for security and on an economic crisis, tied to military defense requirements. He reported that nearly one-third of the emigrants from the Soviet Union preferred to go to the United States, France, or Argentina rather than to Israel. Har's role as a possible absorption center for immigrants has been considerably reduced: an avenue to increased membership has been cut back.

Narkiss went on to report that for the first time in Israel's history more Israelis were leaving the country than immigrants were entering. Emigration from Har has also grown. Exact figures are not available for Har since the status of members away from the kibbutz is often not clear—for example, whether a study leave will turn out to be a permanent leave. Yet we know a significant number of second generation members have left Har and this further reduces the labor force. The emigration from Har to the larger Israeli society or to foreign countries has social-psychological as well as economic implications.

The fact remains, however, that most of Har members have chosen to stay in the kibbutz. The question of why they remain arises after examining the historical and recent economic difficulties and military-political struggles. In attempting to answer this question, we must give consideration to changes in the conditions that have affected the community's development.

During Har's establishment in the prestate years, Socialist-Zionist ideological factors were important in attracting people to the kibbutz. Early settlers were committed to building a Jewish state through the creation of Jewish cooperative institutions. A *chalutz* pioneer spirit combined military heroism with ideals of agrarian labor, motivated the *vattikim*, and bolstered their determination to establish a kibbutz in an Arab-border region. The continual early economic failures fostered the need for mutual aid and served to solidify the community.

From 1948 to the present a transformation has occurred in the community's economy and in its general outlook. With the state established, Har turned its energies to creating economic stability for the community. It was more than a defense outpost. The kibbutz has not only established a stable economic base but has raised its standard of living so it is equal to the average of the larger Israeli society. It has been able to do this through its continual reliance on financial support from national institutions, which, in turn, are dependent upon economic aid from foreign countries and world-wide Jewish philanthropy, especially American.

Today Har is able to offer its members an economic security not enjoyed by the majority of Israeli citizens. This may be a primary reason why some kibbutzniks stay on the kibbutz. Many members who do not have great marketable skills are assured of employment, financial support for their families, and care in their old age. This is no small incentive for community commitment. Others may be unable to imagine any other way of life. The kibbutz experience, apart from the army, may be the only way of life that presents itself to them in concrete, manageable terms.

The advantages gained from the increasing standard of living have also had the effect of eroding the original socialist perspective of its pioneer members. Personal and family domains are supplanting the communal domain as the focus of daily living. One good indication of the withering away of communal socialist concerns is the decreased attention given to May Day on the kibbutz.

Originally, the kibbutz movement strongly articulated its support for the international workers' movement and May Day was a big kibbutz holiday. Israel's deteriorating relations with the Soviet Union and proliferating alliances with capitalist economies have altered the environment of celebration. Within Har fewer and fewer members have pushed for a major May Day celebration. In 1975 in recognition that May Day is no longer a national holiday and that a majority of the membership did not wish to have a large celebration, the General Assembly decided that the kibbutz would work as usual for one-half the day and spend the other half collectively working on community security preparations.

The decrease in socialist passions stands in contrast to a

continuing strong pragmatic Zionist, or national, orientation. In addition to economic security benefits, the other major benefit the kibbutz offers its members is the opportunity to fulfill national needs. Historically Har, as other kibbutzim, fulfilled colonization and absorption functions for the Zionist movement. In recent years Har has fulfilled national economic functions in both the agricultural and industrial sectors. It has continued its military role through members' participation in the Israeli Defense Forces and has remained a symbol of Israeli settlement in border areas. The kibbutz still fulfills symbolic functions of pioneering and nation building that ensure the larger society's continued support and this still evokes a sense of pride in most members.

The social atmosphere of the community that encourages commitment to Har, may be understood by looking at the nature of its celebration activities. Aside from the traditional rituals surrounding Jewish religious holidays, the greatest attention is given to Israeli Independence Day and, a few days earlier, Yom Hazichoron, Remembrance Day. The former marks the celebration of the creation of the Israeli state, while the latter provides a constant reminder of the Holocaust. Together the two celebrations suggest the contrasting definitions of the Jews as the chosen people and the oppressed. In replying to the question of why he remained at Har one member stated: "When I was in Europe during Nazi years I was called a dirty Jew. . . . I rather would have my sons die fighting in Israel than in the gas chamber. In 1967 relatives offered to take the children out of Israel. My sons replied 'Grandpa is crazy, we will not leave our country.' " The celebrations and ceremonies marking Israeli Independence Day and Remembrance Day make certain the connection between the two images is clear, especially for the younger generation.

Har's members participated in a number of events marking

Remembrance Day in 1975. The atmosphere in the kibbutz was one of communal reverence. A brief ceremony was held in the course of military action. Poems were read, a few women stood in the rain crying, and everyone walked back to the kibbutz center in silence. At breakfast a siren sounded at a nationally uniform designated time. The scene at Har was very powerful. The siren sounded. Almost immediately people absolutely stopped all action. Talking ceased, chairs stopped moving, plates stopped rattling. Everyone stood in silence and was "thrown into the past." The whole country was standing still at the same time: a national silence that most people in the United States only know in their immediate families, if that.

Perhaps the most significant indicator of the spirit of the day was the ceremony held at Lachome Ghetto, a large outdoor arena and Museum of the Holocaust period, located near Nahariya. From the arena one could see the Mediterranean Sea and the Galilee Hills. The atmosphere as 10,000 people gathered was a cross between a somber event and a huge picnic, with people meeting relatives and friends. There was music from the Warsaw Ghetto, the Shtetl, and military tunes. Chief of the Army Guren spoke, followed by those who had lost sons in the various Israeli wars. At the end there was a spectacular burning of a wall that had been set up in the field, symbolizing the ghetto. Actors in shrouds moved through the smoke, and then, army troops, carrying torches, marched in singing the 1973 military war song. The whole crowd stood for the national anthem as six lights were lit symbolizing the six million Jews killed in the Second World War, and Israeli flags waved everywhere. The tie between anti-Semitism, death, and Israel was complete. In fact, the activities of the whole day were intended to recall Jewish history and suggest that Jews can rely only on themselves. The ancient prophets of Israel have been replaced by Israeli army officers; the sense of a people as a tribe with its prophets has become, in modern times, a nation-state of people with faith in military heroes.

A week later Har was entirely decorated with Israeli Independence Day flags and pictures. A special dinner was served and included wine and beer, which is rare on the kibbutz. After dinner, tables were cleared away and people started to dance and sing. Songs of military victory were forcefully sung and the chant of "Am Israel Chi" (Long Live Israel) was repeated with great passion again and again. This was the first time since the 1973 War that people felt able to celebrate.

The next morning members went down the mountain to a Jewish National Fund forest for a community picnic. Food, including extra meat portions, was brought down from the kitchen and army troops rolled in on tanks to join the festivities. That night members came to watch a special television program on Israeli history. A television set had been set up in the dining hall in recognition that even members with their own television sets would come to watch the show communally.

The juxtaposition of the silence of Remembrance Day and the gala celebration of Israeli Independence Day illustrates the very active forces of life and death at work in the kibbutz. The eternal struggle between these basic forces continues to unite Har's members in their community setting.

Although the specific form of kibbutz participation in Israeli national development has changed, the fundamental view that community well-being is tied to national security remains. An emotionally based pragmatism underlies the rational support of the kibbutz of the modernization policies of the state. These policies have resulted in the type of industrial organization, the regional networks, and the military preparedness in which the kibbutz has participated.

This emotional pragmatism allows both emotional and rational responses to the life and death events coloring daily existence in a border kibbutz. The question arises, however, about the community this pragmatism will lead to. Has so much been lost of the socialist ideology and communal spirit that it cannot be renewed and then redirected to face other challenges? Perhaps a more significant question at this point in history is: can renewal emerge from within the kibbutz or must the spark come, if it comes at all, from outside the community?

CHAPTER FIVE

From Utopia toward Modernization

It is provided that in the essence of things
from any fruition of success, no matter
what, shall come forth something to make a
greater struggle necessary.—WALT WHITMAN

We live today in a world where the need for constructive utopian vision is acute. A utopian vision indicates possibilities for a different mode of life, for different norms of interpersonal relations and of human organization than prevailing societies permit. The institutions that frame the lives of the majority of the world's populations continue older patterns of domination and reproduce forms of repression.

As a critical survey of capitalist social structure brings forth increasing images of crisis and decline, the models offered by the Soviet Union and other state-socialist countries do not provide the basis for great hope. The lack of genuine utopian thinking and experimentation is a fundamental contemporary issue.

In this moment in human history inventions of a new social order are needed. These are not inventions of a technical nature but rather social inventions that could nourish nonalienating labor, both the reduction and equal distribution of routinized work, and opportunities for individual and collective energies. Moreover, such social inventions will be needed to redefine our relationship with our natural environment, so we can act as caretakers and not destroyers.

It is within this quest for a new economic and political order that the kibbutz presents us with a continuum of promising options, clear limitations, various contradictions, and numerous unanswered problems. The case study of Kibbutz Har documents the formation and evolution of social structures such as job rotation, the general assembly, and communal child care that allow practical experimentation based upon utopian values.

Har's history also demonstrates the constraints placed on the development of these social inventions by nation-state policies, the forces of industrialization, and emerging internal norms of materialism in the place of a socialist-communal ethos. Community tensions between westernized models of development and socialism, between industrial and agrarian economies, between urbanism and rural life, between social responsibility and individual desires, have raised serious questions regarding the future viability of the specific inventions of the kibbutz as well as the general kibbutz experience.

The kibbutz has been an important social experiment for revealing its limitations and peculiarities and its successes in achieving utopian characteristics. As opposed to most utopias, particularly those in nineteenth-century America, the kibbutz was nation-oriented and not retreatist. From its beginning, the kibbutz was the seedbed for various national military, political, and economic institutions. Its web of multidimensional relationships linking the local to the national immediately caused difficulties concerning kibbutz autonomy and identification with the external structure.[1] What has concerned us here is the nature of social change for the kibbutz; what is unique to the kibbutz's development and what are the larger implications of its development for other societies?

Utopian Ideology

The utopian visions of individuals as Proudhon, Landauer, A. D. Gordon, and Buber were evident in early kibbutz ideology and

[1] Rosabeth Kanter, *Commitment and Community* (Cambridge, Mass.: Harvard University Press, 1972), pp. 153-154.

practice.[2] They defined a community organizational structure that was meant to encourage decentralization of power, a sense of mutual interdependence, and opportunity for individual creation. Unlike many other utopias, authority was shared, with no one person acting as a charismatic leader. Closer to a political movement than a religious rebellion, the kibbutzim recognized authority as vested in national political-military institutions.

The kibbutz community attempted to foster an individual's superego without suppressing self-expression. This was of critical importance to the kibbutz ideological approach to the issue of socialist-communalism and individuality. Reflective of the thinking of Rousseau, there was effort to reconcile demands for comradeship with demands for individual freedom. To this end, a great trust was placed in human rationality, and there was a vision of individuals as independent actors. While the early economic conditions contributed to limiting the scope of the individual in the community, kibbutz ideology did not regard this need as unnatural. The educational philosophy of the kibbutz continually stressed the concept of self-reliance for both the individual and the community. The pioneering ethos furthered this theme in the socialization process.

The ideal form of interpersonal relations was defined as community service without great personal involvement. This impersonal communalism became symbolized in the choice of the sabra, or cactus, image for Jews born in Israel: it is tough on the outside but sweet inside. According to kibbutz ideology, individuals meet social responsibilities through self-sacrifice to the common good, not through spontaneous abandonment of self

[2] The following are among the best sources for understanding the thought of these utopian philosophers: Martin Buber, *Paths in Utopia* (Boston: Beacon Press, 1958); Eugene Lunn, *The Prophet of Community: The Romantic Socialism of Gustav Landauer* (Berkeley: University of California Press, 1973); George Woodcock, *Pierre-Joseph Proudhon* (London: Routledge & Kegan Paul, 1956); and for A. D. Gordon, Samuel Kurland's *Cooperative Palestine* (New York: Sharon Books, 1947).

to the group. Sanctioned kibbutz forms of sexuality were connected to this ideological resolution of the tension between communalism and individuality.[3] The loss of self and the intensity attached to free sexuality existed only for a brief time, if at all, in kibbutzim. Asceticism, common to many socialist movements, was evident early in the kibbutz experience.

The means of social control in the kibbutz reflected the voluntary character of community membership and the acceptance of a wide variety of individual personality types. Specific forms of control rested on the force of group solidarity and included mechanisms as verbal warnings, social avoidance, and, in rare cases, expulsion. Nonviolent rather than violent means of conflict resolution constituted the internal forms of social control. These methods were consistent with the overall kibbutz stance toward integrating the individual with the community.

The kibbutz during its first years attempted to realize a number of utopian socialist principles. Increasingly in the last three decades it has accepted modes of development that lead toward more formal and compulsory forms of social organization. The present direction of kibbutz activity is primarily related to the history and the policies of the Israeli state, particularly regarding industrialization. These external factors are coupled with internal community forces in bringing about shifts in kibbutz priorities and in the overall social reality.

Internal Forces

The history of utopian communalism suggests that ideological purity is consistently eroded by the creeping inroads of routin-

---

[3] The recent works by Michel Foucault deserve careful attention by those concerned with issues of dominance: *Discipline and Punish: The Birth of the Prison* (New York: Pantheon Books, Inc., 1975) and *The History of Sexuality*, vol. 1 (New York: Pantheon Books, Inc., 1978). On a comparative note, members of kibbutzim, unlike members of many other communal movements, were not persecuted by the larger society.

ization, political conflict, and the practicalities of daily life. As this occurs an ideological "letting-go" occurs permitting shifts in priorities and methods of organizing community institutions. The passion of rebelling against an old order, of setting up new forms of behavior, is cooled by a settling into emerging routine patterns that soon become well-worn. For kibbutzniks the great pioneering adventure of breaking new ground, of establishing an entire new way of life, provided fertile ground for deep ideological attachment. The *vattikim* of Har were able to synthesize the ideological promise of Socialist-Zionism in their actual experience. They had the historical fortune to give birth to their visions.

The ideological letting-go was perhaps inevitable for the second and subsequent generations.[4] The generation continuum is another issue generally encountered by utopian communities. The children of the founding generation do not share the same catalytic experiences as did their elders. They are more prone to take the emergent community reality for granted rather than to see it as an experiment. For them it is not an experiment but the reality within which they have been reared. The revolt of the first generation is missing from their lives. They can choose to either accept a perhaps interesting, but in any case existing order, or turn elsewhere for direction. In Har's case, we have seen that succeeding generations have tended to become less ideological and politically less active.

An analysis of the ethos of succeeding generations of the kibbutz leads to another conclusion: material success can generate ideological failure. During the Mandate years, the kibbutz barely maintained a subsistence economy. Collective action was just as much a practical necessity as it was an ideological goal. A strong unity of purpose and action both caused and evolved from enforced simplicity. One example of the "failure of success"

[4] Menachem Rosner, *The Kibbutz as a Way of Life in Modern Society* (Givat Haviva, 1970).

has been the changing pattern of communal interaction. At first, there was only one communal building and it housed the communal kitchen and dining hall. The kitchen became the recognized setting for sharing experiences and moreover, became the center for communal nurturing. This was structurally important for the kibbutz's socialist organization for it allowed social trust and social responsibility to be incorporated into daily life. As material success afforded more buildings providing for individual and family privacy and intimacy, the settings for the community-wide sharing and nurturing decreased in importance. More formal and rationalized processes of insuring collective encounters had to be arranged. These new forms have never been able to recreate the spontaneity and everyday promise of collective encounters of the earlier period; but they appear to work well in governing the kibbutz.

The ideological letting-go, the generation continuum, and the failure of material success, are all internal constraints upon socialist communalism. These factors have been important not only in the kibbutz movement, but also in other ideological movements in the past and present. They will undoubtedly operate in the future. They all exist, however, within the context of the larger societal setting. The principal subject throughout this study of the kibbutz has been the overall significance of the relationship between external national forces and local internal change. Change has been continually in response to the emerging forms of Israeli nationalism and industrialization. Perhaps, some of the letting-go of ideological commitment by a second generation in favor of a less taxing, more personal life is an inevitable factor diminishing utopian aspirations.

External Forces: Nationalism

For the kibbutz movement nationalism has been an instrumental force for both Zionist solidarity and socialist disruption. While the kibbutz has been continuously attached to national programs and policies, and has received external economic, social, and political support, socialist values and structures have been undermined by evolving national policies. Before the state's foundation, the kibbutz played a leading role in efforts to build the nation. Nationalist activities by the kibbutz covered a wide range of colonizing efforts. The land settlement, the absorption of new immigrants, the establishment of military outposts, the learning of a common national language, and the initiation of a separate Jewish agrarian economy were part of these efforts. Supported by privately financed organizations of the Yishuv society, particularly the Jewish Agency, these kibbutz activities also produced the foundations for a variety of institutions that became important during the state era. The Histadrut, the Hevrat Ovdim, the Workers Bank are conspicuous examples of countless others.

The kibbutz involvement in nation building proved to be a separate component to socialist-communal ideological directions. Original reverence for manual labor matched the material need of working in new agrarian settlements. Solidarity of the group strengthened both the sense of military threat and the positive ethic of pioneering a community. Even the spatial shape of the kibbutz, its circular patterns around central communal buildings, integrated a communal norm of cohesion with a practical response to the existent military situation. During the Mandate period the kibbutz enjoyed an important degree of local autonomy because of its geographic isolation, the still relatively weak Yishuv infrastructure, and its rejection of political jurisdiction that rested in the British Mandate. The kibbutz was in a position of serving its national aspirations on its own terms. It was the servant of a state to be. It was, in fact, a pioneering elite.

With the establishment of the Israeli state the relationship of the kibbutz toward the nation significantly altered. The powerful influence of the kibbutz remained but its central nation-building functions diminished. The vision of making the Israeli society into one general network of kibbutzim quickly disappeared. In its place was the modern reality of small, local socialist communities existing within a nation-state oriented toward a Western model of development. The overall direction of Israeli political and economic policies became a critical factor in limiting socialist-communal possibilities. The national political structures incorporated centralizing rather than decentralized forms and the national economy invited capitalist investment and Western modes of technology and industrial organization.

The issues of state policy have long been especially problematic for socialists and for kibbutzniks. On the one hand, the kibbutzniks, who emphasize notions of self-sufficiency and a one class system, have had little faith in the concept of the state. They felt central authority should be resisted in principle and that workers should rely on their own resources and solidarity. Rather than assuming a perception of the state as the expression of a general will, these kibbutzniks have largely agreed that the state acted as the executive arm of the ruling class.

However, the kibbutz ideology of Socialist-Zionism was inherently connected to the building of Jewish nationalism, in effect, to the building of a Jewish state. Though many kibbutzniks may have wished that the Jewish state be different from all other states, the signs were evident during the Yishuv period that this would not be the case. The early kibbutz movement, as the rest of the Yishuv, was reliant on capital provided by the wealthier classes in the Diaspora and coordinated by the Zionist financial institutions. Unlike many recent socialist experiments, the land and labor for the kibbutz was not easily available for development. Kibbutz labor was immigrant labor and the land had to be purchased. Immigrant labor and land purchase required substantial capital investment. The financiers of Yishuv colonization were interested in Jewish nation building and not in subsidizing socialist communities.

The Zionist goal of establishing a Jewish state began with the notion that Palestine was a land without a people. The kibbutz never provided a creative response of its own to the issue of an autonomous Palestinian population. In placing primary efforts into nation building, the kibbutz was unable to develop strong communal networks that could have included the *fellaheen*. This is not to suggest that the *fellaheen* would have necessarily been open to such networks. But it remains the case that regional communal efforts were barely attempted. The consequence of the limits of kibbutz socialist-communalism on this issue have been consistent with the state's failure to reach an overall regional accord and unified, comprehensive regional organizations.

Finally, the kibbutz Yishuv experience defined not only future relations with the Palestinian population, but also the kibbutz movement's relationship with international affairs. During the Mandate years, nation-building priorities commanded a great deal of individual and collective attention, but energy, time, and interest increasingly were bounded by an internal rather than external perspective. National particularism rather than international universalism more and more shaped the socialist kibbutz vision. The prestate function of the kibbutz as a military base in a geographically vulnerable area furthered its inward sense of threat from the outside world. On a sociopsychological dimension, internal group solidarity was defined by a militaristic pride and by the threat of death as much as the promise of life and, thus, continues to differentiate the kibbutz from socialist movements and the larger world in general.

The statehood era furthered the gap between the direction of national development and socialist communalism. In the 1950s the revelations concerning Stalin were a severe blow to those looking for viable socialist models. The kibbutz movement suffered terrible splits and recriminations. Simultaneously, national patterns of immigration and capital flow shaped the economic environment of the kibbutz community.

The immigrant groups of the 1950s and 1960s came to Israel at a very different moment in history than the kibbutz *vattikim*. Yishuv pioneering had given way to state subsidized modernization policies. National attention moved from building a rural Jewish peasantry to enlarging a skilled, urban industrial base. State policies resulted in a major reshifting of labor and the resettlement of immigrant groups along with educational programs to bring the newcomers into the dominant *Ashkenazi*, or European, culture.[5]

The incredible population increase from 800,000 in 1948 to over 3.3 million in 1975 politically and economically affected the kibbutz in relation to the rest of the nation. We have seen in the study of Har the ramifications of Ben-Gurion's call for the hiring of immigrant labor by kibbutzim. The Sephardic immigrants had to come to Israel more as a result of a "push" from their former countries than from a "pull" toward establishing a new utopia. Moreover, they were suspicious of socialist endeavors and were often religiously orthodox. They thus were generally uninterested in becoming kibbutz members and often vehemently opposed to kibbutz perspectives. Many settled in development towns near kibbutzim that later employed them.

The kibbutz movement had its own reservations concerning the Sephardic immigrants. The newcomers not only brought with them different ideological and cultural traditions, but also had difficulty integrating into the rather provincial world of the kibbutz. *Ashkenazi* norms were already well-defined in the kibbutz so that when Sephardim did become members (approximately 7 percent of the total kibbutz population were Sephardim), they became "a good culture." The appearance of differentiated patterns of housing became a common social phenomenon.

Relations between the kibbutzim and Sephardim was even

---

[5] David Horowitz, *The Economics of Israel* (New York: Pergamon Press, 1967). Richard Pomfret, in *Trade Policies and Industrialization in a Small Country* (Tubingen: J.C.B. Mohr, 1976), also describes the extent of urban-rural dispersal in Israel, p. 145.

more strongly characterized by a "first" and "second" culture due to the reluctant acceptance by the movement to hire the immigrants as laborers. The existence of hired laborers in the agrarian and industrial sectors of the kibbutz raised ideological problems of a new dimension. For the kibbutz to become an employer of wage labor was a serious violation of its additional socialist-communal values, self-labor, a classless society, and equalitarian job rotation.

From a socialist ideological position, the kibbutz should have resisted accepting Sephardim as hired laborers or accepted them as members because of a national effort to create a classless Israeli society. Politically, however, the kibbutz already accepted the direction of state policy and succumbed instead to acting as employer. The decision to employ hired labor occurred before kibbutz industrialization had been established. Even then national priorities of employing Arab workers and new immigrants had prevailed. Later, the expansion of industrialization exacerbated kibbutz needs for labor.

Changes in the national capital flow were also instrumental in shaping kibbutz material success. In 1948 Israel could be categorized as a less developed country. Per capita income was around $300.00 in 1950.[6] A high, long-term growth rate between 1950 and 1965 resulted in the nation's transformation from a developing to a developed country. By 1970 per capita income was $1,636.00, lower than most North American countries but higher than Italy ($1,587) and close to Japan's ($1,658). This was higher than any other Asian nation except Kuwait.

The steady large inflow of capital has been the major cause of the growth of the gross national product in Israel. Its sources of capital distinguish Israel from other less developed countries. Major sources have been world Jewry, reparations from the German government, and aid from the United States. The first two are not sources for other countries. Between 1949 and 1965

[6] Pomfret, *Trade Policies and Industrialization*, p. 3.

world Jewry contributed $3,558 million, the German government $1,787 million, and the United States government $737 million. Fixed German reparations ended in 1965.[7]

Another distinguishing feature of Israeli growth economy was the character of its original labor force. Of all prestate immigrants, only 13 percent were unskilled and over 90 percent of the males were literate. In addition, the strong ethos of national identification encouraged the work attitudes needed to build a new economy. There are few less developed countries that begin with such a labor endowment.

The kibbutz benefited directly from reparation payments, the availability of state loans and grants, and from the general national rise in production and consumption.[8] Its standard of living shifted from subsistence toward that of the urban middle class. During periods of recession and escalating inflation the collectivized institutions of the kibbutz were better able to withstand the storms than more vulnerable individual family units.

Israel's unequal capital resources provided it with economic advantages unusual for a less developed country, but state policies have become focused on achieving economic independence. To this end, economic policy has concentrated in the 1950s on an import substitution phase and, in the 1960s, on an export expansion phase. Both phases occurred within a framework of modernization. Technology imported from the West was the backbone of import substitution; export expansion was largely concerned with exporting to North America and Europe. The kibbutz economy mirrored these stages through accelerating cash-crop farming and industrialization. By 1961 over 140 of 235 kibbutzim had industrial plants employing over 25 percent of the total kibbutz labor force.

[7] Ibid., p. 4.

[8] The decision of what to do with reparations given to kibbutz members was left to each kibbutz to decide separately. In some kibbutzim the monies were pooled; others allowed individual recipients to keep private accounts.

The Israeli national goal of greater economic independence, similar to that of most less developed countries, has been continually limited by the state's military and political reality. In the prestate period the little manufacturing that did exist largely rested on supplying military hardware for the region rather than on production for civilian use. By 1973 Israel still ranked high in military spending; it was eighth among 132 nations of the world. The disproportionate percentage of the state's budget (35 to 40 percent) earmarked for military and defense needs has contributed to the nation's serious inflation problem and continual deficit in balance of payments. Moreover, the defense budget greatly limits domestic social services: ranked eighth in military expenditure, Israel ranks twenty-third in success at reducing infant mortality, twenty-fifth in public education expenditure, and forty-third in public health expenditure.[9] The state's military and political position as well as its economic position are linked to Western initiatives. Kibbutz transitions, the constraints on socialist-communal directions, must be weighed in this context.

External Forces: Industrialization

The imperatives of the prevailing model of industrialization, including needs for military production, have caused fundamental changes in the social structure of the kibbutz. The history of the origin and expansion of Har's factory has revealed evidence of an increased internal stratification, specialization, the loss of job rotation, and less opportunity for members to influence the work conditions. The division of women and men into the service and wage-producing sectors respectively has been strengthened. Knowledge concerning overall community activity

[9] Ruth Leger Sivard, *World Military and Social Expenditures* (Philadelphia: American Friends Service Committee, 1976).

and plant operations became less shared among the membership allowing more concentration of power and less possibility for direct democracy. Har's General Assembly attendance records document this transition.

While this is not the place for an intensive discourse on the nature of prevailing models of industrialization, the kibbutz experience raises questions concerning industrialism that deserve further study: Are developing countries necessarily tied to the prevailing industrial models? Is a socialist-agrarian ideology, such as that of the kibbutz, inevitably doomed because of the requirements of the international market? In other words, does socialism today require industrialization and if so, in what form?

From its inception, the kibbutz was closely linked to nation-building efforts and never was in a position to determine independently the nature and scope of its economic development. The kibbutz attached itself to agrarian socialism and to possible alternate models of industrialism that did not exist on a national policy level. The state accepted the idea that the international market demanded a certain scale of industrialization and the idea that Israel's primary market ties were with the West. In terms of national political and social organization, the kibbutz never had the power and the strength of ideological commitment to direct state economic policy along the path of its socialist ideals.

Israel followed a direction common to most less developed countries. At first it pushed for import substitution programs. The state's decision, through the Department of Defense, to allow special grants and loans to Har for the renewal of its factory reflected this policy. State military needs were, of course, another important consideration. The success of this economic phase was minimal, but other state policies of full employment and population dispersal were attained.

For Har, as for many other kibbutzim, the import substitution program resulted in an importation of the prevailing model of industrial organization.[10] Its technology, scientific knowledge, marketing skills, and organizational format came from the outside. The imposed structures were alien to the original kibbutz ideology. In sociological terms, Gesellschaft norms pushed against those of the Gemeinschaft, the profane against the sacred, alienation against integration.

Industrialization of the kibbutz since the 1950s has had significant effects on the meaning of work.[11] As the community as a whole has become more materially successful and as more leisure time is created, industrial organization limits a worker's sense of time and space. The imported industrial model demands worker conformity to a particular organization of time and space and lessens opportunity for self-definition. Close attachment to nature, direct manual experience of the means of production, and individual pride in work were undermined as kibbutzniks became industrial laborers and managers. We have seen that the depth of the change touched all spheres of kibbutz life; more time has been spent on individualized, personal modes of consumption and expression. The spirit of inventiveness, critical for future social experimentation, has been discouraged by the nature of kibbutz industrial organization.

The second stage of Israeli economic development, export expansion, increased the scale of the kibbutz industrial effort. A general shift toward more goods requiring skilled labor was

[10] Uri Leviatan, "The Industrial Process in Israeli Kibbutzim: Problems and their Solutions," in *Israel: Social Structure and Change*, ed. by Curtis and Chertoff (New Brunswick, N.J.: Transaction Books, 1973).

[11] Attention on the structure and nature of work and work relations has been proliferating in recent years. Among the most important studies are Andre Gorz, ed., *The Division of Labor* (Atlantic Highlands, N.J.: Humanities Press, 1976); Harry Braverman, *Labor and Monopoly Capital* (New York: Monthly Review Press, 1974) and Richard Edwards, *Contested Terrain* (New York: Basic Books, 1979).

reflected in the boom of Har's metal works factory in the last decades. Growth of aircraft exports, including parts made by Har, was an important element in this shift.[12] During this period the number of hired laborers dramatically increased. By 1970 Har had completely replaced kibbutzniks on the production floor by hiring over 100 laborers. A new managerial class of members has been created. The Weberian image of a world dominated by obedient professional managers and bureaucrats, which had been so far from the early kibbutz ideology of practice, has come much closer to being rooted in kibbutz organization.

The success of the export expansion phase of national development rested on government policies that supported company mergers and market concentration. Relaxation of tariff barriers, reintroduction of export premia in 1965, and consolidation of markets in profitable products all created favorable conditions for growth of Har's factory and those of other kibbutzim. Centralization rather than decentralization has become a principal concept in the state's economic development, and a large expansion of the public bureaucracy has supported this merger movement.

We turn back again to our questioning of the relationship between socialism and industrialism. Are there alternatives to the prevailing model adopted by Israel in the kibbutz? If we take a comparative view, it appears that while no model can be exactly replicated by another nation, there have been a number of socialist experiments relevant for the kibbutz. Principal examples include those in Cuba, Tanzania, Yugoslavia, and China. All of these examples may offer alternatives to the Soviet model and have retained, in varying degrees of success, a significant level of national autonomy.

Tanzania, for example, has attempted to utilize agrarian so-

[12] Pomfret, *Trade Policies and Industrialization*, p. 69 notes the increase in aircraft and parts exports from Israel in recent years.

cialism as the backbone of development policies. When industrialization was introduced, great effort was made to promote national self-reliance and avoid dependence on foreign capital. In the Arusha Declaration of 1967 Nyerere stated that the foundation of Tanzanian development would be agriculture based in the Ujamaa villages. Values of self-reliance, social equality, a sense of an extended family nationhood, and an antiexploitative economy are reminiscent of early kibbutz utopian ideology. The Tanzanian experiment has fallen far short of its socialist goals, however, and the possibility for future success remains a controversial issue. [13]

The Tanzanian experiment provides support for the argument that industrialization, in itself, is not a cure for underdevelopment. [14] In fact, it can spark rather than eliminate unemployment and underemployment. The crisis of urban centers overpopulated with rural immigrants is part of this picture. Modernization following Westernized models also has sapped natural resources of the less developed countries, benefited the wealthier nations, and undermined national independence and local self-control. For the kibbutz and for other socialist experiments, the scale, organization, and products of an industrial effort are problems requiring solutions supportive of socialist goals. At issue is whether industrial and development models of organization can be produced that insure the greatest degree of material well-

[13] At present, perspectives on Nyerere's path of development range from uncritical enthusiasm to ultra-leftist wholesale rejection. Among the more interesting works on the subject are John Saul's "African Socialism in One Country: Tanzania" in *Essays on the Political Economy of Africa* by J. Saul and G. Arrighi (New York: Monthly Review Press, 1973); and Susanne Mueller's "Landing the Middle Peasantry: Narodism in Tanzania," Working Paper, African Studies Center, Boston University.

[14] One supporter of this view is Gunnar Myrdal. See his "Paths of Development" in *Peasants and Peasant Society*, ed. Teodor Shanin (Baltimore: Penguin Books, 1975).

being for the largest number of people in the context of egalitarian norms.

The problems of appropriate models of modernization and industrialization are coupled with the question of whether social organization can develop that gives life to the utopian hope for a creative integration of collective and individual energies. Specific trends of kibbutz development shed light on the possibilities and obstacles facing future socialist experimentation:

First of all, while the kibbutz has continued as part of the agrarian economic sector, it has moved from self-sufficiency farming to cash-crop farming. Today, for example, milk is pumped by machines from cows, sent, untouched by hands, by truck to a regional processing plant, returned by truck to the kibbutz, where, for a price, it fills the common dispenser. The relationship to the land has not disappeared but fewer members work directly with nature. The regional Milouot system furthers the rationalization and capitalization of the agrarian enterprise. The manual labor concept, espoused by A. D. Gordon, is challenged by the new forms of organizing the agrarian sector.

Secondly, industrialization has greatly furthered the existence of hired labor, caused a greater division of labor, and substituted exchange value for use values in work. A managerial and industrial bureaucratic form has entered the community's organization that threatens the socialist concept of worker-controlled enterprise.

Third, military and political instability continues to pose an external threat. Prestate illegal activity in the Yishuv defense force has been replaced by high levels of performance by kibbutzniks in the state's armed services.

Fourth, children of the kibbutz usually remain as kibbutz members; however, attraction to urban life has increased. In addition, the ability of the kibbutz to attract new members from the rest of Israel and abroad has decreased since the 1960s. The limits of new labor power are important considerations to be weighed when evaluating labor-intensive versus capital-intensive economic development.

Fifth, the family has taken on new significance. Children spend more time with parents; women push for more family privacy, partly in response to increasing dissatisfaction at work. The new strength of family ties reflects the sexual division of labor and the fact that while women have become "masculinized" men have not been "feminized." The scope of sexual equality in the kibbutz remains a matter of significant concern.

Sixth, leadership is still rotated but among a small group. Authority remains in the formal structure rather than in the individual personality. However, as in many social movements, charismatic leadership also has had an impact.

Seventh, the kibbutz still controls its elementary and high school systems. Educational philosophy has remained fairly consistent; however, more youth wish to attend higher education not under kibbutz jurisdiction. As more students take exams to enter outside institutions, the kibbutz internal educational programs are modified. The significance of educational and cultural norms for the maintenance of a social order is well known. If internal kibbutz educational policies are diluted, the consequence may be severe for the younger kibbutz generation.

Finally, the relationship between the individual and community has elements of both change and continuity. There is more personal privacy, less communal time, and less of an organic sense of communalism. But communal ritual and solidarity are still present, particularly in times of celebration and distress. Children are still placed in communal child-care facilities during the day; the Sabbath and holidays are still collectively observed. Social control remains nonviolent and membership remains voluntary. The greatest threat to the continuance of collective patterns of interaction appears to be the emerging individualism and materialist value system. The Sabra attitude remains. This attitude, embracing self-confidence, toughness, dedication and inner warmth reveals both possibility and difficulty for further socialist experimentation.

Conclusions

The kibbutz has presented a wealth of experiences, of mistakes, and achievements. What lessons can be drawn?

First, the kibbutz offers no final model for change. While communities can direct themselves to goals of socialist-communalism, no society is static and unchanging. A great challenge confronting socialist efforts to alter existing realities is development of the ability to create working models from the given set of problems such as class, ethnic, and racial divisions of a society. Historical and comparative perspectives are critical for germinating ideas but the concept of a model to fit all socialist movements is not helpful and in the end causes disillusionment.

Next, ideological movements do not exist in isolation but are developed in the context of larger social forces. The direction of kibbutz social change has been shaped by both internal and external forces, acting both independently and interdependently. From the evidence presented one can conclude that a primary factor, if not the primary factor, in kibbutz development has been the nature and structure of Israeli modernization efforts. These modernization efforts encompass national ideology, industrialization, and legitimization of certain forms of social interaction. Modernization has been equated with the West, mass culture, and the death of individuality.

This mode of modernization stands in opposition to kibbutz utopian ideology and kibbutz socialist-communal practices. However, as we have seen, the kibbutz from its earliest days has been linked to nation building and has recognized the authority of national institutions. As the state moved along the modernization continuum, the kibbutz movement did not possess the degree of autonomy, power, or commitment to press forward in an alternative direction. Individual kibbutzim have tended to benefit substantially from general material gains but at the cost of compromising important ideological positions. The study of the kibbutz indicates that small-scale socialist experiments cannot creatively grow or be sustained within a larger opposing culture without, at minimum, suffering major limitations in their ideological thrust.

Finally, the kibbutz experience suggests that the success of socialist efforts depends on new modes of thinking as well as new forms of social organization. There was a tendency in the original formulations of kibbutz ideology to emphasize national identity and class unity. National identity prevailed. The development of national consciousness at the expense of class consciousness has not allowed an approach that links the two modes of consciousness. Independent socialist movements everywhere will have to develop new thinking on this issue.

New thinking is necessary on the problem of integrating local interests with global concerns. The kibbutz increasingly became linked to worldwide and multinational institutions at the expense of losing much of its internal economic autonomy while gaining forms of industrial organization that undermined its original socialist-communalism.

The national military role of the kibbutz with its international ramifications has continually challenged the community's need for peace and long-range security. Fuller coordination of socialist-communalism awaits efforts to solve the regional, national, and international problems that limit kibbutz autonomy.

The integration of individual needs with emerging political-social structures also requires attention. In the kibbutz the delicate balance between individuality and collectivity has increasingly given way to norms of individuality and mass culture. A central goal of socialist-communalism has been to allow full realization of individual potential in an environment of mutual and collective trust. The times we live in gravely repress opportunity to achieve this goal. Yet, seeds for change in the kibbutz and elsewhere remain alive, if not flourishing. New ways of thinking are needed to make them bloom.

Official Exchange Rates for the Palestinian and Israeli Lira in Terms of United States Currency

Sterling	U.S. Dollars
1920-1929	5.00
1930-1932	3.30-3.90
1933-1938	5.00
1949 (Sept.)	2.80

1. On 1 November 1927, the Palestinian pound, the lira, was introduced and had the same value as sterling.

2. Israeli Pound (lira)

Oct. 1949	Lira = Palestinian Pound
Feb. 1962	3 Lira = $1.00
Aug. 1971	4.2 Lira = $1.00
Aug. 1976	8.12 Lira = $1.00

Poems and Songs of Har

These have been translated from the Hebrew by Rabbi Everett
Gendler. Har is a pseudonym for the true name of the kibbutz.

I.

Night stretches out,
and fire from the mountains,
and heroic song
from that place bursts forth.

The fire of my heart is ablaze,
the fire of my heart burns hot.
I am yours Har,
completely and totally yours.

> Our mother,
> cradle of our might,
> defend us!

Should a thousand fall,
with a thousand we shall proudly replace them
until there shine forth on the hills of Galil
a wondrous, luminous day.

Should there be slaughter,
enemies' hands upon you,
we shall once again Har
raise your sheltering walls.

> Our mother,
> cradle of our might,
> defend us!

We shall enlarge your boundary,
we shall open it up.
Ours is the Spring
and the ancient sun.

And you, Har, a wall of steel
during nights of siege,
and a dream of hope
for those to come.

J. URLAND, 1938

II.

What of the night in Har?
In Har what is the word?
Darkness wherever I look,
A massive slaughter in Israel.

Behold, all is lost; and now
Shall we not again build here?
Lord, You surely know!
God, You answer!

Not even one sign have you seen?
Not even a hint of Redeemer?
There is a watching in Har
All through the night, all through the night.

S. SHALOM, 1938

III.

To the heights of the mountains
we have come as companions,
a family of comradely workers.
We shall never turn back!
Here we'll make our place!
The blood of our heart is ablaze,

the blood of our heart is inflamed.
On the borders of the north,
in desolate wilderness
we have fixed a habitation,
we have hewed a window,
a wondrous window
Har! amidst the flinty mountains.

Though results are yet few,
though the way yet be hard,
thus strides forth our people working!
This is the path of toil,
the demand on a people redeemed,
the generation of worthy settlers
who build their houses
with sweat and blood—
We shall build and be built.
Motherland! a nation of workers strides forth!

A. LEVINSON

Glossary

Ahdut Ha—avoda. Post World War I Labor-Zionist party that helped to form Mapai in 1929-1930; later a left-of-center Israeli political party.

Aliyah. Wave of Jewish migration to Palestine; literally "going up."

Ashkenazi. Jewish cultural tradition emerging from Europe and the West rather than from the Mediterranean countries and the East.

Assafa. General Assembly of the kibbutz.

Avoda. Work.

Baghrot. Comprehensive high school examinations for entrance to higher learning institutions.

Chalutz. A pioneer. The term usually refers to prestate Jewish agricultural settlers.

Dunam. Land measurement, equal to approximately a quarter of an acre.

Effendi. Designation for Ottoman official or Arab landowner.

Fellah (plural: fellaheen). Arab peasant-farmer.

Garin. Organized Jewish group of settlers or agrarian workers.

Gizbar. Treasurer in the kibbutz.

Haganah. Underground defense force of the Jewish community in Palestine during the Mandate period.

Hashomer Hatzair. Jewish youth movement first formed in 1913 in Eastern Europe. The organization eventually founded its own kibbutz federation. In the late 1920s, the movement became international and ideologically affiliated with the left-wing-socialist Mapai party.

Haver (feminine: havera; plural: havarim or haverot). Comrade; a term of address for kibbutz members.

Histadrut. General federation of Jewish labor. Founded in

1920, the union consists of 90 percent of Israel's eligible labor force and is a federation of trade unions, communal and cooperative settlements, service organizations, and manufacturing institutions.

Ichud Hakvutzot Vehakibbutzim (referred to in the text as Ichud Federation). A federation of kibbutzim founded in 1951 by the merger of a federation of *kvutzot* (Hever Hakvutzot) with kibbutzim that had been affiliated with Hakibbutz Hameuchad but that left it. This federation is associated with the Mapai party.

I.D.F. Israeli Defense Forces.

Jewish Agency. The executive branch of the World Zionist Organization, concerned mainly with immigration and settlement in Israel.

Jewish National Fund (J.N.F.). A subsidiary of the World Zionist Organization, founded in 1901 to purchase land in Palestine. A land trust, it holds property in perpetuity in the name of the Jewish people.

Keren Halchud. Social Service Fund of the Ichud Federation.

Kibbutz (plural: kibbutzim). Collective settlement; literally, a gathering or community. The term was first used to denote large type of communal settlement as opposed to smaller *kvutza*.

Kibbutz Artzi. Kibbutz federation of Hashomer Hatzair kibbutzim.

Kibbutz Meuchad. Kibbutz federation, founded in 1927 for the larger type of collective settlements; it included small industries during Mandate period.

K.I.A. Kibbutz Industries Association Ltd. An organization jointly representing kibbutz industry.

Knesset. Israel's Parliament with 120 delegates elected under a system of proportional representation at least once every four years.

Kvutza (plural: Kvutzot). Collective settlement of the smaller form, planned to be a "large family." In practice, the kibbutz or large collective has become the preferred form of settlement.

Lena Mishpatit. Kibbutz organizational arrangement allowing children to sleep in the homes of their parents rather than in the communal children's houses.

Lira (Israeli Pound). Basic unit of Israeli currency. See Appendix One for exchange rates.

Mapai. Acronym for the Israeli Workers Party, the largest and most influential of Israel's political parties and the leader of all government coalitions since the state's establishment.

Mapam. Acronym for the United Workers Party. Much of its strength comes from Hakkibbutz Haartzi Federation.

Maskir (feminine: maskira). Secretary of the kibbutz.

Maskiroot. Central kibbutz secretariat.

Meshek. Hebrew term for kibbutz economic organization.

Metapelet. Literally means "some who take care of." In the kibbutz it refers to child care workers.

Milouot. Regional enterprise system of kibbutzim and moshavim in the Western Galilee region.

Moshav (plural: moshavim). Cooperative settlement. It differs from the kibbutz mainly because the land and homes are individually owned while farm implements are collectively owned.

Palmach. Special squads within the Haganah consisting mostly of kibbutz members.

Poalim. Hebrew term for workers. Usually it refers to manual laborers.

Sephardic. Referring to the Jewish cultural tradition emerging from the Mediterranean and East in contrast to the Askhenzai tradition; today over 60 percent of the Israeli Jewish population are from Sephardic backgrounds; they constitute 7 percent of the kibbutz movement population.

Shaliah. Representative of the kibbutzim or other Israeli organization to foreign countries.

Sidron Avoda. Kibbutz work manager.

Solel Boneh. The construction and public works enterprise of the Histadrut.

Tnuva. A subsidiary of the Histadrut engaged in marketing of agricultural produce to which all the kibbutzim belong.

Ulpan. Kibbutz-based program for nonmembers consisting of half-study and half-a-day work.

Vattikim. Original kibbutz settlers.

Yishuv. A term for the Jewish community in Palestine.

Yom Avoda. Literally workday. The term is used in kibbutz accounting to designate the labor cost of the income-producing branches as defined by the ratio of the total number of workdays in kibbutz income-producing branches to consumption expenditures in that kibbutz. It also refers to the earnings per workday in a particular income-producing branch as defined by the net income of that branch divided by the number of labor-days in that branch.

Bibliography

BOOKS

Abu-Lughod, Ibrahim. *Transformation of Palestine: Essays on the Origin and Development of the Arab-Israeli Conflict.* Evanston, Ill.: Northwestern University Press, 1971.

Allon, Yigal. *The Making of Israel's Army.* London: Sphere Books Ltd., 1971.

Amitai, Mordechai. *Together: Conversations About the Kibbutz.* Tel Aviv: Hashomer Hatzair Organization, 1966.

Andrews, Fannie Fern. *The Holy Land Under the Mandate*, vol. 2. Boston: Houghton Mifflin Company, 1931.

Arendt, Hannah. *The Human Condition.* Chicago: University of Chicago Press, 1958.

Arensberg, Conrad M., and Kimball, Solon T. *Culture and Community.* New York: Harcourt, Brace and World, Inc., 1965.

Arian, Alan. *Ideological Change in Israel.* Cleveland: Case Western Reserve Press, 1968.

Arlosoroff, Chaim, Grodzinsky, S., and Schmuckker, Rebecca, eds., *Hechalutz.* Israel: Zionist Labor Party, 1929.

Bein, Alex. *The Return to the Soil.* Israel: Zionist Organization, 1952.

Bell, Colin, and Newby, Howard. *Community Studies: An Introduction to the Sociology of the Local Community.* New York: Praeger Publishers, Inc., 1972.

Ben-Gurion, David. *Israel: A Personal History.* New York: Funk and Wagnalls, Inc., 1971.

Ben-Shalom, Avraham. *Deep Furrows.* Translated by Frances Bunce. New York: Hashomer Hatzair Organization, 1937.

Ber-Borochov, Dov. *Nationalism and the Class Struggle.* Jerusalem: Poale Zion, 1937.

Berle, H., and Means, G. *The Modern Corporation and Private Property.* New York: Harcourt, Brace and World, Inc., 1968.

Bettelheim, Bruno. *The Children of the Dream.* New York: Avon Books, 1971.

Bottomore, T. B., ed. *Karl Marx: Early Writings*. New York: McGraw Hill Book Company, 1964.

Braverman, Harry. *Labor and Monopoly Capital*. New York: Monthly Review Press, 1974.

Bruyn, Severyn. *The Human Perspective in Sociology*. Englewood Cliffs, N.J. Prentice-Hall, Inc., 1966.

Buber, Martin. *On Zion: The History of an Idea*. New York: Schocken Books, 1973.

―――. *Paths in Utopia*. Boston: Beacon Press, 1971.

Cohen, Abner. *Arab Border Villages in Israel*. Manchester: Manchester University Press, 1965.

Cohen, Aharon. *Israel and the Arab World*. New York: Funk and Wagnalls, Inc., 1970.

Cohen, Erik, and Leshem, Elazer. *Survey of Regional Cooperation in Three Regions of Collective Settlements*. Jerusalem: Keter Publishing House Ltd., 1969.

Cohen, Reuven. *The Kibbutz Settlement*. Tel Aviv: Hakibbutz Hameuchad Publishing House Ltd., 1972.

Criden, Yosef, and Gelb, Saadia. *The Kibbutz Experience: Dialogue in Kfar Blum*. New York: Herzl Press, 1974.

Crossman, Richard. *Palestine Mission: A Personal Record*. New York: Harper and Brothers, 1947.

Curtis, Michael, and Chertoff, Mordecai. *Israel: Social Structure and Change*. New Brunswick, N.J.: Transaction Books, 1973.

Darin-Drabkin, Haim. *The Other Society*. New York: Harcourt, Brace and World, Inc., 1963.

Dennis, N., Henriques, F., and Slaughter, C. *Coal is Our Life*. London: Eyre and Spottiswoode, 1956.

Dentler, Robert. *American Community Problems*. New York: McGraw Hill Book Company, 1968.

Deutsch, Andre, ed. *The Seventh Day: Soldiers Talk About the Six Day War*. Tel Aviv: Steimatsky's Agency Ltd., 1970.

Duberman, Martin. *Black Mountain: An Exploration in Community*. New York: Anchor Press, 1973.

Durkheim, Emile. *The Rules of Sociological Method*. New York: The Free Press, 1938.

―――. *Suicide*. New York: Free Press, 1951.

Easton, Loyd D., and Guddat, Kurt H., eds. *Writings of the Young Marx on Philosophy and Society*. New York: Doubleday and Co., Inc., 1967.

Edwards, Richard. *Contested Terrain*. New York: Basic Books, Inc., Publishers, 1979.

Effrat, Andrew. *Perspectives on Political Sociology*. Indianapolis: The Bobbs-Merrill Co., Inc., 1972.

Eisenstadt, S. M. *The Absorption of Immigrants*. London: Routledge & Kegan Paul Ltd., 1954.

————. *Israeli Society*. New York: Basic Books, Inc., Publishers, 1967.

El-Asmar, Fouzi. *To Be An Arab in Israel*. London: Frances Pinter, Ltd., 1975.

Elon, Amos. *The Israelis*. London: Sphere Books Ltd., 1972.

Esco Foundation for Palestine, Inc. *Palestine: A Study of Jewish, Arab, and British Policies*, vols. 1 and 2. New Haven: Yale University Press, 1947.

Fanon, Frantz. *The Wretched of the Earth*. New York: Grove Press, Inc., 1968.

Fein, Leonard. *Politics in Israel*. Boston: Little Brown and Company, 1967.

Foucault, Michel. *Discipline and Punish: The Birth of the Prison*. New York: Pantheon Books, Inc., 1975.

————. *The History of Sexuality*, vol. 1. New York: Pantheon Books, Inc., 1978.

French, Robert Mills, ed. *The Community: A Comparative Perspective*. Chicago: F. E. Peacock, Publishers, 1969.

Freud, Sigmund. *Civilization and Its Discontents*. New York: W.W. Norton and Co., Inc., 1962.

Friere, Paulo. *Pedagogy of the Oppressed*. New York: Herder and Herder, 1968.

Gendzier, Irene. *Frantz Fanon: A Critical Study*. New York: Pantheon Books, Inc., 1973.

Golumb, Naphtali, and Katz, Daniel. *The Kibbuzim As Open Social Systems*. Israel: Ruppin Institute, 1970.

Gonen, Jay. *A Psychohistory of Zionism*. New York: Mason-Charter, 1975.

Goodman, Paul. *The Jewish National Home 1917-1942*. London: J. M. Dent & Sons Ltd., 1943.

Gordon, A. D. *The Nation and the Work*. Tel Aviv: The Zionist Library, 1952. In Hebrew.

Gorz, Andre, ed. *The Division of Labor*. Atlantic Highlands, N.J.: Humanities Press, 1976.

Granott, A. *The Land System in Palestine: History and Structure*. London: Eyre and Spottiswoode, 1952.

Granovsky, Abraham. *Land Policy In Palestine*. New York: Bloch Publishing Co., Inc., 1940.

Halperin, Haim. *Agrindus: Integration of Agriculture and Industries*. London: Routledge & Kegan Paul Ltd., 1963.

———. *Changing Patterns in Israel Agriculture*. London: Routledge & Kegan Paul Ltd., 1957.

Halpern, Ben. *The Idea of the Jewish State*. Cambridge, Mass.: Harvard University Press, 1969.

Handel, Michael I. *Israel's Political-Military Doctrine*. Cambridge, Mass.: Harvard University Center for International Affairs, 1973.

Hanna, Paul. *British Policy in Palestine*. Washington, D.C.: American Council on Public Affairs, 1942.

Hashomer Hatzair Workers' Party in Jerusalem. *The Case for a Bi-National Palestine*. New York: Shulsinger Bros. Linotyping and Publishing Co., 1947.

Hertzberg, Arthur, ed. *The Zionist Idea: A Historical Analysis and Reader*. New York: Meridian Books, Inc., 1960.

Herzl, Theodor. *The Jewish State: An Attempt at a Modern Solution of the Jewish Question*. New York: H. Pordes, 1967.

Hillery, George A., Jr. *Communal Organizations: A Study of Local Societies*. Chicago: University of Chicago Press, 1968.

Himadeh, Sa'id B. *Economic Organization of Palestine*. Beirut: American University, 1938.

Hinton, William. *Fanshen: A Documentary of Revolution in a Chinese Village*. New York: Vintage Books, 1966.

Homans, G. C. *The Social Behavior: Its Elementary Forms*. New York: Harcourt, Brace and World, Inc., 1961.

Horowitz, David, *The Economics of Israel*. New York: Pergamon Press, 1967.

Horowitz, David, and Hinden, Rita. *Economic Survey of Palestine*. Tel Aviv: Jewish Agency for Palestine, 1938.

Horowitz, Irving Louis. *Foundations of Political Sociology*. New York: Harper & Row, 1972.

Huberman, Leo, and Sweezy, Paul M. *Socialism in Cuba*. New York: Modern Reader Paperbacks, 1969.

Hunter, Floyd. *Community Power Structure*. Chapel Hill: University of North Carolina Press, 1953.

Hyamson, Albert M. *Palestine Under the Mandate 1920-1948*. New York: Methuen and Co., 1950.

Infield, Henrik F. *Cooperative Living in Palestine*. New York: Dreyden Press, 1944.

Infield, Henrik F., and Maier, Joseph B., eds. *Cooperative Group Living*. New York: Henry Koosis & Co., 1950.

Ingrams, Doreen. *Palestine Papers 1917-1922: Seeds of Conflict*. London: John Murray, 1972.

Jiryis, Sabri. *The Arabs in Israel*. New York: Monthly Review Press, 1976.

John, Robert, and Hadawi, Sami. *The Palestine Diary Vol. I, 1914-1945*. New York: New World Press, 1970.

Kanovsky, Eliyahu. *The Economy of the Israeli Kibbutz*. Cambridge, Mass.: Harvard University Press, 1966.

Kanter, Rosabeth Moss. *Commitment and Community: Communes and Utopias in Sociological Perspective*. Cambridge, Mass.: Harvard University Press, 1972.

Keren Ha-Yesod Publicity Department, ed. *The Keren Ha-Yesod Book Colonisation Problems of the Eretz Israel Foundation Fund*. London: Leonard Parsons Ltd., 1921.

Khalidi, Walid, ed. *From Haven to Conquest; Readings in Zionism and the Palestine Problem until 1948*. Beirut: Institute for Palestine Studies, 1971.

Klatzman, Joseph, Ilan, Benjamin, and Levi, Yair. *The Role of Group Action in the Industrialization of Rural Areas*. New York: Praeger Publishers, 1971.

Koestler, Arthur. *Arrow in the Blue: An Autobiography*. New York: Macmillan Inc., 1952.

————. *The Invisible Writing: An Autobiography*, vol. 2, New York: Macmillan Inc., 1969.

Kropotkin, Peter. *Mutual Aid*. London: Porter Sargant Press, 1969.

Kumarappa, J. C. *Economy of Permanence*. New Delhi: International Seva Sangh Publication, 1958.

Kurland, Samuel. *Cooperative Palestine*. New York: Sharon Books, 1947.

Lakey, George. *Strategy for a Living Revolution*. San Francisco: W. H. Freeman & Company, Publishers, 1973.

Laqueur, Walter. *The Israeli-Arab Reader*. New York: Bantam Books, Inc., 1971.

Laufer, Leopold. *Israel and the Developing Countries: New Approaches to Cooperation*. New York: Twentieth Century Fund, 1967.

Leon, Dan. *The Kibbutz: A New Way of Life*. London: Pergamon Press, 1969.

Littlejohn, J. *Westrigg: The Sociology of a Cheviot Parish*. London: Routledge & Kegan Paul Ltd., 1963.

Lunn, Eugene. *The Prophet of Community: The Romantic Socialism of Gustav Landauer*. Berkeley: University of California Press, 1973.

Malkosh, Nosh. *Histadrut in Israel, Its Aims and Achievements*. Tel Aviv: Histadrut, 1961.

Mannheim, Karl. *Ideology and Utopia*. New York: Harcourt, Brace and World, Inc., 1956.

Marcuse, Herbert. *One-Dimensional Man*. Boston: Beacon Press, 1964.

Mead, Margaret, ed. *Cultural Patterns and Technical Change*. New York: UNESCO, 1953.

Memmi, Albert. *The Colonizer and the Colonized*. Boston: Beacon Press, 1972.

————. *Portrait of a Jew*. New York: Viking Press, 1971.

Mills, C. W. *The Sociological Imagination*. Oxford: Oxford University Press, 1959.

Muenzner, Gerhard. *Labor Enterprise in Palestine: A Handbook of Histadrut Economic Institutions*. New York: Sharon Books, 1947.

Nahamani, Joseph. *A Man of Galilee*. Israel: Ramat Gan, 1969.

Nettl, Peter. *Rosa Luxemburg*. Oxford: Oxford University Press, 1969.

Nisbet, Robert A. *The Quest for Community*. Oxford: Oxford University Press, 1953.

Nordhoff, Charles. *The Communistic Societies of the United States*. New York: Schocken Books, 1971.

Orni, Efraim, and Efrat, Elishu. *Geography of Israel*. Jerusalem: Israel Program for Scientific Translations, 1966.

Parkes, James. *Whose Land? A History of the Peoples of Palestine*. New York: Penguin Books, 1970.

Parsons, Talcott. *The Structure of Social Action*. New York: Free Press, 1937.

Pinsker, Leo. *Auto-Emancipation*. Israel: Macabean Publishers, 1906.

Pitt-Rivers, J. A. *The People of the Sierra*. Chicago: University of Chicago Press, 1963.

Pomfret, Richard. *Trade Policies and Industrialization in a Small Country*. Tubingen: J.C.B. Mohr, 1976.

Porath, Y. *The Emergence of the Palestinian-Arab National Movement 1918-1929*. London: Frank Cass, 1974.

Prion, Israel. *Development Trends of Spatial Rural Cooperation in Israel*. Israel: Rehovot Settlement Study Centre, 1968.

Quandt, William B., Jabber, Fuad, and Lesch, Ann Mosely. *The Politics of Palestinian Nationalism*. Berkeley: University of California Press, 1973.

Rabin, A. I. *Growing Up on the Kibbutz*. New York: Springer Publishing Co., Inc., 1965.

Redfield, Robert. *The Little Community and Peasant Society and Culture*. Chicago: University of Chicago Press, 1971.

Rodinson, Maxime. *Israel: A Colonial-Setter State?* New York: Monad Press, 1973.

Rosilio, Daniel. *The Regional Structure in the Kibbutz Federation: A Sociological Perspective*. Jerusalem: Van Leer Institute, 1975. In Hebrew.

Rubin, Morton. *The Walls of Acre: Intergroup Relations and Urban*

Development in Israel. New York: Holt, Rinehart & Winston, Inc., 1974.

Ruitenbeek, Hendrik M., ed. *Varieties of Classic Social Theory*. New York: E. P. Dutton and Co., Inc., 1963.

Ruppin, Arthur. *The Agricultural Colonisation of the Zionist Organization in Palestine*. London: Martin Hopkinson and Company Ltd., 1926.

―――. *Memories, Diaries and Letters*. New York: Herzl Press, 1971.

―――. *Three Decades of Palestine*. New York: Schocken Books, 1936.

Ryan, William. *Blaming the Victim*. New York: Vintage Books, 1971.

Samuel, Edwin. *Handbook of the Jewish Communal Villages in Palestine*. Jerusalem: Zionist Organization Youth Department, 1945.

Sanders, Irwin. *The Community: An Introduction to a Social System*. New York: Ronald Press, 1966.

Sartre, Jean-Paul. *Anti-Semite and Jew*. New York: Schocken Books, 1970.

Schumacher, E. F. *Small is Beautiful*. New York: Harper & Row, Publishers, Inc., 1973.

Selzer, Michael, ed. *Zionism Reconsidered: The Rejection of Jewish Normalcy*. New York: Macmillan Inc., 1970.

Shanin, Teodor, ed. *Peasants and Peasant Societies*. New York: Penguin Books, 1975.

Sharp, Gene. *The Politics of Nonviolent Action, Part I: Power and Struggle*. London: Porter Sargent, 1973.

Shatil, Y. *Communal Farming in Israel Land Economics*. Israel: Hashomer Hatzair Organization, 1955. In Hebrew.

Shazar, Rachel Katznelson, ed. *The Plough Woman: Memoirs of the Pioneer Women of Palestine*. New York: Herzl Press, 1975.

Sidel, Ruth. *Women and Child Care in China*. Baltimore: Penguin Books, 1974.

Sjoberg, Gideon. *The Preindustrial City*. New York: Free Press, 1960.

Snow, Edgar. *Red Star over China*. New York: Grove Press, 1961.

Spiro, Melford. *Children of the Kibbutz*. Cambridge, Mass.: Harvard University Press, 1958.

————. *Kibbutz: Venture in Utopia*. New York: Schocken Books, 1970.

Stacy, Margaret. *Tradition and Change: A Study of Banbury*. Oxford: Oxford University Press, 1960.

Stein, Boris. *The Kibbutz That Was*. Washington, D.C.: Public Affairs Press, 1965.

Stein, Maurice. *The Eclipse of Community*. Princeton: Princeton University Press, 1960.

Talmon, Yonina. *The Family and Community in the Kibbutz*. Cambridge, Mass.: Harvard University Press, 1972.

Teveth, Shabtai. *Moshe Dayan*. Jerusalem: Weidenfeld and Nicolson, 1972.

Tiger, Lionel, and Shepher, Joseph. *Women in the Kibbutz*. New York: Harcourt, Brace, Jovanovich, 1975.

Thorbecke, Ellen. *Promised Land*. New York: Harper & Bros., n.d.

Tobias, Henry J. *The Jewish Bund in Russia From Its Origins to 1905*. Stanford: Stanford University Press, 1972.

Tonnies, Ferdinand. *Community and Society*. New York: Harper & Row, 1965.

Truzzi, Marcello, ed. *Sociology: The Classic Statements*. New York: Random House, 1971.

Vidich, Arthur, and Bensman, Joseph. *Small Town in a Mass Society*. Princeton: Princeton University Press, 1958.

Vidich, Arthur, Bensman, Joseph and Stein, Maurice. *Reflections on Community Studies*. New York: John Wiley & Sons, Inc., 1964.

Viteles, Harry. *A History of the Cooperative Movement in Israel*, vols. 2 and 3. London: Vallentine, Mitchell & Co. Ltd., 1967.

Warren, Roland, ed. *Perspectives on the American Community*. Skokie, Ill.: Rand McNally & Company, 1973.

————. *Truth, Love and Social Change*. Skokie, Ill.: Rand McNally & Company, 1970.

Weber, Max. *The Protestant Ethic and the Spirit of Capitalism*. New York: Charles Scribner, 1958.

————. *The Theory of Social and Economic Organization*. Oxford: Oxford University Press, 1947.

Weitz, Raanan. *Spatial Organization of Rural Development*. Tel Aviv: Rehovot Settlement Study Centre, 1968.

Willner, Dorothy. *Nation-Building and Community in Israel*. Princeton: Princeton University Press, 1969.

Wolff, Kurt. *Trying Sociology*. New York: John Wiley & Sons, Inc., 1974.

Wylie, Laurence. *Village in the Vaucluse*. Cambridge, Mass.: Harvard University Press, 1973.

Znaniecki, Florian. *The Method of Sociology*. New York: Holt, Rinehart & Winston, 1934.

Zweig, Ferdynand. *Israel: The Sword and the Harp*. London: Heinemann Educational Books Ltd., 1969.

————. *The Israeli Worker*. New York: Herzl Press, 1959.

ARTICLES AND PAMPHLETS

Agin, A. "The Sons of the Kibbutz in the Army." *Niv Hakvutzah* 19 (March 1970). In Hebrew.

Arendt, Hannah. "The Jewish State: Fifty Years After." *Commentary* 1, no. 7 (1945), 1-8.

Barkai, Haim. *A Model of Kibbutz Production and Factor Allocation*. Falk Discussion Paper No. 742. Israel: Falk Institute, March 1974.

Bein, Yehuda. *Adult Education in Kibbutzim in Israel*. Israel: Authority for Education and Research Kibbutz Movement, July, 1966.

Ben-Gurion, David. *Rebirth and Destiny of Israel*. New York: Philosophic Library, 1954. From an address to a Zionist Conference in New York, 1942.

Cohen, Erik. *A Comparative Study of the Political Institutions of Collective Settlements in Israel*. Jerusalem: Hebrew University, 1968.

————. *Bibliography of the Kibbutz*. Israel: Israel Press Ltd., 1964.

————. "Changes in the Social Structure of the Work Area in the Kibbutz." In *The Social Structure of Israel*, Jerusalem.

Darin-Drabkin, Haim. "Whither the Kibbutz." *New Outlook* 15, no. 2 (February 1972). Israeli Publication.

Diamond, Stanley. "The Kibbutz: Utopia in Crises." *Dissent* 5 (1957), 133-152.

――――. "Kibbutz and Shtetl: The History of an Ideal." *Social Problems* 5 (1957), 71-100.

Fine, Keitha Sapsin. "Worker Participation in Israel." In *Workers' Control*, edited by Gerry Hunnius et al. New York: Vintage Books, 1973.

Galpin, Charles. "The Social Anatomy of an Agricultural Community." *Agrarian Employment Station Bulletin* 34 (1915). Israeli Publication.

Gottschalk, Shimon. "Deviant Communities: A Systematic Analysis of Community Types and of Structural Change on the Community Level." Doctoral Dissertation. Brandeis University, 1972.

Har Annual Economic Reports 1966-1975. Economic Manager's Office, Kibbutz Har and Kibbutz Accounting Office.

Har Weekly Newsletter. March-July 1975. Kibbutz Har Central Offices.

Ichud Hakvutzot V'Hakibbutzim. *Shdemot*, nos. 1-3. Literary digest of the kibbutz movement.

Kaufman, Yehezked. "Anti-Semitic Stereotypes in Zionism." *Commentary* 7 (1949) 239-245.

Lehn, Walter. "Zionist Land: The Jewish National Fund." *Journal of Palestine Studies* 3, no. 4 (Summer 1974). Israeli Publication.

Leviatan, Uri. "The Industrial Process in Israeli Kibbutzim." In *Israel: Social Structure and Change*, edited by Michael Curtis and Mordecai Chertoff. New Brunswick, N.J.: Transaction Books, 1973.

Lockwood, Larry. *Imperialism and the Israeli Economy*. Israel: Middle East Research Center, n.d.

Meron, Hannah. "The Dangers of Group Work." *Education in Kibbutz* (August 1972). Israeli Publication in Hebrew.

Merri, Uri. "Changes in Leisure Patterns in the Kibbutz." Interdisciplinary Research Review (July 1973). Publication of the Federation of Kibbutz Movements.

Milouot. Israel: Milouot, April 1972. Abridged version of *Food and Agricultural Organization Symposium Report* of March 1971.

Milouot and Its Enterprises. Israel: Milouot, n.d.

Myrdal, Gunnar. "Paths of Development." In *Peasant and Peasant Society*, edited by Teodor Shanin. New York: Penguin Books, 1975.

Patai, Raphael. "Musha'a Tenure and Co-operation in Palestine." *American Anthropologist* 51 (1949), 436-445.

Perlmutter, Amos. "Dov Ber-Borochov: A Marxist-Zionist Ideologist." *Middle Eastern Studies* 5 (January 1969), 32-44.

Rabin, A. I. *Kibbutz Studies: A Digest of Books and Articles on the Kibbutz by Social Scientists, Educators and Others*. East Lansing: Michigan State University Press, 1971.

Rosenfeld, Eva. "The American Social Scientist in Israel: A Case-Study of Role Conflict." *American Journal of Orthopsychiatry* 28 (1958), 563-572.

Rosenfeld, Henry. "Process of Structural Change in an Arab Village." *American Anthropologist* 60 (1958), 1127.

———. "Wage and Status in an Arab Village." *New Outlook* 6, no. 5. Israeli Publication.

Rosner, Menachem. *The Kibbutz As A Way of Life in Modern Society*. Israel: Givat Haviva, 1970.

Rossi, Peter H. "Community Decision-Making." *Administrative Science Quarterly* 1 (September 1957), 415-444

Roth, Leon. "Moralization and Demoralization in Jewish Ethics." *Judaism* 2, no. 4 (Fall 1962), 292-303.

Shepher, Joseph. "The Kibbutz." In *Sociology in Israel*, edited by L. Wellner. Westport, Conn.: Greenwood Press, 1974.

Sivard, Ruth Leger. *World Military and Social Expenditures*. Philadelphia: American Friends Service Committee, 1976.

Solcoor Publication. New York: Solcoor, 1976.

Stacey, Margaret. "The Myth of Community Studies." *British Journal of Sociology*, 20 (1969), 134-148.

Steward, Julian H. *Area Research: Theory and Practice*. Social Sciences Research Council No. 68. New York: Social Sciences Research Council, 1950.

Vallier, Ivan. "Structural Differentiation, Production Imperatives and Communal Norms: The Kibbutz in Crisis." *Social Forces* 40 (March 1962), 233-242.

Van Leer Institution. *Symposium: The Kibbutz in the 1970's*. Jerusalem: Van Leer Institution, 1970.

Walton, John. "Discipline, Method and Community Power: A Note on the Sociology of Knowledge." *American Sociological Review* 31 (1966), 684.

Warriner, Doreen. "Land Tenure Problems in the Fertile Crescent in the Nineteenth and Twentieth Centuries." In *The Economic History of the Middle East 1800-1914*, edited by Charles Issawi, 1966.

Wolff, Kurt. "Surrender and Community Study: The Study of Loma." In *Reflections on Community Studies*, edited by Vidich et al. New York: John Wiley and Sons, 1964, pp. 233-263.

"Women in the Kibbutz." *Igeret*. 24 April 1972. Tel Aviv. In Hebrew.

OFFICIAL DOCUMENTS AND ARCHIVAL MATERIAL

Audit Union of the Workers' Agricultural Cooperative Societies, Ltd. *The Cooperative Villages of Palestine in 1938*. Tel Aviv: 1940.

English Zionist Federation. *The Jewish National Fund and its Object*. London: 1908.

Eretz-Israel, the J.N.F. for America—30th Anniversary of the Establishment of the Fund 1901-1931. New York: Jewish National Fund, 1932.

Government of Palestine, Information of the Anglo-American Committee. *Survey of Palestine*. Jerusalem: 1946. Prepared in December 1945 and January 1946.

Great Britain, Colonial Office. *Hope Simpson Report on Immigration, Land Settlement and Development*. Cmd. 3686-87. London: 1930.

Great Britain, Foreign Office. *Peel Commission Report*. Parliamentary Papers Cmd. 5479. London: 1937.

Great Britain. *Report of His Britannic Majesty's Government to the Council of the League of Nations on the Administration of Palestine and Trans-Jordan*. Reports for years 1925-1936. Colonial Nos. 20, 26, 31, 40, 47, 59, 75, 82, 94, 104, 112, 129. London: 1925-1936.

Har Archival Material. *Har's Land Deed*, Feb. 1938; Har *Journal* and

Bulletin, 1966-spring 1975; newspaper clippings 1938-1975; photographs 1938-1975.

Ichud Hakvutzot V'Hakibbutzim. *The Law and Regimentation of the Kibbutz*. Tel Aviv: n.d. In Hebrew.

Israel: Government. *Bank of Israel Annual Report, 1968*. Jerusalem: 1968.

Israel: Government. *Israeli Statistical Yearbooks, 1966-1975*. Jerusalem: 1966-1975.

Israel: Government, Ministry of Labor, Department of Cooperation. *Statutes of the Kibbutz*. Jerusalem: 1966.

League of Nations Association of the United States. *The Palestine Mandate*. No. 7, Oct. 1930.

Milouot. *Milouot 1974 Financial Report*.

Jewish Agency. *Jewish Agency for Palestine: Documents Submitted to UN 1917-1947*.

The Joint Planning Center for Agricultural and Colonization and the Economic Advisory Staff. *Israel Agriculture, 1953/54*. Hakiryah: Israeli Government Printing Press, 1955.

U. S. Congress, House, Committee on Foreign Affairs. *The Jewish National Home in Palestine*. *Hearings before the Committee on Foreign Affairs*. 78th Congress on House Resolutions 418 and H. Res. 419. February 8, 9, 15, 16, 1944. Washington, D.C.: U.S. Government Printing Office.

Index

Paula Rayman is Assistant Professor of Sociology
at Brandeis University.

Library of Congress Cataloging in Publication Data
Rayman, Paula.
  The kibbutz community and nation building.
  Bibliography.
  Includes index.
  1. Kibbutzim—Case studies. I. Title.
HX742.2.A3R39   307.7   81-47152
ISBN 0-691-09391-1   AACR2
ISBN 0-691-10124-8 (pbk.)

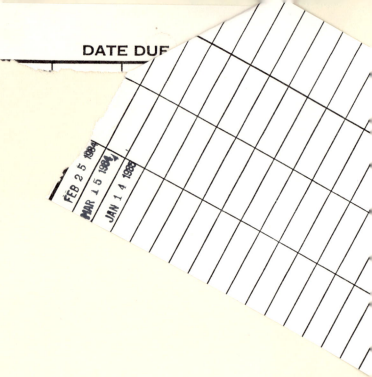

FEB 2 5 1984
MAR 1 5 1984
JAN 1 4 1988